Decreation and the Ethical Bind

Decreation and the Ethical Bind

SIMONE WEIL AND THE
CLAIM OF THE OTHER

Yoon Sook Cha

FORDHAM UNIVERSITY PRESS   *New York*   2017

THIS BOOK IS MADE POSSIBLE BY A COLLABORATIVE GRANT
FROM THE ANDREW W. MELLON FOUNDATION.

Visit us online at www.fordhampress.com.

Library of Congress Cataloging-in-Publication Data available online
at http://catalog.loc.gov.

Printed in the United States of America

19 18 17   5 4 3 2 1

First edition

For my parents,
Soon Bun Yoo and Yong Rang Cha,
and
my daughter,
Laila Grace Holmes,
who have given me everything

CONTENTS

NOTE ON ABBREVIATIONS AND TRANSLATIONS USED

The following abbreviations and translations of frequently cited sources have been used in the text. For consistency, I refer to cited works by their original titles since not all of them have been published in English. Page citations refer to the original, whether or not translations into English are available. The translations into English of works by Simone Weil are my own except for *L'Iliade ou le poème de la force*, for which I use James P. Holoka's translation, *Simone Weil's The* Iliad *or the Poem of Force: A Critical Edition*, and where otherwise noted.

WORKS BY SIMONE WEIL

AD   *Attente de Dieu*. Paris: Fayard, 1966.

CO   *La Condition ouvrière*. Paris: Gallimard, 1951.

CS   *La Connaissance surnaturelle*. Paris: Gallimard, 1950.

CTIII   *Cahiers, Tome III*. Paris: Plon, 1956.

EL   *Écrits de Londres et dernières lettres*. Paris: Gallimard, 1957.

EN   *L'Enracinement: Prélude à une déclaration des devoirs envers l'être humain*. Paris: Gallimard, 1949.

OC   *Œuvres complètes*. Edited by André Devaux and Florence de Lussy. Paris: Gallimard, 1988–.

iv/1   *Écrits de Marseille: Philosophie, science, religion, questions politiques et sociales (1940–1942)*. Edited by Robert Chenavier et al. 2008.

vi/1   *Cahiers (1933-septembre 1941)*. Edited by Alyette Degrâces et al. 1994.

vi/4   *Cahiers (juillet 1942–juillet 1943): La Connaissance sur-naturelle (cahiers de New York et de Londres).* Edited by Marie-Annette Fourneyron et al. 2006.

PF   *Simone Weil's The* Iliad *or the Poem of Force: A Critical Edition.* Edited and translated by James P. Holoka. New York: Peter Lang, 2005.

PG   *La Pesanteur et la grâce.* Paris: Plon, 1988.

PS   "La Personne et le sacré." *Écrits de Londres et dernières lettres.* Paris: Gallimard, 1957.

PSO   *Pensées sans ordre concernant l'amour de Dieu.* Paris: Gallimard, 1962.

PSW   Papiers Simone Weil. Boîte I(I): Correspondance générale. Bibliothèque Nationale Française, Paris.

VS   *Venise sauvée: Tragédie en trois actes.* Paris: Gallimard, 1955.

Certain words—attention, desire, truth, good, necessity, obligation, affliction—appear and reappear with a singular tenacity when you read Simone Weil. Together they compose a kind of refrain for writings with an astonishing range, all bearing the beautifully limpid prose with which Weil has come to be identified. The simplicity of the language, however, as well as the meticulous attention Weil brought to bear upon it, is in contest with a thinking marked by contradictions and abrupt shifts in register. Maurice Blanchot, in a not uncharitable reading, calls it a "thought often strangely surprised."[1] Weil moves willfully and unhesitatingly between philosophy, theology, and poetics, with a total disregard for teleology and disciplinary boundaries. A theory of labor is developed through a contemplation of God, for example. A study of the circumstances of Hitler's rise to power is framed with a Greek myth. The list goes on. Françoise Meltzer paints a vivid picture of Weil's method: "This elision between registers is disconcerting because it refuses to recognize itself as such. It is a kind of brilliant parataxis. . . . It is like Kafka's technique: once you accept that Gregor Samsa is a cockroach, everything else follows logically. In Weil's writings, the reader is frequently confronted with cockroaches, while the writer presses on, deaf to our cries of protest."[2] Those who read Weil with the expectation that the contradictions and contrapuntal strains in her writing will be resolved neatly or at all will be disappointed. And those who argue that they undermine the validity of her thought altogether will not find themselves alone in that estimation. Yet as Blanchot notes, "We are in the habit of valiantly withstanding the shock and constraint of such contradictions [in other philosophers], and I do not see why Simone Weil alone would be disqualified as a thinker because she accepted within herself as legitimate the inevitable opposition of thoughts."[3]

The present study takes as its center point a key "opposition of thought" in Weil's writings, identifying therein the ground for an other-centered ethics: namely, the obligation to preserve the other from harm through a self-dispossession that Weil calls "decreation." Self-dispossession throws one's own creaturely existence into question and necessitates a shift away from an egocentric perspective toward one where the "I" disappears. In effecting one's "disappearance," one does not, however, relinquish one's obligation to the other. Nor is one let go. Instead, the difficulty lies in being bound to the other through this very renunciation of one's "I." The decreative aim of obligation is particular in that it may surpass one's capacity to protect the other from harm and may even redouble the harm upon the one thus obliged. One *has to* give (self-renunciation being the archetype of this donation), but the question becomes what one exactly *has* in the first to place to give. That tension, between one's capacity and one's resources, is exacerbated—even underwritten—by what Weil claims is a common but not equitable exposure to force and consequent destitution. Given that exposure, the answer to the question might very well be *nothing*, although the obligation itself, I argue, remains unfinished. The distinct demand here, to preserve what Weil calls the other's "human presence," may bear upon the one obliged as an impossible demand, then, since it is to be met by one who, in having renounced his "I," has given up his only power (according to Weil) and so, it would seem, can only give more than he has to give.[4] Faced with that demand, one is put in a relentless bind.

Just how this bind both subtends and undercuts an other-centered ethics of preservation that might be derived from decreation is the question with which this book tarries. To be sure, the picture that emerges from my readings of Weil's late writings will seem to complicate rather than shore up the notion of what might be called a "decreative ethics." Simply put, such an ethics is not a given. And what we do get is far from anything prescriptive or practicable—for decreation is opposed to the kind of agency that is identified with sovereign modes of action, even those subject-centered practices that aim specifically to address vulnerability and injurability. It may be a more precise statement to say that Weil offers a way to read the force of claims that express a distinct ethical demand, namely the demand not to be harmed. Reading, in this sense, would then be an ethical orientation that combines the exigency of obligation with the stillness of attention.

In identifying the ethical bind in Weil's writings, this book departs from scholarship on Weil that pathologizes the difficulties to which such an ethics gives rise, particularly that which transposes these difficulties onto Weil's person. Indeed, it is common to find studies that psychologize Weil's thinking by redacting details from her life, effectively reducing Weil's thinking to her biography. Even in its roughest outline, it is understandable why Weil's life might serve as a compelling filter for interpreting her writings: one of two child prodigies (the other, André Weil, a distinguished mathematician) raised in an assimilated and nonpracticing Jewish family in Paris in the context of the two world wars; the Normalienne who engaged in syndicalist activities without ever joining the Communist Party; the teacher who took leave of her profession for factory work, then was later denied her right to teach under the 1940 Statute on Jews in Vichy France; the earnest but clumsy volunteer soldier with the Colonna Durutti who stepped into a pot of cooking oil and had to be rescued by her parents before ever seeing battle; the self-described agnostic who suddenly underwent a mystical conversion experience but refused to enter the Catholic Church; the "saint" who lived her life according to the strictest principles and died at the age of thirty-four from complications stemming from self-induced starvation while recovering from tuberculosis; the Jew who left France to escape anti-Semitic persecution with her parents only to regret to her death having left it behind; the self-appointed modern-day Antigone who was "born to share, not in hatred, but in love," but whose vitriolic statements on preexilic Judaism cut that creed at the knees.[5] Depending upon one's sympathies, it is tempting to conclude that Weil was a saint (T. S. Eliot did, as did Albert Camus), a strange masochist (she figures colorfully as the character Louise Lazarre in Georges Bataille's *Le Bleu du ciel*), or, most contentiously, a self-hating Jew.

Indeed, the temptation to conflate Weil's thought with her life is a strong one. Even in studies that approach her work from a rigorously philosophical standpoint, the "problem" of Weil's life keeps seeping in. Weil's own stated views on the subject do not help to resolve the matter: in a letter that has been dubbed her "Autobiographie spirituelle," Weil claims that the central tenets of her thought are integral to her personal "vocation."[6] Certainly, her conscientious efforts to undertake manual labor (although her training was academic) speak

to her avowed need to have a concrete object and experiential basis for
her studies over purely disinterested and intellectual abstraction. It is
indeed out of these work experiences that Weil's metaphysics of work
would develop.[7] Likewise, in her last major work, *L'Enracinement*,
which envisions the spiritual and political regeneration of postoccupation France, Weil's theorization of a new cultural life for France is
inseparable from ideas concerning actual somatic practices and lived
bodily experience. And it is clear that her last, unrealized project,
staged as counterpropaganda to Hitlerian displays of power and that
proposed the parachuting of nurses to the front lines, would have
included herself among them.

Nonetheless, the transposition between Weil's *bios* and thought is
not as transparent as some of the secondary literature would suggest,
or is at least a terribly fraught one. Considering the challenges Weil's
biography poses for any study of her writings and in view of how it
has subsequently framed Weil scholarship, this study resists any ready
correspondence between the life and the work, although, to be sure,
such correspondences readily abound. How, then, to read Weil's writerly project when her "I" keeps reinscribing itself precisely at the place
where it would vacate itself? But the opposite, maddeningly, is also
true: attempts to correlate the life and the writing are confounded
by the recession of the "I" at the moment it would seem most logical
to insist itself. In a basic sense, we might say that the transformation
of experience in writing, because it occurs as a textual elaboration,
necessarily imposes a distance between the lived experience and its
narration.[8] That distance is especially pertinent when considering
Weil, whose entire lived and written efforts aim at impersonal being,
and whose manifest aversion to relating things "personal" (which she
repeatedly insists is of "no interest") is emblematic of a larger difficulty she faced in entirely extricating herself from the "I" she consciously sought to renounce. For what are we to make of her last
letters where so often that "I" wends its way in? Consider also the
context of those letters, which ever-failingly make appeals for support
of her "Frontline Nurses" project (in which she would risk death in
order to save other lives), and so, imbricate her life precisely with the
worry of "missing" her death (Weil's words)—an imperative to write
met in the crux of an urgent self-dispossession.

Let me end this preface as I began it, with a measure of difficulty. For
someone whose entire corpus is concerned in one way or another with

the effects of force on the integrity of human life, Weil nonetheless sustained some clearly contradictory views. Key among these is her censure of preexilic Judaism.[9] Even with the abundance of fine studies on Weil, attempts to address Weil's polemic against a conception of power and force as she saw it in preexilic Judaism fall short or, more problematically, are hedged by Christian apologetics.[10] There seems to be no good or satisfying way to answer the problem that Emmanuel Levinas calls, most simply, "Simone Weil Against the Bible."[11] Even apart from her gross misreading of the Bible, the fact that Weil did not heed her own consummate practices of intellectual probity which "demands that thought be indifferent to all ideas, without exception . . . equally receiving and equally reserved with regard to all ideas" and whereby disagreement "is simply a reason to suspend thought for a long time, to push away examination, attention, and scruple as far as possible before daring to affirm anything" is itself dumbfounding.[12] Perhaps we would do well to take Weil at her own word here—or in the case of her anti-Judaism, to read Weil against herself—with the idea that from such dissonance we might restore to Weil's thought that "opposition of thought" foundational to the kind of ethics pursued in this book.

"Each being cries in silence to be read differently," writes Weil. What follows, then, is my attempt to read in the late writings of Simone Weil what begs to be read differently, even when or—as this preface has gestured toward—*especially* when one is stopped or at the limits of thinking along with her. It is not an easy task for any Weil scholar, but it is perhaps a necessary one. And to ask the reader to follow along, to engage in the arduous logic of the Kafkan cockroach, is an uneasy petition but one made here nonetheless.

Decreation and the Ethical Bind

Introduction

Simone Weil does not tire of saying that the "I" must be emptied, renounced, reduced to the point it occupies in space and time. "Absolute solitude," she writes.[1] It is perhaps baffling to think that an other-centered ethics of preservation can be culled from the emptying of the "I," as this book will try to do. For it is not obvious that a relationality, let alone a responsibility, emerges from the scene of self-dispossession Weil describes time and again in her late writings, nor is it clear how the other's claims upon oneself—specifically, his claim not to be harmed—might be met under deleterious conditions. Weil says that the claim, expressed in the question, "Why am I being harmed?" (Pourquoi me fait-on du mal?), is the first and last cry of the other emerging from the deepest recesses of his soul in response to injury and force. We might further state that the cry is the very claim of his subjectivity, understood in Weilian terms as his "human being as such" (l'être humain comme tel), which is said to exert "the indefinable influence of his human presence" (l'influence indéfinissable de sa présence humaine).[2] Such a claim is complicated, however, since it makes its demands upon one who, in Weil's view, forfeits the primacy of his own subject position in responding to it. And yet, it is precisely here, at the conjuncture of subject affirmation (the other's) and subject dislocation (one's own), that an ethical obligation to the other is said to emerge.

Weil goes further: the decentering of the "I" is subtended by a more radical dislocation where the "I" itself is said to be "unmade" or "decreated." In Weil's formulation, decreation is the unmaking of

1

the self through the offering of the one thing it can claim, namely, the power to say "I."[3] Decreation would then happen in the withdrawal of a fundamental claim to speech and to sovereignty. In decreating oneself, the primacy of one's own claim of subjectivity might also be said to be "unmade"—a slight semantic distinction from "unmaking" the self of decreation, reflecting a tension in decreation of a renunciation of volitional acts (figured in the offering of the "I") and an interpellation prior to one's choosing (and so, obviating the notion of volition altogether), toward which one might be said to have an "unwilling susceptibility."[4]

The ambiguity of the status of the decreated "I" faced with the claim of the other not to be harmed is at the crux of this book: even if we accept that a kind of ethical directive to preserve the other from harm emerges from the other's cry, it does not provide a clear answer to how that demand might be met in the context of a decreated "I" if it is not exactly the "I" who is addressed and who must respond. The most important feature of this problematic that bears upon decreative ethics, then, is the deconstitution of the "I," which not only shifts the source of ethical norms from which recognition of the other's claim might issue but also puts into question whether such recognition is possible at all. In other words, if the self is not the ground from which ethical action is derived and produced, what exactly underwrites moral action framed by the claim of the other not to be harmed? How might one preserve the other from harm when one is also vulnerable to an inexorable exposure to force? Where are the resources to meet these competing demands to be found, especially if the obligation to the other produces a strain on one's own resources or depletes them altogether? If, as I will argue, an ethical relationship to the other emerges from a common vulnerability to force, need, and destitution, that relationship is surely particular in that it binds the one who is thus subjected to an obligation that may very well surpass his capacity to meet it. It dispossesses him, if you will, of the very capacity that would seem necessary to fulfill the obligation, even as it does not let him go in situating him outside that power.

The response to that claim is further problematized by the precariousness of the form of the claim itself. The cry—"Why am I being harmed?"—is silent or, more precisely, is the expression of what cannot be said or thematized, discernible only in a kind of prelinguistic or extralinguistic vocalization. It is a question that bears the tension between a slightness of form and an emphatic insistence of the intractable demand to be preserved from harm that issues from it nonetheless. Such a claim, then, recalls us to a fundamental vulnerability and powerlessness where the possibilities for speech are severely constrained or nearly entirely undermined, and where speech, when it does issue, might more faithfully be characterized as the rudiments of speech or the fragments of nonspeech, such as we find in hunger, fatigue, supplication, prayer, and the cry. That these fragments figure so prominently in Weil's late writings on impersonal, decreated being suggests the complexities of the address between one who in giving up his power to say "I" has given up a core claim to saying anything and the other whose utterance may simply be too weak or empty to be heard, illustrating a larger problematic concerning the translatability of these claims into the preservation of the other from harm.

But if the claim of the other cannot be seized or situated within recognizable linguistic and epistemological frameworks, how can it serve as the frame for ethical action, let alone for the other's subjectivity, his "human being as such"? For as Judith Butler notes, "a vulnerability must be perceived and recognized in order to come into play in an ethical encounter, and there is no guarantee this will happen."[5] This seems especially true given that the encounter is complicated, as we have said, by a decreated self who has given up its claim to agentic-centered action and speech and by the other who, by reason of injurious circumstances, may be unable to make such a claim but whose very vulnerability insists upon it nonetheless. And so, a running concern throughout this book is to track the exigency that subtends speech in decreation, discerning therein its ethically binding character, the conditions of its production and inscription, as well as those that limit the field of its audibility or shut it down altogether.

The cry of the other, operating as it does at the limits of discursive representation and comprehension, undercuts the certainty and knowingness of the one obliged. In this noncognitive modality, one is rendered helpless, brought to the cusp of failure, dispossessed of one's self-assurance, perhaps even dispensable or substitutable. And still somehow one is called to respond. Implicit in the other's claim upon oneself, then, is the constitution of oneself as a displaced and dispossessed being, confounding because it is also, curiously, the moment of one's relationship to the other. A recurring effort in this study, then, is to bring both the sense of subject-position dislocation and relationality into relief, to begin to think of the way self-dispossession might be a passage to the other.

Whether or not the passage founders under the strain produced by an obligation that appears to engender an impossible demand (namely, to preserve the other's human presence against the limits of one's capacity to do so), however, opens up the broader question of whether or not a decreative ethics is practicable or even desirable. I would contend that it is precisely this tension that a decreative ethics identifies without neatly resolving, either with easy prescriptions or with normative principles of application. And so, one of the underlying aims of this study is to show how decreation opens up—or more exactly, *keeps open*—the question of what constitutes the fulfillment of obligation in the first place, given the competing claims of the one obliged and the one it serves. Decreative ethics, as I am identifying it in Weil's work, does not offer a normative, constructive, or prescriptive model for behavior that is basic to familiar forms of ethical inquiry.[6] The binding force of the claims it answers to is not to be found in a guiding set of principles, nor is obligation in Weil's conception engaged in a positive project.[7] For the decreative aim of obligation is specifically to *preserve* the other from harm, so as to preserve the core of his impersonal being. Accordingly, one does not exactly "do" anything, as it were. And the help that one proffers models a withdrawal of claims to mastery and sovereignty (including the paternalism that arguably underlies the superficially related paradigm of the ethics of care, from which decreative ethics are distinct). It is, simply put, "To not exercise all the power at one's disposal" (PG 53; Ne pas exercer tout le pouvoir dont on dispose).

Weil's conception of the withdrawal of power alters our ordinary way of thinking about power and sovereign modes of discourse—even those who seek to rehabilitate the position of those subjugated—which operate within a binary frame (and so, those who have power versus those who do not). Weil would argue that these modalities fail to recognize a deeper quandary: those who do not have power dream of one day having it themselves and wielding it in turn. It is a vicious circle, Weil argues, in which to inflict suffering and to undergo suffering participate in the same operation of power. To not exercise power where one has it, then, is so radical because it withdraws altogether from the binary model of subjugator-subjugated. That reduced capacity may well jeopardize the prospect of fulfilling one's ethical obligation to the other, but I would submit that it is precisely where one does without power—to align Weil's conception with Maurice Blanchot's formulation ("sans pouvoir")[8]— that a new conceptualization of an ethical force might emerge.

While Weil's core concept of decreation is by now a well-worn term in Weilian scholarship—from the seminal work on her religious metaphysics by Miklos Vetö (to which my own research owes an early and foundational debt) to Anne Carson's brilliant lyrical meditation on decreation and speech[9]—this book offers another treatment: that the concept of decreation gives us a way to read the distinct ethical charge of the other's demand not to be harmed.[10] Certainly, the vulnerability of human beings to force and injury—particularly when wielded by other human beings—preoccupied Weil from her earliest writings. Her conclusion that both those who perpetrate force and those subjected to it are "brothers in the same misery" recalls the Thucydidean formula of power as a kind of automatic mechanism, succinctly described by E. Jane Doering as "the specter of self-perpetuating force." Considering this mechanism, Doering writes, "The problem, as [Weil] saw it, boiled down to finding ways to establish equity between the weaker and the stronger, giving both entities a level playing field."[11] But whereas Doering's comprehensive study (crucial reading for anyone investigating the problem of force in Weil's writings) centers on the question of how to limit and equalize force, my own reading eschews the question of how to establish equity. I ask instead how a different kind of exercise of force—what we might call, borrowing Weilian language, a negative use of power—engenders a relationality between the self and the other without, however, that erasing their relative power.

Significantly, my argument departs from scholarship on Weil that has tended to reduce her thinking to received versions of her biography. For I do not regard Weil's *bios* as a model for an other-centered ethics but as generating questions of subjectivity and language to which a decreative ethics gives rise. To be sure, the competing impulses in Weil's writing—that writing must be absolutely impersonal; that writing expresses an absolutely personal vocation—illustrate the intractable relationship of writing to decreation. In her study of Weil's poetics, Joan Dargan describes that relationship most simply: "Writing is a *via negativa*."[12] And yet, as I seek to show, the "linguistic decreation of the self" (again quoting Dargan) is constantly upset by the stubborn screen of that self precisely at the site of its deinscription, troubling the notion of a linguistic transparency and austerity to which Weil so aspired. The difficulty of that goal is perfectly expressed in this passage from Weil's notebooks: "Writing—like translating—negative—pushing away those words that obscure the model, the silent thing that must be expressed."[13] However, that expression, echoing Emmanuel Levinas, "may be obliged to unsay itself in order to avoid disfiguring the secret it exposes."[14] Weil's own textual elaboration of that unsaying in the passage above seems to suggest as much: writing is invoked in nearly parallel terms with translation (it is said to be "like" translation), and the term that seems to enjoin them is itself negative. Writing, in this sense, appears to be an exercise in decreation.

In locating and affirming an ethics that is not grounded in subjective agency and positive fruition (although that does not imply that it is without concrete implications—the recessive action it proffers is real), *Decreation and the Ethical Bind* seeks to establish a place for Weil in ethics, philosophy, and literature that links her thought to Emmanuel Levinas, Maurice Blanchot, and Judith Butler. It places Weil within a distinct continental tradition of literary and cultural theory in which writing and speech are bound up with questions of ethical appeal and where ethical commitments of writing emerge at the thresholds of loss and injury. In identifying an ethical obligation that emerges from an exposure to force and vulnerability, in further stating that obligation, in Weil's view, responds to a particular demand of the other not to be harmed, I am invoking a distinctly Levinasian term. The formulation of one's response to that demand—in Weilian terms, obligation; in Levinasian terms, responsibility—aligns the two thinkers and reverberates throughout my thinking in this book. Levinas's formulation of the demand of the other, which dispossesses the subject of its centrality and claims of self-identity, resonates with the decreative aims of Weilian obligation, which similarly dispossesses the self. In both cases, the demand binds the one who would respond to an infinite and unconditional obligation that may well exceed his capacity to fulfill it. Moreover, in positing subject formation—both the "I" and the one who makes his demands upon "me"—at the site of its vulnerability, obligation (responsibility) upends sovereign modes of identity and political constitution. What is so unsettling about the Weilian and Levinasian formulations of responsibility is that a fundamental asymmetry between the one obligated and the one served is maintained, even strengthened. But it is precisely here, I would argue, that Weil and Levinas offer us a way to think about subject formation that does not assimilate the one to the other, suggesting a relationality that continually brings one outside oneself.

Judith Butler's work on precarity and injurability informs my discussion of harm, vulnerability, and subject dislocation throughout this book.[15] Taking her cue from Levinas's understanding of the precariousness of life as the foundation of ethics, Butler offers a mode of reading that precariousness—one that is hinged upon one's primary vulnerability to the other—as the basis for an ecstatic relationality that contests notions of the sovereign subject. Butler writes, "As a way of being related to what is not me and not fully masterable, vulnerability is a kind of relationship that belongs to that ambiguous region in which receptivity and responsiveness are not clearly separable from one another, and not distinguished as separate moments in a sequence."[16] That vulnerability, as the effect of an impressionability and impingement by the other, constitutes one's relationship to the other as one of interdependency and prior susceptibility. What we call the "I," in Butler's view, precedes individuation, precipitates sense and knowing, and implies a displacement of the egological.

So, if ethics, upon this view, is understood to be a relational practice, that practice is animated by the seeming paradox of a relational bind that ties us to the other but only inasmuch as it deinstitutes us as discrete entities and profoundly dispossesses us of our presumed centrality.[17] That mode of dispossession aligns with Weil's conception of decreation and helps us to make sense of the difficulty we face here in understanding decreation, too, as a relational practice that curiously binds the self to the other through self-dispossession. For Weil, as for Butler, one's relationship to the other, structured upon the dispossession of the "I," issues from the other's demand upon oneself from which emerges an ethical responsibility. And while both Butler and Weil distinguish between forcible dispossession and a dispossession resulting from one's encounter with alterity,[18] they differ on the mode of responsiveness that arises therefrom, particularly on the role of consent in the latter form.[19] For Weil views that second form of dispossession (what I refer to throughout this book as "self-dispossession" as opposed to forcible dispossession from without) as one's *consent* to being "unmade," an unmaking that troubles the notion of the self involuntarily undone by the other. Consent, as Weil understands it, is not exactly a capacity to affirm having been impinged upon—something that is crucial to Butler's notion of ethical responsiveness.[20] For one's consent to being unmade may very well exceed any capacity we have for it. And in the relational framework, where one is called upon to respond or act, Butler suggests not only that one speaks and acts but that speech and action themselves become possible within that framework. That possibility, so fraught for Weil, and which presupposes at least a horizon of capacity, is another way Butler's account of subject formation departs from the decreated "I" that, I argue, speaks and acts without the power to do so.

We return to the question of what it means to unmake oneself when one is, as Butler puts it, "already undone, or undone from the start."[21] The apparent equivocation of that formulation reflects the double valence in the decreated self impressed upon by a responsiveness anterior to both the self and its encounter with the other and by one that is demanded, even instituted by the encounter itself, by the "you" that draws "me" out of myself. To be addressed by the other in this way is to be profoundly interrupted, not once or forever, but continuously, repeatedly. So the iterative nature of subject formation describes its continual rearticulation in the very encounter and offers here a distinct challenge to the deinscription of the "I" implied in decreation.

The injunction in obligation to give more than one has is echoed in the writings of Maurice Blanchot, whose thinking on the possibility engendered by an impossible demand helps us throughout this book to make sense of the other's claims and the powerlessness upon which it is both founded and founders. Blanchot, whose superb essay on Weil, "L'Affirmation (le désir, le malheur)," is to my mind one of the most assiduous readings to be found anywhere, tells us that the claim to speech arises at the juncture where that claim is rendered useless precisely for the reason that the "I," in speaking, is able to claim nothing. Useless, yes, but somehow necessary. The exigency to speak, or rather the exigency of speech, makes use of and even uses up the one who speaks nonetheless, who understands that he must speak, without being exactly able to even as he does, even if that peculiar incapacity leaves him too weak, unable to assume what he, in speaking, would attest to. The woman who speaks in *L'Attente, l'oubli* is such a person; she speaks without being able to, asks only to "Make it so that I can speak."[22]

Those words resound as a kind of prayer, or, in any case, it reminds me of another prayer, this one found in Weil's notebooks. That prayer, which Weil calls an "example of prayer," is sure to give anyone reading it pause, if not alarm. It asks for nothing short of the complete incapacitation of all one's faculties such that, if granted, would be a mode of existence just this side of death. Of course, that is not something for which one can exactly ask. But I think that it is a way of getting a handle on something that could not be asked for and that, in any case, is undergone with or without the petition.[23] The prayer—that which asks, effectively, for nothing in asking for the impossible—leaves the one who asks behind, with nothing, able neither to capture nor be fully implicated by the very claim of his speech. Juxtaposing Blanchot's notion of a "weak speech" with the weightless extravagance of Weil's example of prayer that asks for nothing it could claim offers a succinct picture of the decreated "I."

An elliptical meditation in Weil's notebooks gives us another picture of decreation, this one imagined from the position of leave-taking:

> I can easily imagine that [God] loves that perspective of creation that can only be seen from the point where I am. But I act as a screen.
>
> I must withdraw so that he might see it.
>
> I must withdraw so that God might enter into contact with the beings whom chance places in my path and so that he might love me. My presence is indiscreet, as though I found myself between two lovers or two friends. I am not the maiden who awaits her betrothed but the unwelcome third who is with the two lovers and who ought to go away so that they can really be together.
>
> If I only knew how to disappear, there would be a perfect union of love between God and the earth I tread, the sea I hear . . .
>
> That I might disappear so that those things that I see may become perfectly beautiful from the fact that they are no longer things that I see.
>
> I do not in the least wish that this created world should no longer be perceptible, but that it should no longer be me to whom it is perceptible. To me it cannot tell its secret which is too high. That I might leave, then the creator and the creature will exchange their secrets.
>
> To see a landscape as it is when I am not there . . . (PG 93–95)

While we are in the habit of thinking of renunciation as a giving up, in Weil's conception, where it is figured both as an offering and as a wrenching of egological centrality, renunciation reinscribes the self at the site of its evacuation through a relationship with the other implied by its offering. Anne Carson gives us a beautifully suggestive reading of that scene of self-wrenching, in which the position of Weil's "I" reflects a more fundamental structure in the imperative to write—or to "tell God," in Carson's words—that strives to be rid of the very "screen" of self that impels it in the first place. Weil calls that originating point (of writing) the "perspective of creation that can only be seen from the point where I am." Carson's reading of decreation in Weil, particularly her view of Weil's "writerly project," informs my own understanding of how the imperative to write (which Weil affirmed as a piece with her larger "vocation") is at once vexed and generated by the screen of the "I."

A NOTE ON METHOD AND BOOK OVERVIEW

My approach to Weil's thought is developed through close and repeated readings of "the silent thing that must be expressed." It is a method that I hope shows not only the complexities of the thing to be expressed but also of expression itself, which is challenged by those very conditions of force and subsequent precarity that demand their expression in the first place. Beyond Weil's stated ideas concerning language, her use of language—caught somewhere between an insistence of the thing to be said and a reticence to expose itself in the saying—reflects a delicate oscillation between the clear urgency to speak and write and the imperative to preserve an essential silence. That tension is beautifully reflected in a striking image from Weil's notebooks: a squirrel running in a cage and the rotation of the celestial sphere (PG 273). "Uneven evenness" is how Blanchot describes the strange synthesis of the restlessness of Weil's lived practices and the perfect stillness of her thought.[24]

For my own part, the method of close and reiterative readings of the themes related to a decreative ethics—self-dispossession, negative action, subject dislocation, etc.—within and across chapters, is likewise meant to at once unsettle and affirm the terms of decreation, thereby enacting a consent to inconclusiveness and nonmastery implied in decreative ethics, as well as disrupting the notion that there is an uncontested story here that unfolds. What does that mean? The kind of reading practiced here will not correct the "difficult coherence" (Blanchot) of Weil's writings with a master narrative.[25] Instead, my intent is to honor the vicissitudes of Weil's thought—however difficult—through a kind of reiterative reading that meets those very dissonances without attempting to resolve them. In this I am mindful of something Ann Smock writes in her introduction to Sarah Kofman's memoir that has guided my own reflections on Weil's writing, that it is "bathed in a lucidity, unclouded by insight."[26] It also recalls us, I think, to the particular claim of speech in decreative ethics where, again quoting Smock, "something speaks that is other than power and other, even, than possibility."[27] It is in that spirit that I employ close and reiterative readings that do not seek narrative fruition or closure, and where reading itself might be an exercise in decreative ethics.[28]

This study looks at texts dating largely from the last four years of Weil's life: the essay "L'Iliade ou le poème de la force"; the play

Venise sauvée; essays and letters published in *Attente de Dieu, Pensées sans ordre concernant l'amour de Dieu*, and *Écrits de Londres et dernières lettres*, particularly "La Personne et le sacré" and "Autobiographie spirituelle"; unpublished letters from the Weil archives at the Bibliothèque Nationale de France; and Weil's notebooks, especially *La Connaissance surnaturelle*. The texts were written at a time of war and displacement, during which Weil was forced under Vichy law to give up her profession as a teacher, fled occupied Paris for Marseille and later left for New York with her parents in May 1942, then went to London to work for the Free French, with the final, unrealized hope of returning to France to fight in the Resistance. In the midst of this upheaval came Weil's mystical experience, although Weil would remain, to her death, outside the Catholic Church. The texts considered here are as representative of the incredible turmoil of this time as they are of the unchanging strands in Weil's thought that remained firmly rooted in Greek philosophy, especially in Plato's notion of the good. More specifically, the texts under consideration are of particular interest for a discussion of an ethics of self-dispossession I am identifying in Weil's work. They feature themes central to decreative ethics: self-dispossession and impersonal being, the withdrawal of power, the exigency of speech, and a conception of address and obligation that emerges out of an encounter with the other's vulnerability and suffering.

The first part of the book examines one's exposure to "force," a complex field of material, physical, and psychic conditions and processes that constitutes the scene of vulnerability and frames the response to the suffering born of this exposure. I consider Weil's claim about the special character of force that, in being assumed and redeployed by those whom it subjects, makes the one who wields it and the one vanquished by it "brothers in the same misery."[29] In pointing out the superior capacity of force to flatten the relative power of humans, I argue that the claim directs us also to the possibility of a new relationality—one that forfeits sovereign modes of power, as defined by the axiom oft-lamented by Weil that "each one commands everywhere he has the power to do so" without that forfeiture thereby signifying an equitable power between the self and the other.[30] For the difference between the one and the other is maintained, even heightened, by this relinquishing of sovereignty. It is in this context of radically unequal and inassimilable terms, outside of relative or specific forms of difference, that we might begin to speak, first, of an unconditional obligation to the other that also does not rest on any particularities of the person to whom one is obliged; and second, how both—the other and one's obligation to the other—are enjoined to the invisible but conjured Other who, in Weil's view, establishes the model for relinquished sovereignty in the first place.

Chapter 1, a reading of "La Personne et le sacré," asks how one might recognize and honor the vulnerability of what Weil calls the other's "human presence," specifically his demand not to be harmed. Weil calls it his cry of innocence. The difficulty of such recognition is deepened by the delivery of the demand, which Weil describes in turns as a silent cry or a nonsensical stuttering and so, which marks the limits of language to express its claims adequately or at all. Its expression, without appeal and without semantic coherence, nevertheless contains an ethical address in the binding character of its summons and the obligation to preserve the other from harm that ensues—even when the demand thwarts one's own plans and imposes limits on one's own volition and desires. For the ethical character of the relationship between oneself and the other emerging from obligation is such that the sovereignty and position of one's own subject position is called into question. That shift, away from an egocentric perspective that accords value to the other in relation to what he might provide for the ego toward impersonal being, is reflected in Weil's notion of decreation, an unmaking of the ego with its voluptuous negation of limits. And so, part of what I seek to show in this chapter is how an ethics modeled on self-dispossession might respond to the demand to preserve the other's "human being as such."

Chapter 2, a reading of Weil's magisterial essay "L'*Iliade* ou le poème de la force," examines the relationship of one's "human presence" to one's subjection to force. I consider how supplication exposes and holds the one exposed to affliction, and argue that it offers a certain opening to the other, even as it marks the precariousness of one's own human being. Referencing Blanchot's superb discussion of supplication ("La Mesure, le suppliant"),[31] I argue that supplication establishes an "uncommon measure" between the two limit-terms facing each other—the one who has nothing but the sacredness of his appeal and the other who, despite that appeal, retains the power to kill—not by virtue of any power the suppliant has, as such, but by laying bare his human presence.

In the middle chapters of the book, both readings of *Venise sauvée*, the obligation to preserve the other's human presence is explicitly dramatized as an account of voice, accusation, and self-justification.[32] Here I focus on the specific economy of obligation, its unending demand against the limited capacity to fulfill it. It seems we are faced with failure, one that is expressed in the economy of unmet sleep and a debt that is the constant reminder of being outbid by the other's claim upon oneself. Under conditions of force, we are given to understand the enunciative moment other than as communicative speech; instead, one finds its broken pieces, its stammering.

In chapter 3, I discuss the breakdown of speech in the protagonist's (barely) articulated promise to preserve the other from harm. The picture of force here is consistent with Weil's reading of the *Iliad*. Force dominates and subjugates those it rules into the "conqueror [who] lives his dream [and] the vanquished [who] live the dream of the other" (PF 66). In a critical moment of the play, its hero, Jaffier, must decide whether or not to lead the insurgency to destroy the free city of Venice. The absolute stillness and silence that accompany his resolve to preserve Venice out of pity for its beauty go against the overwhelming tide of force, violence, and loss. It begs us to consider the particular claim of vulnerability—precisely the claim that Venice in its open and defenseless beauty has upon Jaffier. We know that Jaffier withdraws at the height of his power; when he finally does speak, his speech is constrained by violence and powerlessness. In this chapter, then, I ask about the possibility of disclosure under a particular ethical bind: What is one obliged to say when it conflicts with the soul's preservation of what is secret and inexpressible? I argue that Jaffier's silence at a moment when he is still free to speak is a manner of keeping his promise to the other to whom both his silence and his promise are addressed. Nonetheless, that does not save him from the unfailing sense that in doing nothing he has done too much. In his withdrawal (recul), Jaffier does not make use of the power at his disposal, and the Council's reneging of its earlier agreement to spare his friends (the condition upon which Jaffier gave up the plans for the overthrow) unexpectedly results in his having been made use of. But there remains the trickier question—playing with the possible translations of "recul"—of whether, in unwittingly sending his friends to their death, Jaffier did not also side-step or recoil from his obligation to them. (That is the verdict of his captors.) What plays out, in fact, never puts Jaffier's obligation toward Venice into question, but it does suggest that obligation, bound by love for what exists, is transformed vis-à-vis his friends into an unlivable bind that vexes the obligation to Venice and to his friends alike, and though powerless to save both, releases him from neither one.

How is it possible to honor two obligations that appear to be exclusive of each other? The outcome of the play does not assuage any hope that such equilibrium is possible, even as it may be ethically required. That impossible requirement is the subject of the fourth chapter, a comparative reading of sleep and debt in *Venise sauvée* and Blanchot's *La Folie du jour*.[33] Here I look at obligation as the occasion and structure of a binding which makes nearly impossible the relation of the person to his speech act. If tears and stillness shelter, sleeplessness and debt expose. The exposure is the permanent remainder of the "madness of day"; even blindness cannot excuse you. One must give everything; one must give an account of everything. The difficulty is that the demand surpasses any capacity one has to give. It does not matter that it is not a contracted debt, or that one has already been indicted of having failed to meet one's obligation anyway. One is still obligated, and that obligation, I argue, is unfinished.

The last two chapters of the book examine the decreative charge of the demand through the contrasting poles of destitution and extravagance in the context of Weil's personal experiences. Here I show how the depersonalizing impulse of the demand deinscribes Weil's "I" precisely from the site of its inscription. The decreative aim of obligation, in other words, disowns Weil from those experiences that would seem to be the most personal (for example, her mystical experiences), resulting in a transformation of Weil's lived experience into a narrative experience where that "I" assumes an impersonal and universal aspect (and so, in the case of her personal encounter with Christ, becomes a spiritual autobiography that Weil writes as an *example* of implicit faith).[34]

In chapter 5, I look at how decreation is configured along the principle axes of Weil's Christology, namely, her understanding of Creation and the Passion.[35] Decreation emulates God's relationship to creaturely life that is, for Weil, established first by his withdrawal from the world as an act of love. Consequently, the ethical relationship between oneself and the other presumes a love that seeks to fulfill itself in the form of withdrawal, one that Weil describes as a wrenching or tearing away. The withdrawal, moreover, entails the renunciation of the "I" and its egological claims to centrality and plenitude. Accordingly, decreating the "I" implies not only a deprivation but also a kind of destitution that, however contradictory, underwrites one's love of the other. The contradiction of a fulfill-ment through withdrawal is similarly operative in what Weil calls "the perfect demand" (la demande parfaite), which asks for noth-ing other than what is already, infallibly true.[36] It is reflected in Weil's question—or more precisely, the unasked question—*if she were to ask*, would she be given the sacraments given her unstinting opposition to central tenets of Catholic dogma? The unasked ques-tion that nonetheless does not cease to make its demands known, I would submit, is the deep structure of the petition, formalized for Weil in prayer and illustrated in what Weil offers as an "example of prayer."[37] That prayer, which asks for the total disappearance of one's self as a manner of donation, posits the self only as it exists in relationship to the other and, moreover, to the other's relationship with the Other.

In the concluding chapter, an examination of Weil's last letters, I return to the idea of petition, situating it within the context of an unabating exigency of speech.[38] Levinas's brief commentary on Weil's "example of prayer," which describes it as a singular desubstantia-tion of the "I," offers us a clue to reading Weil's letters. Quoting Paul Celan, Levinas writes that one speaks "in the angle of inclination of one's existence, in the angle of inclination where the creature enun-ciates itself."[39] The singularity of that desubstantiation takes on its full color in these last letters, just as enunciation does its urgency and necessity. Weil explains: "For each person [the good] consists of a succession of acts and events that are rigorously personal to him, and so obligatory that he who bypasses them misses the goal. Such, for me, was the notion of vocation . . . and not to follow such an impulse when it arose, even if it gave rise to impossibilities, seemed to me the greatest of afflictions" (AD 38). Weil's insistence upon the "personal" aspect of vocation takes on a special slant in the context of the cir-cumstances of her departure from France and of her final projects, which Weil understood to be the culmination of that vocation. There the "I" is inscribed at the site of a duty that is impressed or impinged upon it from without. To speak of vocation in the context of impinge-ment returns us to the scene of address followed throughout this book, where one is interpellated by a seemingly impossible demand. And yet, what do we make of Weil ultimately missing her chance to fulfill it? For none of Weil's many petitions to realize her final projects would receive a positive response, while she would die, as she lived, responding to it nonetheless. In this sense, obligation remains, as it began, not so much as the measure of fulfillment or failure, as it is the exercise of impersonal, decreated being.

Just how to give when one has nothing left to give is a question that preoccupies much of my thinking in this book. In one of her final appeals, Weil writes, most simply, that she is near the end of her capacity—morally, intellectually, and physically—and "the limit reached, I'll say that I can no longer give anything."[40] And so, we are met with the limits of what one can give, but does it dispel the end-lessness of an obligation that binds one to the other? To begin, then, to answer for this bind.

CHAPTER I

The Vulnerability of Precious Things

"La Personne et le sacré"

The vulnerability of precious things is beautiful because vulnerability is a mark of existence.

—Simone Weil, *La Pesanteur et la grâce*

In vulnerability, therefore, lies *a relation to the other* that causality does not exhaust, a relation anterior to all affection by the source.

—Emmanuel Levinas, "Sans identité"

In her essay "La Personne et le sacré," Simone Weil describes self-dispossession as a passage from the "person" to the "impersonal"—a passage that would, on its face, seem to negate the very basis of relationality between oneself and the other. But it is precisely there that a relationship to the other is said to emerge.[1] "All those who have penetrated the domain of the impersonal," Weil writes, "encounter there a responsibility toward all human beings. That of protecting in them, not the person, but all that corresponds in the person to the fragile possibilities of passage into the impersonal. It is for them, foremost, that the call to respect the sacred nature of human beings must be addressed" (PS 19–20). Weil situates the relationship to the other where we are least likely to expect it, in the voiding of the "I"—a radical decentering of the ego that would allow the other to make contact with others or, finally, with God. This is not exactly to exempt oneself from contact with God or with others, but it is to withdraw so that one does not act as a "screen" in the way of this encounter. Of this figuration Weil observes in her notebooks, "my presence is indiscreet."[2] As the third, one is always a surplus figure, but that formulation also suggests that the rupture of intimacy between oneself and the other is in some sense necessary. Such a rupture is neither for the sake of a return to a supposed primary narcissism or an egoïc plenitude, nor for the reformulation of the "I" as a larger collective identity ("we"). Weil describes the withdrawal as a negative or recessive action characterized by stillness and attention. This posture of attention then becomes a kind of moral bearing or aptitude (to be distinguished from ability) in the context of the other's exposure to harm and suffering.[3]

Throughout Weil's writings, that exposure is signaled by his cry. Language is undone here. In "La Personne et le sacré," Weil describes the cry as a stammering (balbutiement). Under repeated or sustained exposure to injury, one is eventually reduced to a "state of mute and uninterrupted groaning" (14). In the essay, Weil makes clear the semantic limitations of the cry of destitution and injury in her example of a man who stands accused and who must explain himself to a judge whose superior command of language, in turn, is employed to dismiss the empty (but not meaningless) stammering of the accused's defense. According to Weil, the man is guilty of his destitution, indicated in socially tangible terms by the poverty of his language. Characterizing the appeal made by those similarly exposed to injury, Weil writes: "They are like someone whose tongue has been cut off and who has sometimes forgotten his infirmity. Their lips move and no ear perceives any sound. They themselves soon become powerless in the use of language because of the certainty of not being heard" (36).

To be so defenseless and powerless, to have at one's disposal only the cry that disappears just as quickly into the folds of the senselessness and destitution from which it first emerged—how can such a cry be heard?[4] One is addressed by this utterance that is not only below the level of semantic distinction and intelligibility but of appeal. Given the limits of semantic expression, how might an ethics modeled on self-dispossession—what I am calling "decreative ethics"— respond to the cry of the other, specifically to his demand that he not be harmed? For as Judith Butler reminds us, "a vulnerability must be perceived and recognized in order to come into play in an ethical encounter."[5] Decreative ethics would require a recognition of the other's demand, but any reception is surely vexed by its delivery. Under what conditions, then, might it be met? How might one perceive the demand when it appears to be no language at all, only the ruins of language, the cry but a hollowed reverberation? For the demand not to be harmed, like its delivery, is a negative, empty appeal.

Weil insists that the efforts of one who is addressed in this way must come from something other than his person, his ability, and his volition. In other words, it is not to one's "person" that the appeal is made since it is not exactly one's ability to respond that is addressed as such, nor is it the person upon whom the force of that cry is binding. Who or what, then, is responsible? Surely the vocative dimension of the cry assumes a direction, even as it does not exactly designate who or what is invoked. It could be said that the cry enacts its own limits in failing to designate or find an addressee. Or it might say something about the failure of address itself. But I would like to suggest that the cry of the other tells us something more fundamental about the other that cannot be fully recuperated by his address, but which is nonetheless signaled or enigmatically contained in the very openness of its addressee and the sonorous emptiness of the claims expressed in the cry. Just what measure of recognition is contained in this emptiness, and how, invoking Butler again, does it comport one beyond oneself?[6] And how, in this ecstatic relation—a mode of being that, in Weilian terms, is impersonal and decreated—are we propelled toward an ethical relationality based on that very subject dislocation?

For Weil, that measure of recognition would also entail a recognition that one's own will and desire are limited by material necessity and by the other himself who upends one's sovereignty and self-complacency. The difficulty of recognizing these limits is exacerbated by the imagination, which allows one to forget or even negate those things that stand in the way of one's volition and desire. "There is voluptuousness in everything that makes one forget the reality of obstacles," writes Weil (13). Upon this view, the philosophical problem posed by the imagination is its nearly unlimited capacity to shore up the ego's resources, particularly an egocentric perspective "characterized by illusions that place the subject at the center of space, time, value, and being."[7] Against this mode of voluptuous forgetfulness, I seek to show that an ethics issuing from self-dispossession would affirm an impartial order of things and so, too, would shift their relation to one's own being. What emerges from this shift is a mode of seeing that is an expression of attention; it is a recognition of the reality of human existence, distinct from what that existence might provide for the ego. Recognition of that order is precisely where the ethical imposes itself as a demand by the other to attend to its permanent vulnerability to force and suffering.[8] Such a recognition, in turn, compels one to not transfer one's suffering onto others in the form of injury or in the form of what Weil calls "unlawful love," which is characterized by a desire that destroys its object.

For my reading of harm and vulnerability I look closely at "La Personne et le sacré," an essay that integrates some of the most important themes of Weil's late thought: the precedence of obligations over rights, the constitution of justice, the nexus of obligation and physical and spiritual needs.[9] Judith Butler's reflections on vulnerability and injurability, which invoke Levinasian ethics, inform my reading of harm and one's responsiveness to it.[10] Specifically, I am trying to show how decreative ethics is an encounter with the other from which a responsibility to protect in the other "the fragile possibilities of passage into the impersonal" emerges. Certainly the passage of which I make use here, from Butler and Levinas to Weil, is not a transparent one, nor is it meant to collapse important distinctions between them. They are linked here by what I understand to be central to their respective ideas concerning human life: first, its primary vulnerability to others, and, second, an obligation to the other that emerges, precisely, from this vulnerability.

In her notebooks Weil writes, "The vulnerability of precious things is beautiful because vulnerability is a mark of existence" (PG 181). What kind of ethics can be imagined from this vulnerability? What kind of ethical perspective—freed from the egocentrism of "the person"—can be developed from the kind of impersonal being Weil envisages? Would we find there a distinctly ethical expression of being, one that respects the alterity of the other so that it can neither be subsumed under nor mastered through one's responsibility toward him? Would it compel us toward a mode of being profoundly open to the other, not because of any supposed social harmony (which can lead to idealization, in Weil's view) or because the relationship is reciprocal (obligation, according to Weil, does not belong to an economy of equitable exchange or reciprocity), but because both the self and the other are, finally, vulnerable to harm?

THE PERSON AND THE IMPERSONAL

According to Weil, one's most resilient store of energy is bound up with the "I," which harnesses the energy it takes from the outside world and redirects it instinctively toward its own self-preservation. That is no less true in the case of one's submersion in the collective, where that individual goal takes on a sovereign dimension. There the "I" is amassed under a greater power that holds in common its individual ambitions under the banner of a collective identity and entity, a totality that Weil variously calls "the social," "social matter," or "the great beast," after Plato.[11] The person cedes to the collective as naturally, writes Weil, as does the gram to the kilogram on a scale (PS 43). The collective is the example par excellence of an idealization that supplants the powerlessness of the individual person and legitimizes his interests (however speciously) through his membership. Alluding to Plato's allegory of the cave, Weil writes that the collective is an ersatz good, the only earthly thing that can be taken as an end, "for it possesses a kind of transcendence in relation to the human person" (PG 248).[12] Weil uses this concept of the collective to explain the aura and seductive power of National Socialism, going so far as to confess, "If at this moment I had before me a group of twenty young Germans singing Nazi songs in chorus, a part of my soul would instantly become Nazi."[13] The conspirators in her play *Venise sauvée* likewise dramatize the hyperbolic sway of the collective.[14] Represented on one side by the Venetian citizens who enjoy a free, peaceful, and entitled existence, and on the other, by an uprooted and disenfranchised motley crew who conspire to overthrow the independent Venetian government for the Spanish Empire, the "we" is both the pinnacle and principle of the "I."[15] Their respective claims to get what they deserve is an eloquent enough articulation of the same dream of belonging, employing the notion of inalienable rights to support it. In this context, the restitution of rights is aimed at restoring a fundamental equilibrium; any violence exercised toward this end is understood to be its necessary means.

Weil insists upon the illusory nature of these claims without, however, losing compassion for the destitution that provoked them. Her point is not to dismiss disenfranchisement, forceful displacement, or suffering under brute or continued violence but to argue that the basis of their supposed restitution is itself imaginary: "When someone has harmed us, it creates reactions within us. The desire for vengeance is a desire for essential equilibrium. . . . The search for equilibrium is bad because it is imaginary. Revenge. Even if in fact we kill or torture our enemy it is, in a sense, imaginary" (48–49). The equilibrium is essential and the desire for equilibrium is real, but its object is false, the object being, finally, a self-aggrandizing and self-preserving "I." Weil clarifies the link between self-preservation and harm experienced; the harm that one inflicts outwardly is proportional to the harm that one undergoes: "A hurtful act is the transference onto others the degradation that we bear in ourselves. That is why we are inclined to commit such acts as a way of deliverance. All crime is a transference of the harm in him who acts onto him who undergoes it" (135). One's actions follow naturally from this principle: avoid harm and redirect the harm with which one is confronted. The above passage makes clear the relationship between the "degradation" we bear (a result of the loss of essential equilibrium) and the desire to be relieved of that suffering. To be relieved of it through its transference is a manner of "deliverance." That deliverance comes in the form of hurting another—a false equation, according to Weil, since to inflict harm elsewhere is not to be truly rid of one's own suffering. Under restricted circumstances that redirection still takes place, albeit at the level of imagination. The imagination works to compel present circumstances onto an imagined future where one's desires are fulfilled (and so, one's "destiny" or a "one day . . ."), and thereby alleviates some of the bitterness and reality of what is presently undergone. Nonetheless, the process of transference, as Weil understands it, gives at least the appearance of a solution through the displacement of suffering. Taken in the fuller context of Weil's writings, that displacement is not necessarily, and certainly not primarily, a conscious activity but is rather an instinctive, even animal, gesture of self-protection and preservation. At issue here in Weil's notion of the loss of essential equilibrium is the correlation between aggression and the inclination toward self-preservation.

Weil argues that the restitution of rights is additionally based upon an erroneous conflation between "being" and "having," where self-preservation collapses into self-possession and where both constitute the "I," according to this model. It follows that to be dispossessed of one's rights also throws one's being into question. And so, too, different registers and categories slide into one another: "the rights of man"—is this a political category or an ontological one? Natural or metaphysical? Contingent or absolute? It is precisely to the instability of their constitutive terms that Weil directs her critique of rights. In this regard, the claim of the conspirators in *Venise sauvée* illustrates a belief in the rights of man as an absolute and eternal principle. For Weil, this is an erroneous claim, and not the least because rights are circumstantial, vulnerable to changes in judiciary and cultural temperament, or simply because the notion of inherent rights (of one's "human rights" and of the "respect for the human person") is a historically modern idea. In a related work, Weil traces the notion of "the rights of man" to the French Revolution: "[The men of 1789] only recognized [reality] in the human realm. That is why they began

with the idea of rights. But at the same time they wanted to postu-
late absolute principles. This contradiction caused them to fall into
a confusion of language and ideas that is, for many, apparent in the
present political and social confusion. The realm of what is eternal, universal, unconditioned is other than the one conditioned by
facts, and therein lies different ideas related to the most secret part
of the human soul" (EN 10). According to Weil, the error of French
eighteenth-century rights-based political philosophy (represented by
"Diderot and the Encyclopedists," in Weil's view) is that it bases what
pertains to "the human realm" (and so, to what is finite) upon an
absolute or eternal principle, the contradiction between the finite and
the infinite giving rise to "political and social confusion." In "La Personne et le sacré," Weil appears to conflate the notion of the "rights of
man" in this rights-based tradition with the account of human rights
held by the personalist philosopher Jacques Maritain in his influential
treatise *The Rights of Man and Natural Law.* Like other personalist
philosophers before him, Maritain maintains that human beings are
constituted by what he calls their person (la personne), an inviolable
metaphysical center that grounds their natural rights and is the basis
for natural law.[16] Like his contemporary Emmanuel Mounier, Maritain criticizes the individualism of bourgeois liberalism, the collectiv-
ism of fascism, and the materialism of communism, which he viewed
as impersonal, antihuman, and destructive. Urging a new concept
of community with an explicitly Christian ethos, 1920s and 1930s
French personalism sought to make the person the center of a new
order of Christendom that would be both secular and lay.[17] Here, too,
Weil finds the distinction between the profane and historically contingent and the sacred to be problematically collapsed.

Weil maintains the distinction between the finite and the infinite
without offering a solution to reconcile their difference. Insisting
instead upon their differentiation, she argues that something other
than rights must come to stand in for the human being's relation to
both realms. What is required is something that binds the human
being to the human realm, without being essentially affected by the
tides of circumstance, milieu, or power. The concept of rights fails
according to this criterion because rights, in being contingent upon
the person and so, vulnerable to variable social and political forces
and shifting relations of power, are invariably circumscribed and
conditioned by "social matter." Against this, specifically challeng-
ing Maritain's claim that "the notion of right is even deeper than

that of moral obligation," Weil insists that the notion of obligation is the only thing in the human realm that can be said to be eternally binding and unconditioned:[18] "Obligation is not based upon any *de facto* situation, jurisprudence, customs, social structure, relations of forces, historical heritage, or a presumed historical orientation. For no *de facto* situation is able to create an obligation" (11). For Weil, an obligation cannot be created, as such. For just as much as the object of obligation is always the human being—and more precisely, as we will see below, what Weil views as "sacred" in the human being—the obligation already exists. It is universal, impersonal, and not bound to the particularities of circumstance or convention, or even to the particular individual person it serves—indeed, it is anterior to these. Weil goes so far as to say that the obligation remains intact even when the one served by the obligation does not recognize that any obligation toward him is due: "The object of any obligation, in the realm of human affairs, is always the human being as such [l'être humain comme tel]. There is an obligation toward every human being for the sole reason that he is a human being, without any other condition required, and even when he himself [the one served] does not recognize any such obligation" (11). The object being the "human being as such," obligation is anterior to both the one obligated and the one served by the obligation.

In "La Personne et le sacré," Weil challenges us to rethink the terms of what constitutes human life—away from one's "person" to what she calls "the sacred." For Weil, this move from the person to the sacred is necessary in order to establish the "impersonal" that issues from justice, understood in the Greek sense of equilibrium. Considering the modern juridical notion of justice represented by personalism, Weil challenges the principal terms of the discussion, namely, the person and his attendant rights. She opens her essay thus: "'You do not interest me.' Those are words that a man cannot address to another man without cruelty or without wounding justice." She continues: "'Your person does not interest me.' These words can be used in an affectionate conversation between close friends without hitting upon even the most delicately sensitive nerve in their friendship. In the same way one could say without degrading oneself: 'My person does not count,' but not: 'I do not count'" (PS 11).[19]

What, then, makes it possible to recognize the sacred or impersonal dimension of human beings? Christopher Hamilton suggests that for Weil, it is love which "bypasses all interest in the empirical characteristics of a human being, in what individuates a human being"[20]—a statement that echoes this passage from Weil's notebooks, "Belief in the existence of other human beings as such is *love*" (PG 122).[21] How precisely to think of the relationship between love and its object, and how to distinguish the kind of love that would protect the other from harm or from a desire that consumes or destroys its object—what Weil calls "unlawful love"—is the focus of the discussion below.

THE VOID

Weil envisages the pain of losing one's object of love: "The pain from the death of the other, it is this pain of the void, of disequilibrium. From now on, efforts without object, therefore, without reward" (PG 67; La douleur de la mort d'autrui, c'est cette douleur du vide, du déséquilibre. Efforts désormais sans objet, donc sans récompense). It seems that the loss can only be named negatively, the terse syntax and the absence of the verb in the last sentence conveying the sense of deprivation and suggesting the incapacity of language to also represent or capture the upheaval, even as language seems somehow to bear its imprint. The failure of representation here suggests that while we can be certain of the feeling of deprivation and disequilibrium, we do not know exactly what in losing we have lost, an unknowingness that brings to mind melancholic loss.[22] *It is the pain of the void*, Weil tells us very simply. What, indeed, would restore the equilibrium?

For while Weil accepts that attempts to fill or compensate for loss is a natural and reasonable response to loss, she refuses substitutions for the lost object, as well as a finite term to grief—both of which are understood to be necessary to "successful" mourning in the Freudian paradigm.[23] Substituting for the loss (literally or figuratively) is not only undesirable for Weil but also false. Idealization is one particularly dangerous form that a response to loss might take. The kind of substitutions characteristic of idealization can only be temporary; in Weil's view, they are compensations for what one believes has been lost rather than a sustained and true acknowledgment of what one does not have. As compensations they are a way of lying to oneself and of not seeing the reality of things and of people; without this reality—a nakedness unadorned by one's imagination or compensation—one cannot adequately or truly love others, Weil tells us. Indeed, to bear loss or endure the void it leaves behind without reward would require a supernatural strength. That is a strength one does not have, and yet Weil insists with her characteristic obstinacy that one must nonetheless endure the void. Weil declares unsparingly, "Love is not consolation, it is light" (58). Since there can be no true recompense for loss, all efforts to fill it, recast it, or transform it through the imagination are a form of debasement. Weil maintains that attaching one's desire to a series of objects (as substitutions or displacements) enslaves one to the conditions that our attachment to each object exacts. Weil does not exactly offer an easy solution: she says that one must descend to the source of one's desires to tear away the energy from its object: "That is where the desires are true in so far as they are energy. It is the object that is unreal" (68). But this is said to cause an "unspeakable wrench in the soul at the separation of a desire from its object" (68).

So if loss is experienced as the withdrawal of vital energy and orientation, and if enduring the void further suspends new sources of energy (since enduring the void is to be without recompense for the lost object of love), how are we to sustain our energy? Where is that energy to be found? In losing the object of our love, do we not devastate our store of energy, that force from which we derive the very strength to love in the first place? If "I" do not love without "you," it is not only because we are in some sense inseparable. (That commonplace is true enough.) It is because love's energy comes from without, from the one who gives "me" the energy to love. For Weil, that energy is akin to light—the only energy in the natural world unaffected by gravity. The problem is that one cannot of and by oneself produce one's own food, as does the plant in transforming the light of the sun into energy. One is, of necessity, brought outside oneself; the other must be the very source and substance of one's life and love. One needs the other as one needs food, states Weil. But without that object how can we love or even live, since if loving is as vital to me as food and if I am deprived of it I cannot live? In her essay "Le Passage de la personne à l'impersonnel," Monique Broc-Lapeyre makes clear the connection between loving and living in Weil's texts: "Since childhood, the only way for man to be able to live, is to be loved. The loss of love is the experience of nothingness, an experience so painful that it forces the cry of supreme distress. . . . From childhood, man is in an unconditional and undefined demand for love."[24] It seems that in this equation of unconditional need and demand, we come out on the losing end. Or it may be that in not ceasing to need the other, we are strangely in an uncountable surplus.

Weil suggests that we sustain the absence of our lost love as one "seizes" hunger: "To lose someone: one suffers but his death, the absent one having become imaginary, unreal. But the desire one has for him is not imaginary. To descend into oneself, where the desire that is not imaginary resides. Hunger: one imagines different kinds of food, but the hunger itself is real: to seize hunger. The presence of the dead person is imaginary but his absence is very real; it is henceforth his way of appearing" (69). The question then becomes: How do we stop our desire from attaching to an object? In other words, how do we not "eat" our hunger? Weil maintains that eating and hunger are both direct contacts with what is real. In an oft-quoted passage from her "Autobiographie spirituelle," Weil claims, "The relation of hunger to food is certainly much less complete but just as real as the act of eating" (AD 27). But it is only in hunger, Weil insists, that the representation of the object of our hunger does nothing to diminish or degrade the hunger itself; the hunger itself is always and absolutely real. The obvious conundrum, however, is that it can only be real so long as it is not satisfied. In eating we are like cannibals, writes Weil, consuming and ultimately destroying the object of our desire. Comparing our attachment to particular persons to hunger for food, Weil writes: "We do not love human beings as hunger but as food. We love as cannibals. . . . Human affections are the affections of ghouls. We love someone, that is to say, we like drinking his blood."[25] If we return hunger to the context of loss, how do we resist turning our loss and its attendant void into a form of cannibalism that would devour others? How do we not inflict injury as a mode of satisfying our hunger, that is to say, as both a way of filling the void and as a gesture of self-preservation?

OBLIGATION AND THE UNREALIZED CRY

To sustain one's hunger without food is to desire without an object; this objectless desire is for the sake of the other's life. And so, recognition of the other's life emerges at the intersection of an interdiction (do not eat) and the source and maintenance of that interdiction (hunger). Recognition, then, is the scene of a profound and, it would seem, impossible struggle, since to obey that interdiction to its literal conclusion would ultimately result in one's own death. The interdiction and the implications of its insolubility underscore the profound tension in decreative ethics: that is, how can an ethics impose a demand to preserve the other's life for the sake of love if it is possibly at the cost of one's own?

It is a tension that Weil refuses to resolve, as this quotation makes clear: "One cannot love purely unless one has renounced living. . . . For death alone teaches us what we are, that is to say, that we do not exist, unless it is as one thing among many others" (CS 250). The notion of existing "as one thing among many others" upends one's sovereignty and shifts the perspective from which the self views others and is himself viewed.[26] That posture also suggests the limits of self-mastery and masterability (over the limits to one's volition that is represented by the other and his demands on me) implicit in subject-centered paradigms of political agency, such as personalism, against which Weil wages an explicit critique in "La Personne et le sacré." To desire in this way and subsequently, to exist as one thing among others, does not only necessitate a shift in one's field of relations to others and to human life in general. More radically, we might say that it "put[s] my ontological right to existence into question."[27] How, then, does this constitute a distinctively ethical perspective on human life and human beings?[28] Levinas suggests an initial answer to that question, one that will be developed later in this chapter: "In ethics, the other's right to exist has primacy over my own, a primacy epitomized in the ethical edict: you shall not kill, you shall not jeopardize the life of the other."[29]

In Weil's reading of harm, obligation is conceived as the exigency to protect or preserve what is sacred in the life of the other over his person. "What is sacred, far from being the person, is that which is, in a human being, impersonal. All that is impersonal in man is sacred, and that alone" (PS 16). Weil uses an example of a stranger walking by to illustrate the difference between the person and the sacred: "Here is a passerby in the street who has long arms, blue eyes, a spirit where thoughts pass that are unknown to me but that are, perhaps, mediocre. It is neither his person nor his personality that is sacred to me. It is him. Wholly him. His arms, his eyes, his thoughts, everything" (11–12). She then writes, rather shockingly, "If his person was what is most sacred for me, I could easily gouge out his eyes. Once blind, he would be as much a person as he was before. I would not at all have touched his person. I would only have destroyed his eyes" (12). The passage moves immediately from what constitutes his human life to harming that life. One could gouge out a stranger's eyes and still leave his "person" intact according to Weil's account. So it seems that what is necessitated by obligation does not arise solely from the other's physical vulnerability, nor against my ability to injure him bodily. And yet the question Weil poses immediately following the scenario does not, as we then might expect, take us away from the question of the stranger's injurability. Weil asks: "What exactly prevents me from gouging out the eyes of this man if I have the freedom and if it amuses me to do so?" (12). Weil answers: "What would stay my hand is knowing that if someone were to gouge out his eyes, his soul would be lacerated by the thought that he was being harmed" (12). And so Weil's question has moved us from what constitutes the stranger's sacredness to that of one's responsibility vis-à-vis this stranger. The stranger's right to bodily integrity, we learn, cannot constitute that responsibility. However, responsibility does seem to issue from a certain trespass of an integrity not reducible to his physical aspect but that, more than anything else, makes him permanently vulnerable to such a trespass and is the very point of contact with that trespass.

If I must preserve his bodily integrity—if I must first stay my own hand—it is to save the stranger from crying out, "Why am I being harmed?" (Pourquoi me fait-on du mal?). Responsibility, in other words, emerges from the cry of injurability, of suffering (du mal) under the hand of another, this "you" implied in the cry. Upon this view, then, responsibility implies a relationship between oneself and the other premised upon this address, which itself only seems to emerge in the very cry. In the scenario Weil presents us with in "La Personne et le sacré," it is not even upon hearing the cry of the injured that the "I" is called into being. The responsibility seems to be anterior to an as yet realized cry—Weil calls it the "thought" of being harmed. In the address, the "I" implied in the stranger's "you" seems to emerge from the obligation to preserve him from this cry. Upon this view, we might go further than Weil's explicit statements that the obligation is already under way and say that it is not the moment of the call that is the beginning of one's obligation to the other, even as that moment is when one's relationship to the other must be said to figure. How do we make sense of the apparent tension between the anteriority of the obligation to the cry and its animation in the cry itself? And how do we understand the "you" that is imbricated in the responsiveness demanded by its claims not to be harmed? For it is surely in the encounter itself that the you is strangely enlivened: one is bound to the other's "I" precisely at the moment when that "I" is at greatest risk of being forcefully dispossessed from without and when one's own "I," in its efforts to preserve the other, undergoes its own dispossession.

In this configuration, Weil's persistent claim that we must give up our "I" begins to make sense. Weil writes, "We possess nothing in the world—for chance can take everything from us—except the power to say 'I.' That is what we have to give to God, that is to say, that is what we have to destroy. There is absolutely no other free act that is permitted us, only the destruction of the 'I'" (PG 73). This is not a simple fatalism or nihilism on Weil's part. Understood in the context of the address, to destroy one's "I" is also to destroy the illusion that that "I" exists independently of its relationships with others, figured through the call of the other. To give up one's "I" is to acknowledge and accept that the obligation to the other supersedes any claims of self-possession. Inversely, it is to consent to a state of dispossession necessitated by the other's claim upon "me" in his address. That the other is figured as a stranger (un étranger)—indeed, as a passerby—is no mere accident when we look at it this way. For Weil, the other is fundamentally the one who is strange or foreign to me; for me, he is the primary instance of exteriority. Put differently, the other who needs me (here: who needs me to stay my hand) cannot be mastered by me.

And while the singularity of his need is signaled by his cry for protection against harm, it is never reducible to the particularity of his person, only to the unconditionality of what is sacred, of which his cry signals wordlessly and impersonally: "The cry of pained surprise that the infliction of harm solicits from the bottom of the soul is not something personal. It is not enough to wound the person and his desires to provoke it. It always arises by the sensation, through pain, of a contact with injustice. It always constitutes, in the last of men as in Christ himself, an impersonal protest" (PS 15–16). Weil's description of the cry in this passage as "pained surprise" is worth taking note of here. It constitutes a protest against injustice that is made sensible through pain. Weil situates injustice at the intersection of pain and the upsurge of that pain expressed in the cry. So injustice arises whenever there has been a transgression or violation against the good, which Weil understands to be inviolably sacred. Recalling the biblical admonition to "Become the sons of your Father, he of the heavens, in that he makes the sun rise on the mean and the good and makes the rain fall on the just and the unjust" (43), Weil makes an analogy of good to light.[30] Just as light, available to all, cannot be possessed and so, surpasses capture, the human stands in a nonproprietary relationship to good even as he is not thereby excluded from its being available to him. In other words, he stands in an impersonal relationship to good. Justice is the name Weil gives for such a relationship. In this configuration, the cry is always the cry of one's innocence, that is, of one's unconditional claim to good.

It is also the claim of one who, in his subjection to harm (le mal), undergoes a kind of dispossession other than that constituted by one's nonproprietary relationship to the good. Even as the sacred constitutes what Weil elsewhere describes as the "indefinable influence of human presence" (PF 22; l'influence indéfinissable de la présence humaine), that presence is permanently vulnerable. That precariousness is laid out in the starkest terms in Weil's essay "L'*Iliade* ou le poème de la force," which states very simply the most insidious effects of force: *it can turn a man who is yet alive into a thing.*[31] The state of one who is "yet alive" brings to mind the precariousness of the one who, under continued exposure to force, may one day be unable to utter the cry of his innocence: "Why am I being harmed?" Weil states that such a person is reduced to the level of matter, indistinguishable from, no more precious than stones. For the one under continual injury or exposure to force, the instinct to cry out his pain simply stops one day. "An alternative human species, a hybrid of man and corpse," is how Weil describes one who has suffered thus (23). When one is so degraded, when it seems that one has lost one's barest human presence and the field of audibility has been concurrently shut down, how can the cry be heard?[32] The *Iliad* essay underscores the difficulty of such a derealization: one is diminished—a nothing—or merely a part of a "non-resistant milieu."

The cry of destitution corresponds to the destruction of the "I" from without. But whereas the latter is the form "le mal" subsumes, the cry is always the cry of innocence. Of this correspondence, Weil often invokes the cry of Christ, abandoned by God, "Why have you forsaken me?"[33] Abandonment, in other words, is ineluctably tied to the response implicated in the cry. For Weil, the question, "Why have you forsaken me?" does not seek to understand why one is so destitute. Indeed, Weil argues that the one who utters this cry can no longer even represent to himself the cause or reason for his destitution, nor the relationship between his present condition and his self. He has surpassed the particular limit and order that would allow him to put

things into relationship with each other—an ordering that is the hallmark of thinking and of language, according to Weil. "As when one
is at the limit of thirst," she explains, "when one is sick with thirst,
one no longer thinks of the act of drinking in relation to oneself, nor
even of the act of drinking, generally speaking. One only thinks of
water, water alone, but this image of water is like a cry of one's whole
being" (AD 217).

The cry of destitution, in other words, is an "agonized vocalization," as profoundly wordless and senseless as the cry of abandonment.[34] Concerning the "face," the figure for Levinas of destitution
par excellence, Butler writes that it evokes the "wordless vocalization
of suffering that marks the limits of linguistic translation here." Butler continues: "The face, if we are to put words to its meaning, will
be that for which no words really work; the face seems to be a kind of
sound, the sound of language evacuating its sense, the sonorous sub-
stratum of vocalization that precedes and limits the delivery of any
semantic sense."[35] For Weil, the cry of the other's "whole being" conveys exactly that sense of transgression and semantic limitation, and
it does so immediately, despite its apparent untranslatability. Levinas says of the face that it is "not of the order of the seen, it is not an
object, but it is he whose appearing . . . is also an appeal or an imperative given to your responsibility: to encounter a face is *straightaway*
to hear a demand and an order."[36] The Levinasian face is helpful here
insofar as it helps to explain how one's encounter with the other's cry
is at once an experience of one's own inadequacy, as well as the inadequacy of the cry to its claims: for both the face and the cry issue a
command for preservation (against harm) that exceeds any representation of the very help it demands. The one who cries thus is strangely
possessed by the abandonment itself that yet does not cease to turn
upon a being that has already been vacated from without. If language
cedes, then crumbles here to its proper (its "own") destitution and if,
in one's absolute destitution, one cannot precisely say, "I am alone,
I am hungry, I am thirsty, I have been harmed," what possibility is
there for one's need to be met?

Butler's reflections on translation may help us here. In *Parting
Ways*, Butler asks how a message might be received and so, responded
to, when its delivery is severely constricted or seemingly impossible. In
other words, how might one heed the demand of the other—to return
us to the Levinasian and Weilian scene of the ethical encounter—
when the demand does not exactly fit into a given or appreciable

perceptual or intelligible order? How can it be recognized and so, responded to—least of all, "straightaway," as Levinas argues? The encounter may appear to be a noninterpretive moment of interpellation; it may even be that one is located "precisely at the boundary, as the excrement of established interpellations."[37] And it would seem, if we were to stop there, that there has been no transmission of the message, that one is, in fact, outside of the address. In the conditions of utter destitution described by Weil, when one is all but reduced to a living corpse, it would seem that no address is possible. But Butler insists that there remains even here "some sense of one's addressability": "One *could* be addressed if only the modes of address were hailing in one's direction."[38] And against Levinas's own claims that the demand of the other (which commands one not to kill) is noninterpretive, Butler argues that it cannot precede interpretation or translation. As Butler notes, recalling a point made by Jean Laplanche, "receptivity is always a matter of translation."[39] The idea of translation as Butler articulates it may help us to make sense of the ethical disposition demanded of the one who would respond to the cry of the other:

> What I take from Levinas is the claim that this contact with alterity animates the ethical scene, the relation to the other which obligates me. In this way, the chasm in translation becomes the condition of contact with what is outside me, the vehicle for an ec-static relationality, and the scene where one language meets another and something new happens. . . . If a demand comes from elsewhere, and not immediately from within my own idiom, then my idiom is interrupted by the demand, which means ethics itself requires a certain disorientation from the discourse that is most familiar to me. Further, if that interruption constitutes a demand for translation, then translation cannot be simply an assimilation of what is foreign into what is familiar; it must be an opening onto the unfamiliar, a dispossession from prior ground.[40]

If we return to the scenario with which Weil presents us, the demand to preserve the other from harm and so, also, to protect his passage to the impersonal intersects the other's subject affirmation with one's own subject dislocation. At the crux of one's responsibility, according to the Weilian ethical scene, lies a dispossession that is not unlike the chasm entailed in translation between one language or tradition and another, where that chasm is itself the condition of contact between the two.

The proximity of aggression to the obligation to preserve the other from the cry of pain further deepens the complex intersection of address and responsibility. The related questions, "Why am I being harmed?" and "Why have you forsaken me?," implicate one who astonishingly insists his self at the site of an impingement and aggression from without that threaten to destroy that self. He is at the same time the one for whom I must stay my hand. We looked at the scene of the passerby and the question of what would stop one from gouging out the other's eyes. It seems that the obligation is not only to prevent the other from harm but is also an interdiction on one's own aggression or murderous impulses arising from the encounter with the other's vulnerability. The responsibility, then, is forged from the contest between dispensing with the other's life and sheltering that life. So the precariousness of the other's life is also the tenuousness of one's efforts to protect that life against harm. The tenuousness comes from two directions, according to Levinas, and is summed up by the biblical interdiction not to kill: on the one hand, one must not kill the other; on the other hand, the injunction is against the desire to do exactly that. Levinas writes that "the face of the other in its precariousness and its defencelessness is for me, at the same time, the temptation to kill and the call to peace, the 'You shall not kill.'"[41]

It is not clear whether the desire to harm the other is primary and the injunction issues from it, or whether the injunction at once produces the desire whose fulfillment it also prohibits. Whatever the case, the injunction would seem to maintain the desire in its impossibility, of being named without being realized. That state of "unrealization" might be said to produce an anxiety that cannot be mastered or assuaged by heeding the injunction. The prohibition comes into clearest view if we read the interdiction ("Thou shall not kill") against the cry of the one who might be killed, his "Why are you doing me harm?" Transposing Levinas with Weil here allows us to see that the unrealization and its attendant anxiety do not issue from obeying or not obeying the injunction, that they precede the question of adherence. If one is called upon to not kill the other, one is—and not only by default—simultaneously called to protect the other. But that protection is not subsequent to a conscious decision, just as it is not necessarily commensurate with one's own plans (for example, for a self-centered agency, for self-preservation) and may even thwart those plans altogether.

THE EMPTY DEMAND

Even though the other's fragility would seem to make one's capacity (to protect and to harm) the primary or even sole measure of one's adherence to the edict, Levinas's and Weil's respective readings of vulnerability suggest that responding to the call does not exactly issue from anything one can do. That fragility which, although it can be crushed and brutalized, is of an insurmountable and obdurate transparency that does not yield to one's hands but that still opens itself in its exposure to injury and to violation. "The opening is the vulnerability of the skin offered in its violation and injury, beyond all that can be shown, beyond all that can be, from the essence of being, exposed to comprehension and celebration," writes Levinas.[42]

The vulnerability of the other makes all one's efforts to protect it tenuous—perhaps even useless—not only because one must protect that life but because it may be that one cannot. This failure or incapacity vis-à-vis the other's vulnerability reminds me of a certain claim made by one of the characters in Weil's play *Venise sauvée*: that the city on the verge of a violent overthrow could be preserved not by arms or force but by its beauty. Of course, that claim, made by someone who is ignorant of the city's impending destruction, is touching in its naïveté. But there is a profound truth in that unknowing claim: the city stands ultimately untouched by violence, saved, in fact, by its open beauty. Like beauty, we might say that the open vulnerability of the other is also its naked, empty demand. It does not ask for "something"; it certainly does not ask anything of "me." Rather, it is an open appeal that does not yet disclose anything but nonetheless persists in its demand. One is faced with that demand, unable to turn away from it. Perhaps the anxiety of the one faced with the other's empty demand reflects another failure beyond that of one's desire and capacity. Perhaps the anxiety is the particular form suffering takes when the other's vulnerability, in its openness, takes up anyone who is captivated by that vulnerability so akin to beauty for Weil: "beauty seduces the flesh" (PG 233); it is "a carnal attraction which keeps us at a distance and implies a renunciation" (234). The suffering of anxiety coupled with fear of failure would also be that of being anyone, substitutable by all or no one.

One must be emptied to the point of being a "no one" or an anyone. The full force of this apparent contradiction is brought to bear in this statement from Weil's notebooks: "We possess only what we renounce. What we do not renounce escapes us" (PG 83). Weil dispels the comforting illusions of a possessive model of human relations: "We are attached to the possession of a thing because we think that if we cease to possess it, it will cease to exist" (59). To recognize other-wise, to not exercise our desire to possess the other, is recognition of the self transferred onto things (58; le moi transporté par nous dans les choses). Weil acknowledges the difficulty of recognizing what one does not have; she states that such recognition causes "anguish equiv-alent to that which would be caused in reality by the loss of all loved beings" (86). Weil calls recognition of this order consent. It always falls short of or on this side of what one can accomplish; it comes out on the side of losing what one does not, in any case, really have. But how can having nothing underwrite our preservation of the other from harm?

TOWARD A DECREATIVE ETHICS

Weil argues that decreating the "I" must be understood as a creative act, one that might even be said to participate in divine creation. In Weil's religious metaphysics, the creative act of dispossession is mod-eled upon Creation, the Incarnation, and the Passion—each under-stood by Weil to be an abdication of God's power and consented withdrawal from the world.[43] Dispossession, then, would be both anterior to the self and the very structure of the self based on the model of creation, understood by Weil to be the supreme instance of dispossession. Consequently, dispossession would be the basis of all relationality, understood not on the model of possession but upon what must always, and finally, dispossess us. Creative power, as Weil describes it, is therefore an absence of power, if we understand that term to designate a force or capability. It implies a renunciation of power, and its very exercise (creation) is the withdrawal of plenitude or presence. To participate in this act of creation likewise requires one's withdrawal—a paradox that, if we follow Weil, is first sum-moned by the fissure between love and its object (so, between God and Himself and between God and creaturely life) and necessitated by divine creation (that is, God creating something other than Him-self). The decreated, then, is not on the side of being or having; it is on the side of absence, nakedness, and destitution, which Weil states is signified perfectly by our birth and death.[44] "In so far as I become nothing, God loves Himself through me," writes Weil (PG 84). Again, in her notebooks, Weil writes that God does not love "me," he only loves himself: "Creation is an act of love and it is perpetual. At every instant our existence is God's love for us. But God can only love Himself. His love for us is love for Himself through us. Thus, He who gives us being loves in us the consent to not being" (81).

If we place Weil's comments about disappearance in the context of the creation story, then God would provide the ultimate model and condition for both love and violence. If, however, the existence of the world represents the emptying of God's divinity from Himself and the Passion represents an "unspeakable wrenching in the soul at the separation of desire from its object" as acts of love, then it would seem that one is vanquished neither by love nor by the violence implied in decreation. If one consents to that form of love which is always anterior to one's person, and if that love is said to be "that which alone is exempt from force and which preserves him" (PS 24), then love for the other would respond to a specific need in the other to be preserved from harm. In this sense, love would not merely follow from a conception of a generalized absence of God but would be experienced precisely in the encounter with the other and the irreducibility and specificity of his needs. The universality of Weilian obligation, then, neither precludes nor undermines recognition of either the particularities of circumstance or the systemic structural inequalities that constitute a complex force field within which the human being lives. In his reading of Weil's conception of love and decreation, Rowan Williams writes, "What is to be loved is surely the absolute contingency, the mortality, of a person: the object freed from the future that our egotistical imagination longs to project, the object or person as radically vulnerable to destruction by time and chance."[45]

Weil does not conceive of the encounter with the other along easily configured lines. On a first reading it would appear that it is no encounter at all. In a perplexing set of meditations in Weil's notebooks, we read: "If I only knew how to disappear, there would be a perfect union of love between God and the earth I tread, the sea I hear . . ." (PG 94). It is not exactly that my presence is too large, but insofar as I am there at all, "I blemish the silence of heaven and earth by my breathing and the beating of my heart" (94). It is hard to read these statements without the suspicion that self-effacement is not also an act of massive self-violence. And there is perhaps no other way to read it, since one's encounter with the other is the scene of a violence that must be suppressed or redirected elsewhere. One response

to Weil's statement might be to argue that such violence can only produce a form of narcissism that feeds off of self-contraction. For if the
kind of love Weil imagines here demands that one cede one's power
and place for the sake of the other, and if, as we have seen, in love and
through love one must cease to "eat" the other, how does that not by
necessity produce an unbearable attrition?

But we must be wary here of too quick a response: the disappearance Weil writes of must be understood, I think, in the context of a
set of meditations on a form of violence that is, however seemingly
contradictory, an obligation to limit it. The limitation, I have been
arguing, is the limitation of violence and the limitation of the kind of
desire that makes the other the condition or the goal of one's desire.
Not of desire, as such, since love's energy issues from desire, and that
is a vital energy that one absolutely cannot do without. For Weil, to
act through love is of necessity to act through a form of passivity that
does not accomplish anything exactly, since what is produced from
passivity is nothing. Now to say as much does not mean that one acts
passively, or that this "nothing" is either annihilation or unreal. One
must act, but that act must proceed from the consent to being nothing. Again, that consent is nothing other than the consent to a certain
destitution: that of having nothing.

THE VULNERABILITY OF PRECIOUS THINGS

The other's vulnerability is the site of a relationality founded on the
subservience of the one obligated to the one it serves. Weil writes in
"La Personne et le sacré" that one is called to heed the cry of pained
surprise—a cry that can all too easily be reduced to a stammering
or even to oblivion but that always recalls a fundamental innocence.
One is interpellated by this cry, and it requires a response implicated
by this address. If the address presumes a relationship to the other, it
is defined by difficulty, even impossibility—indeed, animated as much
by an interdiction as it is by an obligation. With Weil we begin to
understand that when it happens, it is through a crushing vulnerability to injury and to failure. The impossibility lies not in its being
something that happens, for exposure is permanent, and one's obligation is unconditional. As we have seen, Weil goes further: she tells us
in L'Enracinement that it is the sole obligation relative to the human
that is not submitted to any condition. That this obligation remains
whether or not the cry has been heard—for the cry of the injured or

the one threatened with injury may be broken, unrecognizable, or even silent—might well testify to the duress of the one who cries, but it does nothing to mitigate one's obligation to the other. To return to that with which I began, the obligation is unconditional, even as it submits one to the profound and intractable contingency of the one undergoing suffering. The profound difficulty lies in the submission of the one who, in renouncing his "I" to the other, also exposes himself to vulnerability, failure, even to death.

That is how one is bound to the other, in the fragile passage of this offering that presumes a kind of failure: my relationship to the other is as much defined by what I cannot do as it is by what I must do. We might say, most simply, quoting Bracha Ettinger, that "failure is the measure of what has been recognized."[46] That resonates perfectly with what I think might be called a decreative ethics. We opened this chapter with Weil's statement that the "vulnerability of precious things is beautiful because vulnerability is a mark of existence." To recognize this vulnerability implies a failure, a failure that is even beautiful, but beautiful in that it cannot defend itself against the cry of the other. That is the ethical bind: that, bound to the other by an unconditional and unconditioned demand ("Why am I being harmed?"), one must nonetheless undergo and sustain an unconditioned desire defined by its unrealization and that presumes the destruction of one's "I." If we follow Weil, it is the only thing that one can offer.[47]

CHAPTER 2

Uncommon Measure

*"L'*Iliade *ou le poème de la force"*

The wretchedness of our condition subjects human nature to a moral form of gravity that is constantly pulling downward, toward evil, toward a total submission to force.

—Weil, *Réflexions sur les causes de la liberté et de l'oppression sociale*

The true hero, the true subject, the center of the *Iliad* is force. The force that men wield, the force that subdues men, in the face of which human flesh shrinks back.

—Weil, "*L'*Iliade ou le poème de la force"

Force has the power to transform a living human being into a thing, Simone Weil tells us bluntly in "L'*Iliade* ou le poème de la force."[1] It finds its apogee in war, where that dehumanization is made to seem natural through the operation of power that submits the weaker to the stronger. In a related essay, Weil notes: "One cannot even begin to form any clear ideas on the relationships between human beings as long as one has not put the notion of force at their very center."[2] Weil's comments in "La Personne et le sacré" detailing the effects of force upon human livability and injurability shed some initial light on the nature of those relationships. There Weil notes that wars are "intoxicating: they empty human lives of their reality and seem to turn people into puppets,"[3] a nod to Plato's allegory of the cave and the humans who are chained to the illusions they take to be real.[4] In the case of war, Weil argues that the greatest illusion is the belief that force can be "owned," especially when the tides of circumstance are in one's favor and one wields power for a time.

The operation of power—that it submits the weaker to the stronger; that it can be wielded—recalls a famous historical anecdote related by Thucydides to which Weil often referred in her

last writings and which heavily informed her argument in the
Iliad essay.[5] In his *History of the Peloponnesian War*, Thucydides
recounts the refusal of the small city of Melos to side with the
Athenians in their war with Sparta and the subsequent destruction of the city by the Athenians. Here is Weil's translation of the
Athenian response to the people of Melos who claim that the gods
would side with their just cause and protect them: "We only examine what is just when an equal necessity exists on both sides. Where
there is one who is strong and one who is weak, what is possible
is executed by the first and accepted by the second. . . . We believe
with regard to the gods, but we are certain with regard to men,
that always, by a necessity of nature, each one commands everywhere he has the power to do so."[6] Those are words that might just
have easily been spoken by Achilles. In "L'*Iliade* ou le Poème de la
force," Weil highlights Achilles's pitiless response to a young Trojan warrior begging for mercy at his feet:

> Come, friend, die also yourself! Why do you complain so?
> Patroclus too has died and he was a much better man than you.
> And I—do you not see how comely and tall I am?
> I am of noble lineage, my mother a goddess;
> but for me, too, there is death and a harsh destiny.
> There will come a dawn, or an evening, or a midday,
> when some warrior with his weapons will strip away my life,
>   too . . . (21.106–12)

The logic of the Athenian position seems to prevail in Achilles's
response, for Achilles is undoubtedly the stronger one, and the Trojan
will not be spared.

And yet, in acknowledging his own sure death at the hands of
another, Achilles recognizes the inability to ultimately master or
own force. It is a recognition of the superior strength of force as Weil
conceives of it here and throughout her writings: as an agent of the
regulative principle in the universe known in the Weilian idiom as
"necessity" composed of opposing tensions that tend toward equilibrium and immobility (Weil borrows from Heraclitus and Anaximander here), force has the capacity to immediately flatten or equalize
the relative power of humans—a totalizing effect that Weil characterizes as its "blindness" and "symmetry."[7] In Weil's reading of the
Iliad, then, it seems that force necessarily puts into question one's
capacity (pouvoir) and power (puissance). This, for Weil, is the basic
and sobering truth of the *Iliad*, that "every human being may at any

moment be compelled to submit to force," just as all are subjected to necessity without exception (PF 25).

"Such is the nature of force," Weil writes. "Its power to transform human beings into things is twofold and it cuts both ways; it petrifies differently but equally the souls of those who undergo it and those who ply it" (35).[8] Weil's remark that force leaves no one untouched—both those who wield power and those who must submit to it—suggests that the peculiar power of force is found additionally in its capacity to transform those affected by force into agents of force who, in turn, assume and redeploy it. That continuous redirection of force is aptly described by E. Jane Doering as "the self-perpetuating mechanism of force that catalyzes force in others."[9] And as we saw in chapter 1, that mechanism seeks to displace the suffering born of one's exposure to force and reflects the profound need for an essential equilibrium upset by the rupture of competing energies that comprise a complex force field.

In what may be the essay's most breathtaking claim, Weil writes, "Here is born the notion of a destiny under which executioners and their victims are similarly innocent: conquerors and conquered are brothers in the same misery" (31). That is an astonishing claim, to be sure. And we may understandably have serious reservations about the idea of a shared misery or similar innocence, especially when one party has inflicted harm or suffering upon the other, or is in a position to do so. But I would submit that it is precisely here, in this position of radically uneven power born of one's exposure to force, that the key to resisting the notion of commanding power everywhere might be found and a relationship to the other that does not seek to harm him might emerge. The dual and outwardly contradictory aspects of force—that it flattens the relative power of humans; that it is assumed and redeployed by those subjected to it—calls our attention to the terms of the relationship between those who wield force and those who are "vanquished" by it (Weil's term), both "brothers in the same misery."

The question for us, then, is how exactly this shared—but different—submission to force results in a new relationality, one that forfeits sovereign modes of power as expressed in the Thucydidean formula. Put simply, how might an equilibrium between unequal terms or forces be found? Is there a way to achieve equity or, failing that, find a common measure between unequal forces or incommensurable terms? Is there, in other words, a kind of "counterforce," one that does not partake in power, as such, but works precisely by the force of its weakness? I propose that the answer to this question of equilibrium might be found in the example of supplication, a relationship that initially appears to shore up rather than mediate between unequal terms. For supplication is itself an absurd mediation between two limit-terms of radically unequal power, and it does so through an absolute exposure of the two positions: the suppliant comes with nothing but the offer of his life, and the one supplicated has that life in his hands regardless of that offer. Supplication does not make the two terms commensurate—indeed, it maintains, even firms up the distinction of power between the suppliant and the one supplicated—but it acts *as if* an equilibrium or common measure were possible. That is what I would call its "uncommon measure." It is a way of reading Weil against herself, in a sense, if we accept Doering's claim that Weil's overriding question was how human beings might limit and equalize force in the context of their shared vulnerability.[10] For my approach does not seek to show how force might be limited, as such, but understands that claim to direct us to how a negative or weak force—one symbolized by the posture of the suppliant with nothing but the offering of his life—becomes a counterweight to a force that demands everything.

MORAL GRAVITY

"L'*Iliade* ou le poème de la force" opens with warriors struck down in battle, demonstrating the blindness and ubiquity of force, its downward propulsion, and its power to literally render "man into a thing" by turning him into a corpse. Time and again, the *Iliad* describes corpses dragged behind the chariots while the "unmastered" horses charge ahead without being steered. The transformation of men into things is evident in the first passage from the *Iliad* that Weil translates:

> . . . the horses
> made the swift chariots thunder along the paths of war
> in mourning for their blameless drivers. On the earth
> they lie, much dearer to the vultures than to their wives.
>   (11.159–62)

From the very outset Weil suggests that one's "own" force is not something that can stand up against a greater force that can strip one of one's power at any given moment.

There are the fallen men, and there are those who are dragged along the ground, trophies of battle for their killers.[11] The most spectacular instance of this is Achilles driving the slain Hector behind his chariot, mistreating the body again and again for twelve days.[12] It is one of the most haunting images of bodily exposure and degradation in the *Iliad*:

> Then, when he had yoked running horses under the chariot
> he would fasten Hektor behind the chariot, so as to drag him,
> and draw him three times around the tomb of Menoitios' fallen
> son, then rest again in his shelter, and throw down the dead
>   man
> and leave him to lie sprawled on his face in the dust.
> (24.14–18)[13]

Here Achilles still understands himself to wield force; his taking the reins of his horse and dragging the body of the defeated shows this in all its mercilessness. The act of dragging a human body as one would any other thing of no value or that could offer no resistance is part of the process of stripping that body of its human presence. Done for the moment, Achilles "throw(s) down the dead man and leave(s) him to lie sprawled on his face in the dust." A dead man can be treated as indiscriminately as a piece of meat—What indeed, asks Weil, distinguishes this human from a thing?[14]

But there is also the one who is not yet killed and dragged to the earth. In Weil's reading, the blood that darkens the earth and the warrior who treats another human being like inert matter are both metaphors for the descending movement of force. It is consistent with the analogy Weil makes elsewhere of the movement of force to the downward propulsion of gravity, a key concept in Weil's moral philosophy. Briefly put, Weil's conception of gravity transposes Newton's formulation with the idea of entropy, which describes energy transformations and the tendency for energy to "degrade" or become lower in quantitative value.[15] Weil uses gravity as an explanatory model: just as gravity is one of two forces that "reigns over the universe" (the other is light), Weil argues, "one must always expect things to happen in conformity with gravity."[16]

"All the *natural* movements of the soul," she continues, "are governed by laws analogous to those of physical gravity" (PG 41).[17] In other words, Weil employs the notion of physical gravity to illustrate a *moral* inclination or tendency to submit to force such that one's energies result in a similar "degradation"; the difference, of course, is that the qualitative value implicit in the degradation of energy in Weil's concept of moral gravity is entirely absent in the physical phenomenon of entropy. In the former, there are high values (the highest is toward the good) and low values (toward evil) associated with the "work" of energy. Specifically, Weil is interested in how the value of energy available to a human soul "degrades" until it is no longer capable of doing work specific to itself (that is, the work of thought).[18] By contrast, in the latter, there are neither positive nor negative values; there is simply more or less energy available for performing work. Ann Pirruccello notes that for Weil, however, "the "indication of value [in physical phenomena] points to a similar slide downward on an ontological scale." The passage is worth quoting at length:

> A place on the value scale corresponds to a kind of thing, and since entropy points away from the supreme good which is represented as a kind of thought and which represents ultimate reality, it must be interpreted as an attraction towards becoming what is furthest from that highest transcendent love and reality. For Weil, that furthest point is just inert physical matter neither capable of thought nor possessed of energy forming the conditions for thought or love in any but the most indirect and distant way. The mechanism accounting for this is called "gravity" by Weil. This is the case, apparently, because we comprehend physical gravity as a downward force, while Weil makes it clear throughout her writings that "upward" is the figurative direction of the Good which is the highest value and reality. Physical gravity thus becomes a symbol for a moral mechanism which makes human beings "devolve" toward the less perfect in thought or love, analogous to the way a satellite, fallen from its orbit, falls faster and faster until it becomes so hot that is burns up and is destroyed.[19]

According to Weil's theory, the effect of moral gravity determines what we can expect from others just as it determines what we receive from them. And so we might say that Hector submitted to death in the way he is (his dead body dragged along the ground behind Achilles's chariot) is the effect of a "moral gravity" in Achilles.

THE POWER TO REFUSE

The vanquished brought to their knees offers another picture of this descending movement: "They for their part, in danger of being reduced to nothing in an instant, imitate nonentity. Pushed, they fall; fallen, they lie on the ground, so long as chance does not prompt someone to raise them up" (PF 22). By contrast, those who feel invincible move and act without opposition or resistance. They rush forward (the spears plunging through the neck of the enemy; the throats of youth slit as "naturally" as flowers are cut for a tomb) or celebrate and rest in leisure. "He who possesses force moves in a frictionless environment," Weil writes; "nothing in the human matter around him puts an interval for reflection between impulse and action. Where reflection has no place, there is neither justice nor forethought" (27). Indeed, the strong and the weak do not appear to occupy the same space; they do not even appear to belong to the same species. And yet Weil insists that in the *Iliad* the sense of fear and invincibility goes through the *same* human depending on the tide of war and the favor of the gods—depending, that is, on a balance of power that affects everyone, just as all are, without exception, subjected to gravity.

Between one day and the next, however, the permanent vulnerability to force can be forgotten. Weil argues that for those who kill under force, thinking—specifically, the thought that arises in the "brief interval" between the sense of invincibility and the act of killing another—is severely diminished or impossible. "*Nothing* in the human matter around him puts an interval for reflection between impulse and action," writes Weil (27; Sans que *rien,* dans la matière humaine autour de lui, soit de nature à susciter entre l'élan et l'acte ce bref intervalle où se loge la pensée).[20] That is because there is nothing to resist or inhibit his course of action: the one who will die under his hands is someone who cannot influence the course his killer will take. He is diminished—"nothing"—or merely a part of a "frictionless environment" (un milieu non résistant). In other words, he who is effectively dead although he has not yet been killed has lost a quality basic to his humanity. He has lost his "indefinable influence of human presence," which inhibits the range of actions that another might otherwise have vis-à-vis his milieu: "Human beings around us have by their very presence a power, belonging only to them, to stop, to inhibit, to alter each action our body traces. . . . But this indefinable influence of human presence is not exerted by those whom a moment of impatience may rend from life before even a thought has time to condemn them to death. Before them, others move about as if they were not there" (22). Weil also comments, in a closely related essay on justice, on the inhibition issuing from the power of human presence:

> In other words, only obstacles set a rule or a limit for human action. These are the only realities with which it comes into contact. Matter imposes obstacles according to its own mechanisms. A man is capable of imposing obstacles by virtue of a power to refuse which he sometimes possesses, and sometimes not. When he does not possess it, he

constitutes no obstacle, and hence no limit either. From the point of view of the action and agent he simply does not exist. . . . Anything within the field of action which does not constitute an obstacle—as, for instance, men deprived of the power to refuse—is transparent for thought in the way completely clear glass is for sight. It has no power to stop, just as our eyes have no power to see the glass.[21]

In his reading of this passage, Peter Winch identifies the "power to stop, to inhibit, to alter" another's actions with "the power to refuse." When the other possesses that power, one hesitates upon being confronted with him (even if unreflectively) and pursues a course of action that seems called for by the encounter with the person who has effectively influenced what action is finally decided upon.[22] It is in that "indefinable" power that a person is said to inhibit or refuse the actions of another. Now this depends upon a basic condition, that one is recognized as human and so, as having the power of exerting that "human presence." In the context of those who, if they are not already reduced to "things," are said to "imitate nonentity" out of fear, what human presence can we say they bear? And in the scenes of supplication that Weil discusses in "L'*Iliade* ou le poème de la force"—where, to quote Blanchot, "the suppliant is not weaker or the weakest, he is so low he is utterly beyond reach"—what can we say of that power to refuse?[23]

BALANCING IT BY THE MIDDLE

Given the freedom of action of those for whom the balance of force is in their favor, the conceit of the warriors who are winning in battle is to think that they themselves wield force and that, in wielding power for the moment, they thereby control force. "They forget one detail: that all is not in their power," insists Weil (PF 29). They are blind to the circumstances that have brought them there, believing their position to be held by virtue of their own power. We might further say that they believe the freedom they enjoy to be unlimited (as against the laws of equilibrium) and so, also, free to act in this manner. But, asks Weil provocatively, would not the same be said of the vanquished if suddenly free? Would they not assume the posture of the strong just as easily and as unthinkingly?

In arguing that force is indifferent to the relative power exercised by humans, Weil suggests that force is also fundamentally indifferent to the one who suffers. Whether this indifference of force to the one who bears it through his affliction also entails a certain transposability of suffering is less clear. The following quotation is highly suggestive, but it does not offer any clear answer: "Such is the character of force. Its power to transform human beings into things is twofold and operates on two fronts; in equal but different ways, it petrifies the souls of those who undergo it and those who ply it" (35). Weil argues that force extends its "reign" through those under its constraints; they, in their turn, exercise these constraints through their actions and thoughts toward others—a kind of automatic displacement of energies intended to restore an essential equilibrium, which instead creates what Doering calls "the self-perpetuation of force." And yet, to say that neither power nor suffering can be owned and that under force both positions are provisional and transferable (so that the one in power might give place to one in suffering, and vice versa) is not quite the same thing as saying that this is a transposable relation. What is the relation of the one to the other? It is not only that one suffers; all suffer, as Weil's essay makes clear.

Moreover, in Weil's reading, suffering isolates and estranges one from all places. "The man who finds himself on all sides the weaker is solitary even in the heart of cities, even more solitary than the man lost in a desert," writes Weil (25). In this sense, I would say that there is no suffering that is exclusively one's own because suffering is precisely that which dispossesses the "I" of its self-possession. To say "my suffering" well indicates the inexpressibility of suffering or its always inadequate expression and suggests its exclusivity. But it is precisely that affliction estranges the self from its self, and it heightens, perhaps makes insurmountable, the distance of the "I" from the other, from all others. Suffering and so long as one is in suffering, one is doubly estranged, but neither can one get away. As the poet Edmond Jabès puts it: "Suffering is without place. When we say that its place is in us, we mean that we give pain a provisional place."[24] The one undergoing suffering hosts affliction, gives it a place within himself, while he is himself outside of any place—an estrangement represented for Weil most hauntingly in the scene of Hector, alone, outside the walls of Troy. One is away from one's home, an enduring metaphor for a primordial loss of protection and security. One is vulnerable to an outside, and in that defenselessness, it would seem that one is most alone. In this context of profound social, political, and moral disequilibrium—where one has been forcefully dispossessed from without and where one perpetuates force oneself—the idea of justice is difficult to fathom, unless it is to understand it as the prerogative of those who wield force for the time being. (That is the lesson of the Athenian Realpolitik in the incident cited by Thucydides.)

And yet, Weil insists with an unfailing persistence upon justice and a shared sense of suffering. Weil takes her cue for political justice from the idea of equilibrium, stating that "equilibrium alone destroys, cancels out force" (PG 262). Drawing from Greek science, Weil considers the dynamic equilibrium of forces, in their harmony and respect for limits, to comprise a kind of justice—a concept of justice she extends beyond material forces to include human beings and "social matter." In this, Weil follows Anaximander's definition regarding the regulation of competing energies: "Order is equilibrium and immobility. The universe, submissive to time, is a perpetual becoming. The energy which moves it is the principle of rupture of equilibrium. But, nevertheless, this becoming, composed of the ruptures of equilibrium, is in reality an equilibrium because the ruptures of equilibrium compensate each other."[25] That order, which Weil calls "necessity," is the regulative principle or the principle of regular order of the universe (Weil suggests that it is both). Force, as an agent of necessity, has the capacity to shift and transform the complex interaction of competing energies that compose what we might call, following Françoise Meltzer, its "force field."[26] And yet, force not only maintains energies in a dynamic equilibrium; it can also overextend the limits constitutive of the regular order of the universe, thereby jeopardizing its "justice." Pirruccello comments: "A model of necessity must reveal ever-present balance amidst the world of flux, a balance which suggests harmony or mediation. Moreover, according to the ancient view Weil adopts, the effects of material forces possess a tendency towards exceeding their spatio-temporal limits. These effects tend to expand in space and time further than is their due or limit according to necessity, and away from the conditions of balance and unity."[27] What, then, can put things back in balance?

We know from chapter 1 that the displacement of suffering in the search for equilibrium is not a solution. That process of transference merely redirects the effects of force rather than countering its tendency to exceed limits. A possible answer is found in book 8 of the *Iliad*, symbolized by Zeus's golden scales and characterized by Aeschylus thus: "The law protecting those whom force would crush merges with the law that holds the world in equilibrium and whose symbol is the scales of Zeus."[28] At the highest point of Mount Ida, Zeus surveys the human drama below with an empirical eye until noon, "when the sun god stood bestriding the middle heaven." He then "balanced his golden scales, and in them he set two fateful portions of death . . . and balanced it by middle" (8.68–72).[29] As Maurice Blanchot puts it, following René Schaerer's reading of the scene, the notion of justice issues from "an essentially unstable composition of two differences," the one horizontal, represented by the arms of the balance, and the other, the vertical line of the divine gaze.[30] To balance it "by the middle" requires finding that central point between the two axes: the one, in which fates are poured out according to common measure; the other, emanating from the one set completely apart (the divine), in which fates are judged by a terrifying impartiality, represented by the image of the two urns "positioned at the threshold of Zeus, where are held the gifts he grants, the one sort bad, the other good" (24.527–28).[31] The point for Weil is that both urns are poured out according to a divine justice, "raised up by the middle," to quote Blanchot again.[32] The symmetry of the two is not to be found in an equity of force, for Zeus's decisive action happens at a moment when the two sides are already "exactly equal."[33] It is rather in the dynamic equilibrium of an absolute difference—an uncommon measure, we might say—that we can speak of the blind symmetry of forces.

How might this concept of divine justice be enacted by humans, given our susceptibility to moral gravity and the tendency of human energy (specifically, desire) to exceed limits and so, to disrupt equilibrium? It is a question that preoccupied much of Weil's thinking, particularly in the late essays on war. A possible answer to that question, I think, is suggested in the central encounter of the *Iliad*, the scene of supplication between Achilles and Priam, and it will be the focus of the discussion below.

SPEECH OR DEATH

In her notebooks Weil writes, "the attitude of supplication" is that "I must necessarily turn to something other than myself since it is a matter of being delivered from oneself" (PG 44). This characterization may at first seem at odds with those suppliants cited in Weil's essay on the *Iliad*. For it seems that they do not free themselves but are helplessly delivered over to the other through their act of supplication. In other words, it seems that one is bound to the other through supplication, although, to be sure, that bind is a peculiar one: for one delivers oneself over to another who may or may not dispense with one's life. Here is Hector at the mercy of Achilles: "I beg you by your life, by your knees, by your parents" (22.338). Weil tells us that Hector's supplications are "in vain." More devastating is her assessment that they only appear to increase the triumph of the victor. But such triumph is bitterly short-lived, as we have seen in Achilles's response to Lyocaon, who is begging for his life:

> Come, friend, die also yourself! Why do you complain so?
> Patroclus too has died and he was a much better man than you.
> And I—do you not see how comely and tall I am?
> I am of noble lineage, my mother a goddess;
> but for me, too, there is death and a harsh destiny.
> There will come a dawn, or an evening, or a midday,
> when some warrior with his weapons will strip away my life,
>   too . . . (21.106–12)

This is one of the most breathtaking passages Weil translates from the *Iliad*. It problematizes the relationship between the one who suffers and the one who has the power, however provisionally, to make him suffer. We see that it is possible to say to another, as Achilles does of his beloved Patrocles: "But he was better than you, and you live on." Achilles's ruthlessness may not surprise us here, but his acknowledgment of his *own* certain death at the hands of another is important. It reminds us of another of Weil's favorite passages from the *Iliad*: "However, that these things should have happened, accept them despite our pain / And our hearts in our chests, submit them to necessity" (18.112–13).

In each instance of supplication highlighted in Weil's essay, the suppliant is alone with the one who can either take or spare his life. The suppliant's petition is devastatingly simple: *I beg you by your life, by your parents, at your knees.* But insofar as it is addressed to the other, the petition engages each one—both the suppliant and the one supplicated—to go beyond himself in order to heed the other. The "power to refuse," then, implicates both the suppliant and the one supplicated: the suppliant implicated through exposure, the other as the culminating figure of this exposure. In this sense, the one supplicated is witness to the exposure such that he cannot extricate himself from the unwanted responsibility that that entails. Equally, but not in equitable power, the suppliant's life is tied to the other's by virtue of his power to spare that life. Their lives are further enjoined to the invisible but conjured Other—the divine Other, to be sure, in whose name and under whose auspices of power the suppliant dares to speak. More than that—and with a powerlessness from which he curiously draws his strength—the suppliant also speaks in the name of all the others, those whose impossible presence (for they are not there or cannot be there and as such, are figures of divine transcendence through their very absence) the supplication also invokes. And so, when Priam addresses Achilles "in the words of a suppliant," it is by invoking such a figure: "Achilleus like the gods, remember your father" (24.485).[34]

The chapter begins with the gods debating whether Hector's corpse should be returned to the people of Troy. While there is some intercession on the part of the gods, in the end it is Priam alone who must go retrieve the body of his son from his enemy.[35] Not unimportantly, Hector's corpse is the image of exposure: he is left to rot outside, food for vultures.[36] Weil's translation begins where Priam's speech has ended:

> He spoke. The other, thinking of his father, desired to weep;
> Taking him by the arm, he pushed the old man away a little.
> Both were remembering, one Hector slayer of men,
> And he huddled in tears at Achilles' feet, against the earth;
> But Achilles wept for his father and then too for
> Patroclus; their sobbing filled the hut. (24.507–12)

Priam's speech moves Achilles to tears. Priam, there to claim his son's body so that this last might be given a proper burial, reminds Achilles of his own father. Weil's translation of the Greek text begins with the one who speaks and who, in speaking, makes a claim that could not reasonably be made given the balance of power. Weil does not give us the content of the claim, although as readers of the *Iliad* it can go unmentioned for Weil's analysis.[37] *He spoke.* There is a sublime economy to these words that surpass narrative description. "He spoke" goes through the terrible risk of death for Priam. By divine favor Priam made it across the Achaean camps, but what can protect him now, alone and vulnerable to the great Achilles?

Again: Priam is alone, and he speaks. "What, then, finally gives him a chance?" asks Blanchot, referring more broadly to the relative positions of the suppliant and the one supplicated. Blanchot answers: "It is the fact that he speaks. The suppliant is, par excellence, the one who speaks." It is the particular mystery of the suppliant—a lowly and debased being, "so low that he is beyond reach"[38]—at the knees of the one supplicated, that he would, in this radically unequal posture and power, still come to the other and address him. If the suppliant comes to the other with nothing other than his lowliness and his speech, how can we begin to understand this encounter, especially as Blanchot describes it, as a face-to-face (vis-à-vis)?

Blanchot, quoting Edmond Beaujon, reminds us in his essay "La Mesure, le suppliant" that "suppliant" is translated from the Greek word meaning "he who comes."[39] In the case of Priam, he leaves his home and crosses the threshold of another man's home. He comes alone, dispossessed of his son and soon, we know, of his home. He comes to Achilles not as a king but as a stranger. And in his crossing the threshold and his absence of protection, he passes a boundary in a double sense. He is "separated from all force. . . . The suppliant and the stranger are one; both are cut off from the whole."[40] Or, returning to Weil's essay, as a suppliant, Priam is "nakedly exposed to sorrow, without the armor of power that had shielded [his] soul, with nothing to separate [him] any longer from tears" (PF 28). He is unprotected and without protection (that is, he does not *have* anything and he is *outside* anything that would tip the balance of power), and he speaks. He speaks in his powerlessness, and Achilles responds in his power. That is as it can only be: the fact of the address does not change their relative power. Blanchot goes further: "It is a matter of firmly establishing the fact of inequality, and even more, the fact that there is no common measure between the two limit-terms facing each other."[41] Priam speaks at the knees of another who at any moment may kill him; that vulnerability does not change regardless of Achilles's decision. His "I will not kill you" is always in the context that he can; that is what the suppliant and the one supplicated both know with a certainty.[42] It aligns with Weil's stunning description of this posture: "The act of kneeling. Supplex et supplicium. To kneel is to offer oneself for whipping, beheading, or any punishment; it is to place oneself most conveniently for the sword" (OC, i/4 114).

Recalling "the power to refuse," Winch offers a compelling reading of Weilian supplication. But it is one with which I ultimately disagree:

[Weil] means something like this, perhaps: that sometimes one is in a position where one's refusal is seriously taken notice of by others and sometimes not. Thus Priam, because defeated and completely in the power of the Greeks, no longer has the power to refuse. That means that nobody is going to take any notice of anything he says. But it *also* means—and this is important to Simone Weil's discussion—that he himself will no longer attempt either to give or withhold consent. His falling on his knees is not an expression of consent; it is an

acknowledgement of the fact that he is no longer in a position to give
or withhold it."[43]

By contrast, I would suggest that although the suppliant is at the
mercy of another's power, he preserves a power conferred precisely
by the lowness of his position. It is a "weak" power, to be sure; it has
no power to kill or transform the relations of force, as we have seen.
And, indeed, he is in no position to give or withhold much of anything. But he does preserve his ability to consent *through* his subjection to "necessity" (understood in the Weilian sense). The suppliant,
in other words, is not "inert matter"; he is not a "thing" at the knees
of another. He speaks, and the force of that weak speech is the force
of his offering itself: a life that is *already* at the mercy of the other,
regardless. That is the audacity of his offering and the absurdity of
what he affirms in his supplications.

Again: *He spoke.* Although the suppliant's speech does not over-
turn the relative power between the two limit-terms, so long as he
speaks we know he is not dead, although he is so low that he can
only be counted as "separate." Yet he bears his human presence in
his speech in a way that might not be otherwise possible. Blanchot's
comments in this regard are illuminating: "Through speech, he, the
very low, is in relation to the very high and, without breaking down
the distance, makes his powerful interlocutor enter into a space they
do not yet have in common but that is between-them. This between-
two (empty and sacred) is the very space of the middle, the mysterious "median thing." . . . [It is] speech attending the invisible."[44] In
attending the invisible, supplication invokes the invisible presence of
the other human being (l'autrui) who bears the trace of the divine.
Indeed, he speaks, and it is for the one who in his death cannot speak.
And unable to grieve (unburied and, so, in a state of suspension, Hector cannot be properly mourned), Priam is twice dispossessed of son.
His own demand to Achilles is an empty one: he speaks for the other
(Hector) and for all the others who cannot be there with him (his
kinsmen). So it is the other (the other who is no longer even present
or who is only present in his infinite absence) who makes the demand
upon Priam to dare to speak in his name. When Priam speaks it is so
he might be in "a silent conversation between one who mourns and
one whom is mourned"[45]—a conversation such as it is elaborated by
Blanchot as an "entre-tien," a holding or preservation of speech that
is a between-speech, that cannot be shared (in the sense of common-
ality) because the other's death has excluded that possibility. But the

other's death that eludes one (in that death is ultimately not shareable) holds that self, maintains it in the present of infinite dispossession.

That is the gift of the one who in his death offers something that he could not offer in his life and that he cannot ever give himself in his own death. Blanchot writes that in such a conversation one shares "the solitude of the event which seems to be the possibility that is most his own and his unshareable possession in that it dispossesses him radically."[46] In other words, the death of the Other is simultaneously what is proper to him (it is never "my" death and, as such, excludes me), but insofar as death can never be experienced as such (it excludes the possibility of the experience) it exceeds any mastery. Thus, what is properly one's "own" is precisely that which dispossesses the self. One is maintained only in this infinite dispossession; it is the only possibility of a now (maintenant) since one's own death is precisely that which cannot be experienced in the present. And it is the fact of being exposed to the death of other (and so, his finite existence) that makes this possible. In his essay on Blanchot's *La Communauté inavouable*, Joseph Slugia calls this incongruent possibility the "impossible experience" of death, and it is arguably at the center of all supplication.

Priam's supplications to Achilles only heighten the operation of this "impossible" experience. Priam is begging not only for his own life but for his son's "life" (since, according to Greek custom, Hector's death is suspended without proper burial; Hector "lies yet forlorn" [24.554]).[47] It suggests that in supplication the one who speaks does not speak for his life, or even for the life of the other, but so that the death of the other might be recognized. That his speaking is a *speaking for* is precisely the form his relation to the other takes and that opens oneself up to the other's death. To be sure, Priam has come to Achilles loaded with gifts, but it is finally his own life that he is ransoming for his son's—a wild economy (ransoms are always the pretense of an "exchange") given that for the one supplicated it is not a choice between the one life and the other. Before Achilles releases the body, he accepts the ransom from Priam, "innumerable spoils for the head of Hektor" (24.579), then addresses his beloved Patrocles, killed by Hector: "Be not angry with me, Patroklos, if you discover, though you be in the house of Hades, that I gave back great Hektor to his loved father, for the ransom he gave me was not unworthy. I will give you your share of the spoils, as much as is fitting" (24.592–95). On a quick reading it appears that the ransom has put things back in balance, for as great as Hector is said to be, so, too, the gifts are deemed "not unworthy." But what I would like to suggest instead is that Achilles's pledge to the memory of Patrocles is not of an equitable exchange (the return of his killer in exchange for a share of the spoils) but of an offering that illustrates the wild economy of supplication itself: that is, an affirmation of total difference between the one who comes with only his speech or his death and the other who might acknowledge the first or cause the second. In this respect, the lavish gifts that Priam bestows are merely the symbol of the gulf that separates the two. It is also an economy that recalls the substitution of the other's death for one's own as the only one that can be experienced, whether or not one kills or is killed.

After Priam speaks, we are told that Achilles, "thinking of his father, desired to weep" (songeant à son père, désira le pleurer). What emerges between what is spoken and the other who, in his infinite absence, cannot be addressed as such? Weil translates the Greek as "songer"—a word that does not exactly mean to think or to dream but that means something in between. So this word that is neither to think nor to dream is the word that binds Priam's speech to Achilles's own father. In other words, something comes to intercede, and the intercession is at the threshold of what cannot be done and what must be done, and of what cannot be spoken and is said nonetheless. In this way, "songer" names the threshold between thinking and the unthinkable act of supplication in which one knowingly puts oneself in the easiest position to be killed. Separate, and yet both Priam and Achilles cry, each for their "own."

Yet, no word or intercession of the gods, no heart or strength, can prevent Priam's fear in the face of the great Achilles. For it is Achilles who, knowing in advance that Priam would come to ask for the body of Hector and having already "agreed" to the return out of respect for the gods, must still grant that to Priam in their meeting. Of all the power at his disposal, the one most required in this encounter is that which would allow Achilles to recognize Priam's "human presence." By contrast, the only thing required of Priam is to consent to the likelihood that vis-à-vis Achilles, he bears no such presence. We know that Achilles pushes Priam. It is not a strong push, but for one brought to such misery, Weil argues, anything can reduce him to nothing, a word or even a look can do this. Here is her commentary on the scene: "Not through insensitivity does Achilles push to the ground the old man clutching his knees; the words of Priam, calling to Achilles' mind his own father, have moved him to tears. He simply finds himself as uninhibited in his attitudes and actions as if, instead of a suppliant, an inanimate object had touched his knees" (PF 22). Commentators have noted the infelicity of Weil's reading here; the *Iliad* tells us that it is a gentle push and that Achilles is full of pity for Priam. But such an objection misses the more profound point that Weil is trying to make here, one that is still surely faithful, since it recognizes the notion of an absolute difference maintained in supplication.

In Weil's description, Achilles pushes Priam to the ground as one who pushes a thing to the earth, "as if he were not a suppliant." That qualification is important, and here Weil's reading suggests that even the sacredness of the suppliant may not be honored when a certain limit has been exceeded, equilibrium has been disrupted (the equilibrium that the "middle space" of supplication is supposed to ensure), and moral gravity has taken hold. Indeed, Priam goes too far in his supplications when, soon after invoking the gods, he asks Achilles to no longer delay returning Hector's body (24.553–58). Achilles's reply leaves no doubt of Priam's audacity, "you must not further make my spirit move in my sorrows, for fear, old sir, I might not let you alone in my shelter, suppliant as you are" (24.568–70).[48] Another way to put it, recalling our earlier discussion of justice, might be that the middle point of "an essentially unstable composition of two differences" has given way to supplication's far side: an either-or that admits no such mediation or harmony between unlike terms. It's *speech or death*, says Blanchot. And Priam, we know, has said as much as he can. And to grant the suppliant's request (as Achilles ultimately does) does nothing to eviscerate the inequality that sets them apart but that also binds one to the other—even though that other is one's enemy.

UNCOMMON MEASURE

That bind is illustrated in the most quietly extraordinary moment in this scene of supplication. After the body has been ransomed and prepared for its homecoming, Achilles invites Priam to share a meal with him, recalling the story of the grieving Niobe, who, exhausted from crying, also eats. Here is the passage, as translated by Weil:

> Since even Niobe of the lovely locks thought to eat,
> she whose twelve children perished in her home,
> six sons and six daughters in the bloom of their youth.
> Apollo slew the boys with his silver bow

in his wrath against Niobe; Artemis who loves the arrows slew
   the maidens.
All because she had likened herself to fair-cheeked Leto,
saying "she has two children; I, I have borne many."
And those two, though they were only two, had made all the
   others die.
Nine days they lay in death; no one came
to bury them. The people had become stones by the will of
   Zeus.
And on the tenth day, they were buried by the gods of heaven.
But she thought to eat, when she grew tired of tears. (24.602–
   13)

Weil's commentary immediately following the passage relates the suffering particular to the death of a beloved to the loss of one's "inner
life":

Such is the realm of force: this realm extends as far as that of nature.
Nature also, when essential needs come into play, effaces inner life
and even the grief of a mother.
   No one has ever described with such bitterness the misery of man,
which renders him unable even to comprehend his misery.
   Force wielded by others dominates the soul like an excessive
hunger, since it comprises an unending power of life and death. (PF
24–25)

Weil is clear: force dispossesses one of that which seems to be one's
ownmost (one's children, one's inner life). In its seemingly limitless
capacity and scope, force is said to dominate, take, and eviscerate.
There is no indication that something comes to fill in for the resulting emptiness or even that such an emptiness can be comprehended.
Nonetheless, it seems that the emptiness is still the site of a desire for
something that would come to fill it, even if it is felt despite oneself
and against one's capacity. For the one who has lost everything is still
subject to an outside that does not cease to enter him in the form of
force and need.
   That is how hunger enters here, and it pits one's moral life (here:
the capacity for grief) against the inevitability of necessity. Throughout her writings, Weil frequently cites the myth of Niobe, who,
defeated by hunger, must submit to necessity. "Those moments when
one is compelled to look on mere existence as the sole end represent
total, unmixed horror," is how Weil characterizes such submission.
She continues: "'Niobe also, of the beautiful hair, thought of eating.' That is sublime, in the same way as space in the frescoes of

Giotto. A humiliation which forces one to renounce even despair."[49] In his commentary on Weil's reading of the passage, James Holoka writes, "Despite Niobe's love for her children and her psychic turmoil, she could evade nature's appetitive processes no more than she could defeat death to save their lives."[50] The mother who eats despite her sorrow is the one whose very love is rendered inconsequential. It is not that in eating she has ceased to love. It is rather that necessity renders that capacity secondary, even useless.

Elsewhere Weil states that Niobe's fault does not lie in the audacity of a claim to surpass the gods but in the fact of counting her children—a statement that becomes suggestive in the context of the scene of supplication in which the story is recalled. Niobe counts her children, and the punishment for her boast is the death of those children. Scholars have noted the similarity between Priam and Niobe as it is told in the *Iliad*.[51] Both have had their children taken from them, and for days they are left unburied. The trajectory of their stories moves from a model of self based upon possession to one based upon having nothing. Niobe's response to the loss of her children suggests more than a dispossession from without; it suggests a radical form of destitution, not the least of which tears and hunger, in their marking the threshold of pain and livability, are perhaps its most vivid manifestations.

Weil likewise describes the meal between Achilles and King Priam as marking such a threshold, circumscribed by loss and necessity. "And now, let us not forget to eat," says Achilles, recalling Priam to the level of need. "Sublime words," Blanchot says very simply.[52] The meal is literally an instance of incorporation, but does it make the two enemies any less strangers to each other? We know that it does not; they remain enemies, and the destruction will continue. The fundamental inequality that characterizes the relationship of the suppliant to the one supplicated is maintained, even strengthened by this meal. Blanchot writes that there is no common measure between them, but I think this shared meal also begs us to consider the limits that chiasmically bind the two together. Those limits are here given in the form of need; eating, in this regard, is a submission of both men (*all* men, says Weil) to a hard necessity that conjoins the two by virtue of that shared submission. It is a moment when relative power is confounded; it is where force is unquestionably the "true hero" of the narrative.

And what do we make of the fact of its being recalled in the form of a *story* framing the shared meal? I want to suggest that the story does not just frame the shared meal, but that, in a sense, it becomes the very substance of that encounter. Here, at this sublime juncture where the story told is (the same as) the event of telling it, is where desire and necessity meet in "the most terrible, the most beautiful" convergence.[53] "And now, let us not forget to eat," says Achilles, commencing the story. So it seems that at the middle point—that measure that we have said holds the difference of two opposing terms—we find language. What Blanchot writes about Simone Weil is just as true here: "Language is the place of attention." And attention, Weil tells us, breaks through the monotony of force and the downward propulsion of moral gravity.

THIS BRIEF MOMENT, LUMINOUS

There is a time when Hector must face his death at the hands of Achilles. All alone and outside the walls of Troy, Hector is, in Weil's reading, "awaiting death and trying to brace his soul to face it" (PF 30). Weil calls this moment "luminous." Here is her translation of the scene:

> Alas! if I go behind the gate and the rampart,
> Polydamas will straightaway shame me . . .
> Now that I have lost my men through folly,
> I fear the Trojans and the Trojan women in their trailing robes,
> and I dread to hear it said by those less brave than I:
> "Hector, overconfident in his strength, has destroyed his coun-
>   try."
> . . . Yet if I were to put down my curved shield,
> my good helmet, and, leaning my spear on the rampart,
> if I were to go to meet famed Achilles? . . .
> But why does my heart counsel me such counsels?
> I will not approach him; he would have no pity,
> no respect; he would slay me, if I were thus exposed,
> like a woman . . . (22.99–100, 104–7, 111–13, 122–25)

Weil notes that "Hector evades none of the pain and shame that befall the luckless. Alone, stripped of all the prestige of force, the courage that kept him outside the walls does not keep him from fleeing" (30). Weil's translation continues:

> Hector, at the sight of him, was seized by trembling. He could
>   not steel himself to stand firm . . .
> . . . It is not for a ewe or an ox hide
> that they struggle, the usual race-prizes;

> it is for a life that they run, that of Hector, breaker of horses.
> (22.136–37, 159–61)

What good is Hector's legendary strength against another who is not only stronger but single-mindedly driven to avenge the death of a beloved? There is the fact of being outside the walls of one's home: it is the symbol of one's separation. It is also a succinct picture of what it is to be exposed and vulnerable to the outside. In such a state of displacement where the boundary of protection has been effectively eviscerated (Hector cannot by this point turn back), the soul recoils—what can make such a soul face its death? For death is certain, but to *await* one's own death is to be without all and any certainty. Recalling our earlier discussion of Blanchot, one's own death is precisely that which cannot be experienced. Death that takes place outside the walls of one's home situates one in a certain position vis-à-vis death. To face one's death—to be so "resolved"—is, paradoxically, as much an open vulnerability as it is to take the part in what is already yours. To be "resolved," in this sense, is outside of any notion of self-sufficiency or capability, something that Hector ultimately acknowledges after the barrage of self-questioning.

Trembling and stripped of even the prestige of power, and yet, Weil tells us, Hector is a man "facing" his death. The facing breaks through the monotony of affliction and the totality of force; it is but a brief instant, "soon lost under the empire of force":

> A tedious gloom would ensue were there not scattered here and there
> some moments of illumination—fleeting and sublime moments when
> men possess a soul. The soul thus roused for an instant, soon to be
> lost in the empire of force, wakes innocent and unmarred; no ambig-
> uous, complex, or anxious feeling appears in it; courage and love
> alone have a place there. Sometimes a man discovers his soul during
> self-deliberation, when he tries, like Hector before Troy, to confront
> his fate all alone, unaided by gods or men. Other moments when men
> discover their souls are moments of love. (36–37)

Something happens in this brief moment—Weil calls it "luminous"—that is unlike the relentless monotony of force. As with the body bending in supplication, it seems that the one facing his death is without protection, "unaided by gods or men." What prevents the soul from being crushed or torn apart? The answer would seem to lie in the soul's "resolve": the moment when the soul is still. Its stillness is first imposed from outside, for the soul is still subject to necessity and to force. But it is in its awaiting death—first, in its recognition of the reality of things as they are, unadorned by the imagination, the soul consents to the force that will result in death; second, in the knowledge that one's own death is precisely that which can never be experienced in the present—that a different kind of stillness emerges.[54] It is how the soul under force does not also succumb to a moral gravity; through one's consent to limits, force's descending movement is interrupted, even if only "briefly." This consent, where one consents to one's ultimate dispossession ("one's" death, "all alone"), is to descend "by a movement where moral gravity has no part" (PG 44). Weil writes that it is in this self-dispossession, so unlike being forcefully dispossessed from without, that one finds one's soul.[55]

SANS RIEN

Weil writes of those subjected to force: "They are nakedly exposed to affliction, without the armor of power that had shielded their soul, without anything [sans rien] to separate them any longer from tears" (PF 28).[56] In this sense, tears are not simply an affective response to force but, more exactly, mark a state of dispossession. That forced dispossession, we have seen, is such that one no longer exerts what Weil calls the "indefinable influence of human presence" that would make others respond to one differently than they would to a thing (22). Of such a person, Weil writes: "He is living, he has a soul; he is nonetheless a thing. Strange being—a thing with a soul; strange situation for the soul. . . . That a human being should be a thing is a logical contradiction; but when the impossible has become a reality, the contradiction lacerates the soul" (20, 23). A person's soul under these conditions is torn; to return to our earlier quotation, he is without anything (sans rien) that might separate him from tears. It seems, then, that there is something about tears that exceeds our customary understanding of them as an expression of suffering or of one's experience of pain in suffering. In Weil's description, tears are situated on the other side of a protective boundary that has been surpassed or obliterated.

If, as we have been saying, force exposes one to affliction and if it brings one outside oneself by virtue of that exposure, is one also brought inexorably to a relationship with the other human being (l'autrui)? Weil's reading of the Iliad underscores this quandary: under conditions of force one is exposed to an outside and yet, in its extreme manifestation, force leaves one too debased, a "living thing" seemingly incapable of having a relation to the other, a "strange being" even to oneself.[57]

And yet, if it is true that one is "nakedly exposed" to force, it is perhaps also true that such exposure becomes a certain opening to the other. The kind of opening I am thinking of here comes from Emmanuel Levinas: "The opening is the baring of skin exposed to injury and to violation. The opening is the vulnerability of the skin offered in its violation and injury, beyond all that can be shown, beyond all that can, from the essence of being, be exposed to comprehension and celebration."[58] Can we also say that tears of exposure are a kind of offering to the other, of and through that very exposure? The offering, constituted in the first place by the opening (itself a site of injury or injurability), conjures another to whom the offering is made. We can go further in saying, following Levinasian thought, that the baring of the skin is an invitation to be taken up by the other, even though, as we have seen, the other vis-à-vis the one thus exposed is someone who can harm, even kill.

We have seen Weil's stunning example of that posture in her definition of supplication: "The act of kneeling. Supplex et supplicium. To kneel is to offer oneself [se présenter] for whipping, beheading, or any punishment; it is to place oneself most conveniently for the sword" (OC, vi/4 114). Upon this view, exposure is not solely an impingement from without but a raw openness at the very site of one's limits or boundaries. Both Levinas and Weil describe the posture of the one thus exposed as an offering. And for the one without anything to protect his soul but the very tears that mark this loss of protection, the only offering he can make is his being "without anything" (sans rien)—an equation that is perplexing, even absurd. It is the puzzle of offering nothing (one's being without anything) as a counterweight to a power that might be characterized as demanding everything (one's life).

Like gravity, force brings all things down; it spares no one and is reiterated by humans in the form of moral gravity. Under what power is one able to rise against it? "We have no power of rising," Weil writes. "We have only the power of lowering. That is why to lower oneself is the only way of rising" (CS 58). Lowering oneself is not constituted by any power one has at one's disposal but by one's human presence laid bare. Such is the one who is alone, facing death. As is the suppliant, whose bent back embodies the descending movement of gravity and who, in his absolute exposure, establishes the relation of necessity between the one who can kill and the one who can be killed. Weil writes that his heart is "frozen" by the immanent contact with death (44). And yet, in offering himself to death, the suppliant "puts oneself near that which gives life" (OC, vi/4 114). Without changing the relations of necessity, supplication establishes an uncommon measure between the two limit-terms facing each other: the suppliant challenges the one supplicated to pity him and so, also, to refuse the force of moral gravity.

CHAPTER 3

Stillness and the Bond of Love

Venise sauvée

> And what happens in his soul remains mysterious.
>
> —Weil's notes to *Venise sauvée*

> As soon as Jaffier recognizes that Venice *exists* . . . To believe that something exists and to destroy it, there has to be a truly imperious duty.
>
> —Weil's notes to *Venise sauvée*

Simone Weil's notes to *Venise sauvée* offer a snapshot of the play's movement:[1]

> In the 1st act, a single rhythm—the momentum of the con-
> spiracy.
> In the 2nd, two—this momentum and Jaffier's stillness.
> In the 3rd, stillness. (18)

The first act sets up the political intrigue of the play and introduces its main characters and their stake in the conspiracy of the Spanish Empire to overtake the independent city of Venice.[2] The conspirators are composed of officers and mercenaries who live and work in Venice without enjoying the rights of citizenship; their homelands having been absorbed into the Spanish Empire, they are permanently uprooted (déracinés). They include Renaud, driven by the prospect of political and personal glory; Pierre, military leader of the conspiracy; and Jaffier, Pierre's best friend. On the side of Venice are the Secretary of the Council of Ten and his daughter, Violetta, symbol of Venice's beauty and innocence. The Machiavellian prowess of Renaud is counterpoised from the outset to the disinterest and political detachment of Jaffier, who has joined the conspiracy purely out of friendship for Pierre. The second act introduces a counterpace to the exalted mood of the first act. There is a slowing down of the play, but it is not exactly situated at the level of plot. Something enters suddenly

and wordlessly toward the end of the first act and continues its presence in the second; it cannot quite be marked, save for a change in the
expression of Jaffier's face upon hearing Renaud's rallying speech to
the soldiers encouraging a merciless sacking of Venice. Renaud notes
the change in Jaffier's face, perceives it to be a sign of fear, and tells
Pierre that Jaffier must be killed to ensure the success of their plans.
Pierre, of course, vouches for his friend and calls upon the additional
testimony of officers concerning Jaffier's ability and integrity. He even
campaigns successfully for Jaffier to assume his leadership when he
is called away unexpectedly for official business by Venice's Council
on the eve of the planned overthrow. In the end, however, the plot is
unsuccessful, Jaffier having decided out of pity for the city to tell the
Council in exchange for his friends' lives. They are nonetheless tortured and executed, and Jaffier, the only one spared, throws himself
into sure death. Dawn rises upon the fair city saved from destruction.

The play hinges upon the exercise of force yet ends with the preservation of Venice. The one who "saves" Venice is no hero in the
banal sense of the term: in saving Venice, Jaffier betrays his friends
and sends them to their deaths. In the eyes of Venetians like Bassio,
he is "a thousand times more odious because he also betrayed his
accomplices, his own friends" (105). But Jaffier is the play's hero in
the tragic sense—something that the Secretary, despite everything,
recognizes to the end in maintaining Jaffier's "great courage, impetu-
ousness and pride" (104). Weil calls Jaffier's decision his "resolve," a
term that evokes the freedom fundamental to both his determination
to save Venice and his recognition of its reality, which precipitates
that determination—a recognition (anagnôrisis) that is tragic in Aristotelian terms so far as it is "a change from ignorance to awareness of
a bond of love or hate."[3] What Weil writes in "*L'Iliade* ou le poème de
la force" resonates here: "Sometimes a man discovers his soul during
self-deliberation, when he tries, like Hector before Troy, to confront
his fate all alone, unaided by gods or men. Other moments when men
discover their souls are moments of love."[4] Surely Jaffier represents
this other moment of the soul's discovery.

That awareness of the bond of love, emerging out of the recognition of what really exists, is tragic because in it Jaffier must encounter the limitations of that love to accomplish all that it set out to do.
Unable to save both Venice and his friends, Jaffier wishes for nothing but his own death. "The pain, shame, and death that one does
not wish to inflict upon others falls upon oneself," writes Weil in her

notes to *Venise sauvée* (15). It is a succinct statement of what Jaffier suffers as a result of the limitations of human love against what surpasses its power and so, of all it cannot do. Of course, to say as much speaks to power in its social and political incarnations; it is central to the development of the plot and is surely that against which Jaffier must weigh his actions. But the limitations of Jaffier's love are also in the bond itself—the one that binds him to his friends while making him responsible for their welfare beyond his capacity. It is certain he wants to save his friends and never does he ask that his own life be spared as well. What is doubtful is that he can do this against the competing obligation to prevent the destruction of Venice.

"Out of pity, I renounced everything in order to spare [Venice]. . . . The power that I had, pity forced me give it up" (115; 120), says Jaffier, a captive at this point in the play, waiting to be escorted out of Venice. To spare (épargner) Venice from destruction upsets the notion of wielding power as an inevitable outcome of force. At the height of possibility, on the eve of a perfectly planned coup, there comes the incredible decision not to wield force. This apparently negative action or nonaction, then, goes against the Thucydidean formula we have been following throughout the first two chapters that "each one commands everywhere he has power to do so"—a renunciation of power that is represented in *Venise sauvée* as stillness.[5] Jaffier's stillness arises when he is free to act, and yet the stillness is not exactly an action since it requires the renunciation of his power to act. Nor is the stillness an utter passivity since it requires his consent to acting without power. To act without power partakes of a different economy altogether, disrupting both the mechanics of the transmission of violence that submits the weaker to the stronger and the self-perpetuation of force that ensures its continued transmission.[6] Those mechanics are again followed in this chapter, this time in view of the bond of love Jaffier feels for Venice's blank, unmarked innocence—something that surpasses linguistic capture but produces an urgency to express it nonetheless. For the negative use of power seems to be inextricably tied to a certain stillness of speech, at once pressing "the silent thing that must be expressed," as Weil puts it, and preserving its essential silence.[7]

Indeed, renouncing power seems to also cost Jaffier the power of his speech. His words fall upon deaf ears when he is disarmed and physically powerless; from raging to near inchoate muttering, he finally falls silent. He is powerless (sans pouvoir)—as Maurice Blanchot would put it—in the double sense that he is without might (puissance) and without capacity.[8] And yet that powerlessness produces an obligation to speak. The anguish of this is the ethical bind into which Jaffier is put: for speech remains exigent even when one is without the power to speak or the ability to do so. Nowhere is this more troublingly the case than when Jaffier fails to answer Pierre's anguished cry as the latter is being led to his torture and death. It may be the sole instance in the play where Jaffier's innocence falters, for this curious muteness comes at a time when there is nothing yet to stop him from speaking out.

The idea of speaking without power begs us to consider the particular claim that helplessness and vulnerability have—exactly the claim that Venice, in its open defenselessness, has upon Jaffier. It recalls Blanchot's idea that speaking without power produces a duty to preserve language, or more precisely, to speak a language that preserves something so foreign to power that no form of power whatsoever, even one that seeks to destroy and master, can touch it. Importantly, Jaffier's decision to renounce his power is coupled with a stillness of spirit reflected in his relative silence in the first two acts, a silence only broken by his private meditations on Venice's beauty. "And what happens in his soul remains mysterious," writes Weil of Jaffier (18). There the wordlessness, emerging as it does in the context of force, is yet curiously untouched by it; its containment is wholly unlike the muteness in the third act that is inseparable from Jaffier's captivity—and so, his literal immobility. There, speech first rages against, then falls silent under its raw interdiction.

How, then, might we begin to understand "what happens" in Jaffier's soul when it is unspoken and, as Weil insists, still? It cannot be understood through the outcome of Jaffier's decision, if by this we mean something that has changed or progressed, or that is evident or measurable, for the play ends as it began, with the start of another day in the free city of Venice. Nor can it be understood by what is said or done in the play itself, for what Jaffier expresses with regard to what "happens in his soul," outside of Weil's private notes to the play, amounts to almost nothing. And what he does might be better characterized as a refusal to do anything. "Action would be like a language. . . . We communicate something by an action. Underscore this in *Venise sauvée*," notes Weil (16). The difficulty of this statement is the one pursued in this chapter: that is, What does Jaffier's decision to preserve Venice tell us? And how would it anyway, being the most unmarkable of actions in the play, one that in giving up everything, actually does nothing?

DÉRACINEMENT, ENRACINEMENT

The picture of force in *Venise sauvée* is consistent with Weil's reading of the *Iliad*: force dominates and is a determining factor in one's relationship to the other. It is taken to be the natural order of the world and is accordingly submitted to in one of two ways. In the first, one understands oneself to be the "natural" master over others through the exercise of power. In *Venise sauvée*, the naturalization and mastery by force are facilitated by claims of belonging; as in Weil's reading of the *Iliad*, one wields power as though one owns it. Force takes on an almost unlimited capacity, socially, psychically, physically; in its most deceptive and subtle form it dissimulates its violence, seeming to be peaceable, as the calm of Venice illustrates. In contrast, all those who live in Venice but who are not its citizens live in a permanent state of uprootedness (déracinement), lacking the social and political consideration attendant to belonging.[9] Critically, those represented in this second form of submission to force are seduced by the prospect of assuming mastery in turn; it is their principle motivation or drive, as Renaud's rallying speeches to the soldiers make clear. For that is the seduction of force in Weil's view: even those who are without it dream of one day having it at their disposal, just as they would retransmit the violence they suffer given the opportunity.

The official reason for the overthrow of Venice is in no way at odds with the personal motivations of the conspirators. Those who operate enthusiastically under its dictum and who are thereby absorbed into the larger collectivity imitate the logic of war. Just as the accumulation of power requires and is itself the continual result of its deployment and reenactment, the conspirators aim to extend its reach. But as we saw in chapter 2, they do not, nor will they ever own force. Nonetheless, it can be said that their lives are determined by force and the physical and psychic violence that are intractable to it. The conspirators are shadows among the citizens of Venice who do not recognize them and who tacitly sanction the violence of this nonstatus.[10] Violetta, symbol of the city's virtues, says: "Father, I have always thought that I could not love an outsider. How would he understand me, he who did not know the happiness of having been born a member of such a city?" (VS 82). Violetta's question surely exceeds her awareness of its import; that is perhaps only as it could be since she herself has been born into such a city and its happiness, and thus, according to Weil, belongs to a "human milieu of which one is no more conscious than the air that one breathes."[11] That happiness does not simply consist of belonging to a larger social entity; it cannot be said that those fighting for the Spanish Crown do not normatively belong, but they do not, as Weil would insist, *naturally* belong to it. If the free city of Venice can be said to be innocent, Weil's representation does not permit us to think that the city's innocence extends blindly to its citizens. By the play's end we are given to reflect that the innocence of Venice is made up of its supreme and magisterial indifference; it is the particular blindness and intransigent violence of its citizens who by this fortune of birthplace also believe themselves innocent. Venice—including its citizens—will be preserved irrespective of its supposed merits contra any expectation (the Venetians' and the audience's) that not being harmed is a result of virtue.

J. P. Little argues—in contrast to Richard Rees's reading that *Venise sauvée* is fundamentally a story of redemptive suffering (through the figure of Jaffier)—that the play is "an artistic expression of the theory embodied in *L'Enracinement*."

> In these late writings the religious questions which were preoccupying [Weil] increasingly are allied to the social conscience which had always been present, but which the terrible events of the occupation and the fall of France had intensified and matured. One of the main tasks which she set herself during these last anguished years was the search for a viable order of society, and this led her to an increasing awareness of the role of society in the life of the individual. It is this awareness which we find in *Venise sauvée*, in addition to the theme of redemptive suffering, which Sir Richard Rees considers to the predominant in the play. Certainly Jaffier's role as redeemer which he performs by breaking the cycle of evil and bringing the full consequences down upon himself, is of first importance; but the background of the function of society against which this drama is set is too fundamental to Simone Weil's thought to be ignored.[12]

Indeed, from her notes we know that Weil did intend for *Venise sauvée* to reproduce her theory of *déracinement*. Following Little, my reading takes social uprootedness, with the violence and mechanics of suffering that it entails, as its point of departure. I depart from Rees's argument that Jaffier breaks the cycle of evil: when dawn rises on Venice it is not the start of a "new beginning," only the start of another day, this one the same, unmarked by the night's proceedings. In fact, practically nothing *happens* dramatically: Jaffier's "resolve" is unseen and, indeed, practically unwritten and literally in a state of permanent incompletion, "inachevée," due to Weil's untimely death, as the editor's notes to the play put it.[13] To say that Jaffier breaks the cycle of evil and that his suffering is redemptive is, in a certain sense, a more generous reading than what the play itself affords, for Venice is that which cannot exactly be given, although the very near success of the coup reminds us that it can be taken over at any moment. And although its beauty gives infinitely, it does so indifferently, without regard for one's status or merit.

THE DREAM OF VIOLENCE

It does not surprise us that in response to seeing Jaffier's face "turn pale and become decomposed" (pâlir et se décomposer), Renaud proposes to Pierre that Jaffier be killed. Renaud takes the changed look to be a sign of fear and a failure of resolve, factors most detrimental to success of their plans. Killing him is the only possible solution, a "necessary" cost in war, he reasons.[14] "What is a single human life when one is about to change the world?" (VS 39). While such violence is reasoned to be "a passing evil for a lasting good," from Renaud's speeches we also understand that a certain pleasure or gratification is inextricable from its execution (36–37). As Renaud describes it, the license to destroy is not only a necessary form power takes under conditions of war; it is also intoxicating.[15] He describes how the ragtag group of mercenaries is stirred by the mere prospect of destroying Venice: "And tonight's undertaking will give them neither fortune nor glory; afterwards, as before, they will be soldiers. One must give them this city as a plaything for one night, or even for the following day. . . . They must have full license to kill all those who resist them and even those who do not. Only such a license gives their actions this devastating character that brings with it victory" (63). It is surely a political calculation on Renaud's part to reward the soldiers' efforts in this way. But as he shrewdly notes, it is also the dream of inflicting outward the violence they have sustained. Renaud's long monologue in the second act is a clear example of placing the unlimited (what Weil calls "the dream" in *Venise sauvée*) upon what is essentially a limited domain (what Weil calls "the real" or "what really exists").[16] Upon this view, the dream is always what one does not yet have but for which one orients one's entire present. And here, too, violence is intractable from the prospect of its realization. "The conqueror lives his dream, the vanquished live the dream of the other," is how Renaud puts it.[17]

> Men of action and initiative are dreamers; they prefer dreams to reality. But, through arms, they constrain others to dream their dreams. The conqueror lives his dream, the vanquished live the dream of the other. All the men of Venice who will have lived through the night and through tomorrow will remain without knowing whether they are dreaming or awake until their death. But, starting tomorrow, their city, their freedom, their power will appear more unreal than a dream to them. Arms make the dream stronger than they do reality; it is this stupor which makes one submit. Starting tomorrow, they must believe themselves to have always been submitted to the Spanish Empire, to have never been free. The sky, the sun, the sea, the stone monuments will no longer be real to them. As for their children, they will be born uprooted from any homeland. But it is necessary that the shock be violent so that they might be forever stripped of their sense of what is real. . . . Your will, your fantasies, your dreams are their master and must henceforth be their only reality. You will be one of those men whose dreams the people are constrained to live out. . . . Their lives and their deaths will only be in service of your dreams. Is there a more glorious destiny than this? Such is the sweet fruit of victory! (66–68)

Renaud's long monologue generates the play's momentum in the first act; it frames the logic of the coup, for the lowest mercenary to the most politically ambitious officer, and gives the rationale for the violence necessary to achieve their goals.

The above passage illustrates Weil's understanding that to inflict suffering and to undergo suffering are part of the same operation of necessity. Indeed, what Weil writes in her essay on the *Iliad*—that executioner and victim are " are brothers in the same misery . . . in equal but different ways, [force] petrifies the souls of those who undergo it and those why ply it"—has brutal resonance here (PF 31, 35). Renaud's pleasure at their anticipated victory—and the pleasure he assumes Jaffier shares with him—no doubt reveals the irresistible force of violence upon those who suffer it and who, given the opportunity, would transmit violence in turn. For the mercenaries, the image, if not the fact, of transmitting that violence is enough to sustain them for some time; their dialogue, limited to a few lines in the play, concerns their anticipated pleasure in raping the noblewomen of Venice.

Weil succinctly describes the particular mechanics of this transmission of violence in her notebooks. The following passage also suggests that the mechanics of suffering also have to do with powerlessness and with a certain "telling" of pain by the one who suffers:[18]

> Human mechanics. Whoever suffers seeks to communicate his suffering—either by mistreating others or by soliciting pity—in order to diminish it, and he thereby truly diminishes it. He who is at the bottom, whom no one cares about, who does not have the power to mistreat anyone (if he does not have a child or someone who loves him), his suffering remains within him and poisons him. That is as imperious as gravity. How does one free oneself from it? How does one free oneself from that which is like gravity? (PG 46)

In Weil's account, the one in suffering looks for a way to communicate his pain and, depending on his relative ability and power, can either transfer his own suffering to another in mistreating him or can solicit pity. In both cases, the suffering seems to be lessened by means of this transference; it is a manner of "saving" oneself. There is a need to communicate one's suffering and to have that suffering received or at least recognized in some form, but under conditions of acute suffering the possibilities of adequately communicating—or of a communication at all—are severely diminished.[19] The need remains unfilled and imperious, "like gravity," writes Weil. Mute suffering, suffering that cannot find expression, Weil argues in "La Personne et le sacré," poisons the soul. The question becomes, How one might free oneself of suffering if not by imparting that suffering elsewhere? (Comment s'en délivre-t-on?). And for the one who does not appear to count, what can such a person do to redress his suffering?

And while this transference may be sufficient to relieve the suffering for a time, it is wholly insufficient to guarantee any lasting effect. The one who suffers from affliction—that is, the one who is "marked" with suffering, as Weil says in "L'Amour de Dieu et le malheur"—cannot be so easily released through these means since an unconscious memory of it is awakened when one is confronted with suffering anew.[20] The affliction redoubles upon the one who is utterly powerless to transfer his pain elsewhere. There is in this notion of redoubling the sense that undergoing affliction is also an accumulation. That is to say, time enters into suffering but in such a way that it obliterates both its length and spontaneity. It functions to bring life to a standstill or to the limits of what can at any moment be endured, just as it returns in such a way that it seems never to have left.

The afflicted one is left with little but his imagination or his bitterness to shore up his self if he is to persist in this suffering without help or relief. Weil argues that for such a person the dream—if not the possibility or actuality—of allaying that pain elsewhere can be as vital as food or sleep.[21] In *Venise sauvée*, the courtesan offers the most developed portrait of such a person: her thirst for revenge stems from the need to diminish her suffering by returning the violence and humiliation she has endured at the hands of the Venetians, a mirroring that is reflected in her words. Asked by an officer about her hatred of Venice, she recounts the injustices she has suffered under it—broken promises, her father's murder, social degradation. By reason of these external circumstances she has been forced into sexual trade.[22]

The courtesan plays a small but decisive role in *Venise sauvée*: not only is she an obvious counterpart to Violetta (the only other woman represented in the play), but she is, tellingly, the only specific example of violence undergone by the conspirators in the first two acts. Moreover, the importance of this particular form of violence, that is, the sexual violation and trade of the body, provides a stark metaphor of the economy of violence. The suffering is not only experienced passively but is undergone to the point that one's body is no longer one's own, and so would ultimately vacate passivity of its meaning and sense. Not surprisingly, the courtesan's revenge will be to inflict the same suffering on the wives and daughters of the men who have used her: "All those men who have violated me, I have kept their names. I want their wives and daughters to be turned over to the soldiers. As well as those women and daughters of government officials. What pleasure, tomorrow, to see the survivors choking with shame and to mock them without them daring to respond!" (VS 75–76). It is important that this suffering should be transferred onto their loved ones whom they would be helpless to save. Their inability to save them, combined as it is with a crippling fear and shame, would reenact the courtesan's experience of humiliation. In the imagined scenario, the pain is symbolically and literally lodged in the throat, a choking that suggests the impasse of the courtesan's own impotence. On the one hand there is the one who suffocates from an unspeakable shame; on the other is the irrepressible and derisive pleasure of the one who can cause this suffering with impunity—both, "brothers in the same misery" (PF 31).

SPEAK, STILLNESS

Renaud sees the change in Jaffier's face but fails to see what has happened. And how could he? Whatever it is has come about without visible expenditure, including the expenditure of language. Or more precisely, it has come in a decomposition, in the expression of a face without composure, in the recognition of something hitherto unseen. If it has come from an effort of attention, as Weil suggests, we need to ask ourselves what kind of obtainment this is exactly, since whatever has come about is nothing, really, to be had. To the question of what Jaffier's face betrays—in the sense of both giving up and of revealing—is the answer, quite simply, *nothing.* Nothing that isn't already there, nothing other than the open beauty of Venice, something that is invoked repeatedly throughout the play by its sky.

After Renaud's speech concerning the necessary sacking of Venice, Jaffier says, "I am altogether penetrated by the truth of your words, and I will conduct myself accordingly" (VS 68). What is this certitude? The relationship between certitude and attention outlined in Weil's essay "Réflexions sur le bon usage des études scolaires en vue de l'Amour de Dieu," may help us here.[23] Thought is to be suspended so as to leave it available, empty, and penetrable by the object of one's attention. Weil describes the object of one's attention as naked and the one who is attentive as the one who, in his readiness to receive the object, waits for it: "The most precious goods must not be sought after but awaited" (AD 93). Awaiting (l'attente) is thus a posture of maintaining oneself in proximity to the thought (itself empty) of the object (itself naked).

The tension between maintaining proximity without (possibly ever) making contact is commensurable to the qualities of desire. The certitude is not in the actual receiving—for Venice's beauty, we have said, cannot be "had," only recognized—but is rather in the rapport itself. And so, for example, when Jaffier and Violetta wax poetic on Venice's beauty, it is beauty that brings together their desire. This desire is the certitude itself. Weil describes their intimate exchange as one of the "culminating points" of the play (VS 85). Here Jaffier's characteristic reserve falters: "No man could make something like Venice. God alone could. The greatest thing a man can do which comes closest to God, since he cannot create such marvels, is to preserve those which exist" (85). This comes after Violetta's rhetorical question to Jaffier that culminates in an apex of emotion: "Who would want to, for so little gain, destroy something so beautiful, something so unique! Harm Venice! Its beauty defends it better than soldiers, better than the protection of the government! Isn't that so, Mr. Jaffier?" (84–85). Weil's notes following this exchange are telling: "All this is interrupted [coupé] throughout with Jaffier's replies. He agrees with Violetta in a tone of voice mixed with light banter and enthusiasm. Progressively, from reply to reply (in couplets?), Jaffier's tone moves from banter to love for Venice. There must be a painful resonance in everything he says there" (85). Since Weil never completed this scene, we can only imagine what Jaffier's replies to Violetta might have looked like: "coupé" does not suggest a "cut" but rather a movement that exceeds, then is contained by the other's words. The couplet form suggests the movement, a "pas à deux" between Jaffier and Violetta, who, from their respective positions—one belonging to the city and one who is to uproot all those who do—share a love for its beauty. As Weil envisioned it, the voice of the other would enter, bringing reprieve and solicitude to the monologue, and would culminate in one of the play's most tender and sorrowful scenes. With the play in its unfinished form, we can only say so much and have perhaps exceeded the limits of what is given us. For Weil cautions, "But even this expansiveness is contained" (18).

We might begin to make sense of the tension of a "contained expansiveness" by reference to what Weil calls elsewhere the promise of the nuptial "yes": "'I want.'—That is like the 'yes' of marriage—'I do.'"[24] A performative reading would claim that attestation, desire, and action culminate in the "yes"; it is both the affirmation and actualization of the obligation to the other in its enunciation. It signifies an absolute present and one's being present to it (that is, the "yes" cannot be spoken by anyone else; one is singular and nonsubstitutable), and yet it seems to exceed its very presentness in the implication of duration that could not be otherwise spoken for or claimed so absolutely or, perhaps, at all. However, there is an irreducible tension in the "I want" and the "I am resolved," and again in Jaffier's final words, "how beautiful the city is," since they are affirmations that do not really say anything and leave us wondering what exactly has been done and when, if at all, that has transpired. The "yes" might also be said to destabilize the boundaries between private and collective language, and consequently, between one's obligations to the individual person and those to the collectivity. One's "yes," so deeply private, is in the context of the law attested to by others. The address would be affirmed, then, by these others who have the ability to contest the impending promise. Nonetheless, Weil insists that there can be no concordance between private and collective language. "The language of the public space is not that of the marriage chamber," writes Weil (AD 58). For Weil, the language of one's resolve is secret and mysterious.

Likewise when the reality of Venice enters Jaffier's soul, it does so secretly and "at once" (VS 68; du premier coup). In her notebooks, Weil states that "for all of the 2nd act, Jaffier's speech . . . is *entirely* double-entendre. And what happens in his soul remains mysterious" (18).[25] It is an exquisite evocation of what happens but which cannot be spoken of as an event, as such. Attempts to circumscribe it fail: to call the encounter by the name of "pity," as Jaffier does, only confirms that something has taken place; it does not by itself say what that is. A further question arises here: How do we account for the dissonance between the immediacy of the recognition of Venice's reality and the problem of its being fully knowable and speakable—and this last despite its already having been seen? What Jaffier says to Renaud immediately before his decision to save Venice suggests how the object of his resolution—the most apparent thing of all (in that it is, quite simply, what can be seen)—"cannot simply be spoken."[26] And yet, that difficulty in speaking coincides with Jaffier's first open comments on the city: "When I see this city, so beautiful, so powerful, and so peaceful, and when I think that in one night we, a few obscure men, will become its master, I must be dreaming" (65–66). And so, what begins as the immediacy and certainty of what is seen in its present reality ends with its near dissolution in the imagined future, an unreality that is characterized as dreaming. The truth of knowing what he sees, in other words, emerges from the directness and presentness of its referent ("this city, so beautiful, so powerful, and so peaceful") and is immediately lost upon being displaced onto an unknowable, because imagined, future occurrence ("when . . . we will become its master"). In a more general sense, I would suggest that Jaffier's words, particularly the "when" (quand) of his narrative, marks the equivocality of that moment of sight: both the certainty of its occurrence and the inability to seize it, the "when" of dreaming delineating its transformation into an unreal event.[27]

Later alone, Jaffier ponders:

The city is still happy this evening in its splendor;
For one evening its people remain undisturbed and proud.

This last sunlight alone covers it with its beams;
If it knew, it would stop out of pity.
But neither the sun has pity for the city, alas, nor do I.
Is it permitted me to be as insensible as the sun,
Me, whose eyes see what kind of city will perish? (94)

Eyes that see, what is permitted them? And what is required of them? "I see clearly what I have to do, I am certain of succeeding and am perfectly resolved. . . . I will execute my decision with great firmness to keep my friends from all danger. Nothing can weaken my resolution," Jaffier continues (96). And so, the passage above moves from Jaffier's stillness to his responsibility. Seeing the reality of Venice, its profoundly defenseless beauty, produces at once the resolution to preserve it. It seems that the preservation, as a kind of sheltering, is its own containment. Unlike the dream of power, Jaffier's resolution to protect Venice, as he would "keep his friends from all danger," is a way of containing the sense of limitless expansion common to the machinations of power.

I think we can better understand Jaffier's recognition of Venice's defenseless beauty through Emmanuel Levinas's notion of the face.[28] The face goes against the idea that one commands everywhere one has the power to do so; to "see" the face of the other is to give up one's power. In speaking of the face, we are speaking of something that cannot be captured and that offers itself precisely in its exposure to the other. The vulnerability of its exposure is what composes the face and what holds it together in its composition. The face of the other, which cannot offer anything but its sheer exposure, might be understood analogously as a naked destitution, "as the extreme precariousness of the other."[29] In other words, the face is what cannot be identified as such; it escapes any strict determination of its presence, including those attempts at linguistic capture. Moreover, its exposure can be neither "revealed" nor "unmasked" since it is already there, even though what is there cannot be assumed nor seized by the one who is faced with it.

This inability only incites the desire to consume, apprehend, possess, or even destroy the face that, in its extreme nakedness, according to Levinas, is the very injunction to protect or preserve it. And so, the injunction arises from the place of desire and, as such, entails an other who both solicits and thwarts that very desire. Put slightly differently, in the face is that which does not fail to summon you or to bring you to a summons but which paradoxically requires a certain retreat or withholding of oneself (recul). Read in the context of what Jaffier must do in *Venise sauvée*, I want to suggest that such an encounter also puts into question what one has to give, in the two-fold sense of what one has (and so, what one can master and possess) and what demands this giving over (and so, what one must give). The turning point of the narrative—that is, Jaffier's anguish at the prospect of Venice's destruction and his resolution to preserve it—begs us to consider both senses of what one has to give. Nothing is so clear as this as when in the final act we see Jaffier, reduced to a certain nakedness, a traitor "twice over" according to his captors, clutching his bag of gold, wishing for nothing now but sleep as for oblivion and as for death.

To be sure, Violetta waxes poetic on the beauty of the city; there is no time when her speech is not carried by it. There are others who seem to be awake to this beauty; indeed, ordinary citizens of Venice claim, "For us, Venice is as dear to us as it is to the nobles; Venice belongs to us as it does to them" (134). But rather than enjoin it to Jaffier's, their understanding seems too insular and exclusionary, almost self-congratulatory. For do they not at all times believe they to belong to it? And it to them? A certain attachment to the city and to its beauty pervades their entire outlook. But to see beauty, that is, to be alive to what is outside of you, is different. Beauty touches you at a remove; this contact is constituted through detachment and the impossibility of possession. Beauty gives, but this giving is singular in that "it only gives itself, it never gives anything other than itself."[30] In other words, one cannot make a claim on beauty; it is for beauty to make a claim on you—but it is a claim that claims nothing. Or more precisely, it is a claim that does not claim anything. Its plenitude lies in this very emptiness: "it alone is good in and of itself but is so without our finding in it any particular good," writes Weil (AD 157).

Both the face and beauty have this in common: a nakedness and open vulnerability that cannot be contained even in conditions of extreme brutality, not even by the very hand that would seek to protect it. For Weil, a certain powerlessness constitutes one's relation to beauty; "man does not need to renounce the command of matter and souls since he does not possess the power to do so" (147). In her essay "Formes de l'amour implicite de Dieu," Weil draws the relation between beauty and its exposure in the order of the world (l'ordre du monde), arguing that together they constitute a contact with the love of God. In Weil's view, the contact is real but indirect since God has withdrawn; in creation (that is, the world, including human beings), he renounced a part of his divinity. Creation is itself this renunciation, and this renunciation is the love of God. We, who are not divine, who cannot take "one step upward," are yet capable of a similar act of love. That act is a renunciation of our false divinity, of all that we imagine is in our power. It is to open ourselves and empty ourselves of our attachments and so, to suffer the void left by the absence of all that is imaginary. In her notes to *Venise sauvée*, Weil writes:

> Things are unreal for us when they are understood as "values." But illusory values also strip reality from perception itself through the imagination that encompasses it. For illusory values are not deduced but are directly read in the sensation to which they are tied.
>
> As such, only perfect detachment permits us to see things nakedly, without this fog of illusory values. That is why it took ulcers and shock before Job could see the beauty of the world. For there is no detachment without pain. And there is no pain suffered without hatred and without lies unless there is detachment.
>
> (That *Venise sauvée* might reproduce this movement.) (16–17)

In the void that, for Weil, is inseparable from suffering, one receives the world and its naked beauty. That is how Violetta's "daylight" (rayons du jour) is for Jaffier the same "clarity of day [which] causes me suffering" (131); the day, indifferent to both this joy and this suffering, exists.

SPEAKING FROM THE POINT AT WHICH IT CAN SAY NOTHING

We began with Weil's notes on the play's rhythm: the passionate mood shared by the conspirators turns inward onto the figure of Jaffier, who expresses this passion in astonishing wordlessness.[31] His outbursts of regret in the final act only seem to magnify the silence. But there his silence emerges from a different context: he is isolated from his friends, a powerless, unarmed captive.

The Secretary tells his valet, Bassio, what Jaffier's reaction will be upon learning the Council's decision to execute the conspirators despite its promise to the contrary:

> He will first explode with anger; therefore, along with two of your men, guard him well, and disarm him before he can draw his sword. When he sees that his anger is of no use, his anguish will explode. After he's complained enough, he'll shut up; then he'll try to persuade me. In vain he'll exhaust the little that remains of his strength.

> Then he'll fall into a deep despondency. In this state, it will be easy
> to escort him out of Venice. Despite his great courage, impetuous-
> ness, and pride, I'm not worried, for there is no man, however strong,
> proud and impetuousness, who is not overcome when he is made to
> feel that he can do nothing. (VS 104)

This is a terse and accurate account of what follows. Twice, in
response to Jaffier's continued demands to know why the Council
has not honored its promise, the Secretary tells him: "I have told you
all that I had to say. I have nothing to add" (123). Against the Secretary's decisive silence, we see Jaffier at the edge of speech; his cries
do nothing to change that. If anything, his pleas only serve to harden
the Secretary against him. Nonetheless, through his behest, Jaffier is
spared death for his decision to come forward about the conspiracy.
He is given a bag of gold and will be let go outside of Venice once his
friends—those Jaffier had chosen to save—are tortured and killed.

Not incidentally, the scene of torture in the third act happens off-
stage. Just before the prisoners are led away, Renaud cries over his
aborted dream ("Who, who are they to have stolen my destiny from
me" [110]); an officer uselessly claims his innocence ("It's not my
fault, it's not me, I was dragged along" [107]). And Pierre cries alternately to himself, alternately to the missing Jaffier whom he imagines
has suffered a worse fate:

> My God, if only his voice were here suddenly,
> If I touched his hand, if his eyes were upon me!
> How do I leave this life without ever again seeing him?
> I desire him in vain; he is nowhere. Everything is empty. (112)

In their totality, however, their cries are addressed to a terrible void;
"alone, in the hands of [their] executioners," they are hauled off
unceremoniously to their deaths (112). Jaffier appears onstage as the
officers are being carted off but without their seeing him. They are at
a distance, one that Jaffier seems only to compound by not answer-
ing their cries even though there is not yet anything to stop him from
doing so. In this sense, Pierre's words, that "[Jaffier] is nowhere," are
true and must make us wonder at Jaffier's retreat from the situation.
Thereafter, all that he is really witness to are the men's cries under
torture.

From her notes we know that Weil intended to place Jaffier in the
tradition of Greek tragedy where the hero is "perfect" (25). In what
does this perfection consist? Weil's play makes us think that it has an
intimate relationship to silence and stillness, transformed in the third

act from one's consent to powerlessness to an ethical bind far from one's choosing. Jaffier's situation here shows the limits of what one can do out of love for the other. The passion of Jaffier is that the "pain, shame and death that one does not wish to inflict upon others falls upon oneself" (15). Indeed, in Jaffier we see the stamp of the Greek tragic hero's silence—or "near silence," as Walter Benjamin so clearly tells us in his essay "Oedipus, or Rational Myth." What Benjamin writes of Sophocles's Oedipus strikingly resembles Jaffier's situation after he has unwittingly led his friends to their deaths: "Screaming with the pain inflicted by his own hands—he utters speeches in which there can be no room for thought, for reflection. It is true that he is insatiable in his need to keep repeating the horrific events. . . . But it is this very speech that makes him fall silent inwardly; and in the same vein, he wishes to become like the night." Benjamin then quotes from the tragedy words that could just as easily and no less portentously have been said by Jaffier:

> Could I want sight to face this people's stare?
> No! Hearing neither! Had I any way
> To dam that channel too, I would not rest
> Till I had prisoned up this body of shame
> That I might be blind and deaf.

"And how could he [Oedipus] not fall silent?" Benjamin continues. "How could thinking ever free him from the entanglement that makes it impossible to decide what is destroying him—the crime itself, Apollo's oracle, or the curse that he himself lays on the murderer of Laius? Moreover, this silence characterizes not just Oedipus alone but the hero of Greek tragedy in general."[32]

Jaffier's anguish finds its deepest expression in his silence following his vain entreaties to the Secretary. This silence is manifestly different from the Secretary's: for it is upon being repeatedly heard by no one that he falls silent. Jaffier takes this situation further, linking speech with being: "Alas! *I am nothing*, and everyone around me is deaf" (123, emphasis added). At first Jaffier keeps talking, since "As soon as I keep silent, my loss will be complete. I will no longer be able to do anything" (125). The first time Jaffier uses this expression is after he has been disarmed; disabused of any lingering illusion that he wields power, Jaffier changes course, thinking that "without doubt there are words that will succeed in making them yield" (125), but to no avail.

For us to know that he speaks in vain, as Jaffier himself will soon learn, does not lessen the exigency to speak. Against one's will and one's power, and putting into question both capacities, one is delivered over to the other without appeal. I would suggest that the powerlessness is not solely the result of being disarmed and is qualitatively different from the renunciation of power in the second act. The two aspects of Jaffier's immobility take their shape from their very incommensurability with one another: absolute stillness—signaled at the highest moment by wordless attention—comes when one has renounced one's power. His subsequent capture, when he is divested of any lingering illusion that he wields power and when he can no longer speak, is in contest with the imperious need to speak. In other words, Jaffier's silence undergoes a complete change in the third act: his reticence or reservation in the first two acts, and particularly in the second, where, as Weil notes, "Jaffier's retreat is supernatural" (19), undergoes a brutal transformation as his speech, at turns delirious and frenzied, at turns knotted and choked, emerges from the helplessness of what he cannot do. "I gave them all my power," he cries. "I can do nothing" (119). No one will listen to his entreaties, and his friends will be tortured and killed.

And yet he speaks, and so, to whom? Following what I have been suggesting in the first two chapters, his speech supposes the one to whom it *would* appeal. The address is a bringing to bear upon another who is absent and so, who cannot respond as such, but whose presence is nonetheless reanimated in the form of this absence. Words remain, in all their intransigence and uselessness; they stumble and redouble upon themselves. The hypnotic effect of repetition speaks closely to Jaffier's desperation and despair. A homonymic reverberation of the stopped tears that gorge the throat, the plaintive cries of one who, unable to speak it justly or adequately, returns again and again to the same words. They are the cries of a being that "wants to speak from the point at which it can say nothing."[33] Jaffier cries:

Oh, my friend. Where is my friend?
. . . .
I would like, I would like to save you.
I gave them all my power.
They have disarmed me. I can do nothing. (118–19)

Jaffier posits his friend where he is not. In asking where his friend is, there is already the realization that he is lost to him and that the wish to save him must remain in the historical present of the address itself. Only the address keeps open the possibility of such an apostrophic gesture. But to keep it open, one needs to return to the site of the loss and transform it as an opening or an open question. "I would like to save you"—here the object is posited but only in the context of a radical uncertainty over what can be done, and so, puts the object into question. The desire is untouched, but can the object of one's desire be "saved"? The "failure" of the object in the first instance turns upon the failure of the one who posits it, that is, of what he would like to do, what he can do, what he has lost, and what he has voluntarily given up.

We also witness the desperate signaling to presence of Jaffier's words to his friend in his cries to the Secretary: "You to whom my hope rises as it would to God, / You who will set my friend free" (124). Can one's own presence be brought to bear upon the other in calling the other? Does it do so in Jaffier's entreaties to the Secretary? The other is addressed constantly, manically; sometimes it is still in the register of an order or threat: "You don't answer? You don't even answer? . . . Speak to me! Speak to me!" (122–23). The Secretary leaves Jaffier without responding further, and Jaffier's continued pleas to his captors to bring him to the Secretary are unheeded. The solicitation, finally, is not for the Secretary; it is for the possibility of address itself, for the "you" that might receive his words.

Imagine, then, Jaffier's anguish at hearing Pierre cry out to him as he is being led away to his death. Can we say that these words have been received at the moment when Pierre has spoken into the void and Jaffier, in hiding, nonetheless hears these words? Are these, as Weil writes, "cries without response"? (21). Weil seems to point to this problem of reception when she writes in the prefatory notes regarding repetition and its relation to helplessness: "The power of simple repetition, as observed in the Spirituals. Repetition to the point of becoming sick to the very nerves. To be applied in *Venise sauvée*. In the scene of those condemned to death. And in the insults to Jaffier" (22). It may be, then, that the reception happens at a distance—here, at the crossroads between a separation by force and separation by withdrawal—and that this distance is itself the condition of its happening.

But as I read this again I think that the more difficult thing to fathom and accept is that there is no reception. While that may be a more brutal reading of the scene, it is not, I think, an ungenerous reading. His agreement with the Council does not, finally, matter. And what he has given up, in a different sense, also does not matter or count toward anything. Given that his friends' lives have not been spared, it seems hardly possible to call this a "redemptive" suffering, as Rees suggests. Again: Jaffier's cries are without answer. He cries into the void out of an imperious but ultimately empty need to speak. Then he falls silent. Perhaps the only response is to repeat and redouble the cry itself, and that what joins them here, what allies them at the end, is precisely the cry. For Pierre, it is death that silences the cry. And Jaffier, who is left alive despite himself, can only cry after his friend, a wail that repeats itself without saying anything new and without the capacity to change anything.

"I will become mad if I have to be subjected to so many looks. For pity's sake, go away all of you, I don't want to go mad," begs Jaffier, before eventually falling silent (129). Upon first seeing him with Bassio, a fellow Venetian asks, "And that thing there looking at the ground, what is that, then?" (134). Upon learning of the near-events of the previous night and Jaffier's part in them, the craftsman's apprentice asks incredulously, "We're going to leave one of these dogs alive?" And then to Jaffier he says, "Raise your head, dog! I want to see the eyes of a coward. Come on! Look at me" (135)—an absurd order to attest to one's presence under circumstances which all but negates that possibility.[34] One does not, it seems, have pity for something that is too close or too abject—a stark contrast to the pity Venice's untouchable beauty inspires.[35]

"Why doesn't he say anything? I'd like to hear his voice. Let me hit him to make him cry," exclaims the apprentice (136). What can preserve speech so that its stillness is untouched by even the most extreme conditions of brutality? "Tell me!" is the order of his captors. Jaffier, just before his eyes are "soon without sight," says most simply: *how beautiful the city is*. It is surely an attestation inadequate to what is there, yet giving cohesion to what has surpassed him. If Venice still exists, if it is ultimately untouched by violence, it is not exactly because of something Jaffier did. In his renunciation of all power, he ultimately does nothing, takes part in nothing. We are left with the beauty of Venice; it is the Venice that Jaffier will no longer look upon. Venice: night has made way for its morning. Another day begins.

I began this chapter by inquiring into love's bind, where Jaffier is powerless to save both Venice and his friends. Recall Jaffier's prescient words, spoken when nothing yet had happened, that the best one can do is to preserve the things that exist. Jaffier does not "save" anyone or anything, and it might be said that he actually fails to do so. Preserving something partakes of a different economy altogether since it doesn't need Jaffier, doesn't need anyone, only needs to be left alone or untouched. More radical than a substitution in that it could have made use of anyone, not just Jaffier. And more mysterious in that it is indifferent to, even dispenses with the one who, in a singular moment of recognition, was utterly stopped by beauty, bound to it endlessly thereafter.

CHAPTER 4

Unfinished Obligation

Venise sauvée *and* La Folie du jour

> There is never in this universe any dimensional equality between an obligation and its object. The obligation is infinite; the object is not.
>
> —Weil, *L'Enracinement*

There is a moment in *Venise sauvée* when the hero breaks down helplessly.[1] He is disarmed, his body exposed to his captors, his speech reduced to an empty stammering, then, finally, to silence. He has revealed the plans for the overthrow of the free city of Venice out of pity for its defenseless beauty. In exchange, he has been assured that his friends involved in the plot will not be harmed. The promise is not honored, although his own life is spared, his impunity measured in the bag of gold he is given. Of course, this impunity is given without having been asked for, and the debt he has incurred in his treachery is unpayable. The demand of his captors that he speak—always against the force of his silence (the only "force" he has by this point in the play)—amounts to the demand to explain himself. Earlier, when Jaffier still speaks, when his speaking is a cry for his friends, he tries in vain to do just that. It is still at a moment when Jaffier understands himself to have acted justly and is incredulous that Venice's Council of Ten will execute his friends. But the fact that the Council does not honor its word to spare his friends neither annuls nor mitigates Jaffier's own obligation to them. His being subjected to circumstances outside his own power that ultimately make impossible the fulfillment of his obligation does not make him any less responsible for its object. Put this way, the obligation is unfinished.

This chapter takes up the question of fulfilling this obligation in *Venise sauvée*. I am specifically interested in the obligation as the occasion and structure of ethical binding. Here the one obligated is subject to the bind and the other, strangely, appears untouched by it or indifferent, even though it is from his vulnerability that such a bind emerges in the first place. The obligation is infinite while the object is not, according to Simone Weil. From this incommensurable relationship emerges another one between the one obligated and the one to whom one is bound. And the obligation being infinite, can the one obligated, in his finitude, answer its demands? In *Venise sauvée*, the bind of obligation ultimately has a strangling effect, making it nearly impossible for Jaffier to speak adequately or, finally, to speak at all. All the while there is the demand to speak and there is the demand to be accountable for one's speech, "to be as good as one's word," as they say. In the insistence that one tell what happened is already the slippage from giving an account to an accounting that exceeds one's capacity to meet it. Under such circumstances, the twin poles of speech—here, between what one gives and what one owes—turns upon a narrative structure that seems as much to "unsay" as it does to tell anything at all, thereby eliding attempts to circumscribe those very events that are supposed to constitute the "story." For nothing, we know, really *happens* in *Venise sauvée*, and "what happens in [Jaffier's] soul remains mysterious," writes Weil.[2]

Speaking is untethered by any reason to do so, in any case, because one has already been indicted of having failed to meet one's obligation. It seems that the accusation is not so much the description of the failure as it is its instantiation and reanimation. "Day that does not pass. At the heart of the time that passes, nothing goes on, nothing comes up" is how Emmanuel Levinas puts it.[3] (And all the while, the unambiguously brilliant and unmarked transparency of Venice's beauty, with nothing to reveal or to say, goes on and is always there.) The failure to meet the obligation has already taken place once one has been accused; the one who seeks to fulfill the obligation from this point onward is, in this sense, too late. And yet the obligation stands; not having been met, it is, nonetheless, not finished.

Sleep and debt are the two figures of which I think Weil makes use to explain unfinished obligation in *Venise sauvée*; it is also at play in Maurice Blanchot's *La Folie du jour*.[4] Through a comparative reading, I inquire into the relationship between sleep, debt, and obligation—an obligation that, if we return to Jaffier and his bag of gold, outbids the one bound by the obligation. Jaffier's captors misread what this gold means, taking it to be a sign of compensation for an act of betrayal. "We don't need to ask why he betrayed his friends!" cries one of them knowingly. But from the point of view of compensation, whether it is understood to be a rendering of an equivalent, or whether it is taken as an amends or remuneration for loss, the bag of gold cannot put things back into balance. And for Jaffier, who did not exactly do anything, as I have said in chapter 3, but whose unaccomplishment results in his friends' deaths anyway, what kind of reparation would even make sense? "Finally, it's over. I would like to sleep now," says a defeated Jaffier, reduced to near silence at this point in the play (VS 139). How are we to understand this seemingly simple statement—one that does not exactly withhold its sense but whose meaning is all the more stubbornly unresolved for passing over what precisely happened? What is "it" that is said to be over, according to Jaffier's self-understanding? Whatever it is, I would submit, is not quite finished, although there can be no doubt that it has made thorough use of Jaffier, who is really done for, wishing for nothing more than sleep's release.

The Council did not keep its word, but what is at stake—the heart of the play's moral dilemma—is whether Jaffier kept his. "Keeping one's word," a common expression for keeping one's promise (tenir parole), can be taken further. In *Paroles suffoquées*, Sarah Kofman draws a series of stunning correlations: first, between killing and "forgetting" the Other (Kofman's quotations), and second, between the power to kill and keeping one's word. "Among [the multiplicity of] powers is that of killing, of 'forgetting' the Other," she writes. "And the correlative power of *keeping one's word*, the task for which nature raised and educated man."[5] I would like to consider these correlations in Weil's play and in view of her statement that to harm the other is to get something from doing so. That statement comes from her notebooks; it is not developed as such, and it ends with a question that takes on a greater urgency in the context of our reading of *Venise sauvée*: "What has one gained?"[6] The power to kill assumes a power to harm the other or, as Kofman suggests, the power to "forget" the other. But to not harm the other, does that mean that one has thereby "remembered" the other? Something stands in the way of their easy transposition. A better way of understanding the connection between not harming and not forgetting the other has to be found elsewhere. Perhaps the man who keeps his word—that is, who does not forget the other—is the man who has something to give. What that something is or is not remains shrouded in mystery, however, shadowed by the prior urgency of the question of what one *has to* give.[7]

Let me try to explain by returning to the passage I quoted from Kofman. The French for keeping one's word is "tenir parole," and there are some related idiomatic expressions, such as "Il a tenu parole" (He was as good as his word) and "C'est un homme de parole" (He's a man of his word), which suggest a link between the person and speech and between the speech and what the person has. A synonym for that expression, "Il n'a qu'une parole" (His word is his bond), suggests both the strength and transparency of that link. And yet, "Il n'a qu'une parole" vacillates between singularity and evanescence, between being and having. If one is one's word, and if under conditions of force one's word is in some way not honored, it seems that one's being, too, is endangered. If one is one's word, and if this word also constitutes in some sense what one has, then it might be negatively put that without one's word one has nothing.

One does not hold speech, one holds speech *with another*; one does not keep one's word, one keeps one's word *to another*. That is, an other is implied in this relationship between one's word and one's being. And yet, if there seems to be a transparent relationship between one's speech and one's being, that relationship is nonetheless interrupted by a third element whose exteriority destabilizes and cuts through the dyadic structure. For as Kofman makes clear, one's relationship to the other is conditioned upon a dispossession, a radical and indestructible alterity born of the power to kill and from which one might possibly speak a language preserved from power—a fragile possibility, as the deaths that result from Jaffier keeping his word surely attest to. In that sense, both *Venise sauvée* and *La Folie du jour* are stories of what did not happen: one's own missed death and the death of the other. Between the question of betrayal and the question of fidelity is again the question of an unspeaking speech that we have been tracking throughout this book: what can one say, after all?[8]

THE GATELESSNESS OF SLEEP

When Jaffier is certain that his friends have been killed, he says, most simply, "Finally, it's over. I would like to sleep now" (VS 139). An enigmatic statement, all the more so for its apparent simplicity. Jaffier, we know, does not sleep then; it seems he does not sleep throughout the whole play, although others do, and he himself encourages them to do so. We know that by this point in the play he cannot; he is taunted by his captors, never left alone long enough for sleep. He is exposed in a manner that prohibits the total exposure that is, nonetheless, sleep. So two kinds of exposure are involved in sleep, one that can be said to properly belong to it and into which the sleeper falls, and one that confronts the one who cannot sleep. Is there something about sleep itself that makes sleep impossible? Or does this impossibility arise from elsewhere, from something that is not internal to it?

In *Venise sauvée* sleep passes almost imperceptibly, sliding past like night that never comes but only *is*. The action happens through the night, breaking off at the dawn of day. There are numerous places (which on a first or second reading can go by unnoticed) where one is sleeping or will sleep, where one is advised to sleep or when one cannot sleep. What are we to make of this interplay of permission and prohibition? Night is at once a great, perhaps the greatest, equalizer, suggests Jean-Luc Nancy in his beautiful meditation on falling into sleep: "Everyone sleeps in the equality of the same sleep—every living being."[9] Furthermore, night is inseparable from and is itself the time of sleep. It is deeply shared in the sense that it leaves no one untouched, but it is also the time when one might be said to be most alone, even from oneself, when it perhaps does not even make sense to speak of "one" or "myself," or even "self." In the "cover of night," we say, but night is also the time of an incomprehensible uncovering: one is vulnerable to an outside from which one has receded but has never quite left.

Being left in night finds its mirror image in what has been called the "gatelessness" of sleep: "One does not cross over into sleep; one is instead just suddenly *there* . . . . There are no gates through which to enter sleep. And their absence is part of our experience of sleep. When we are again awake, we can verify that we did not enter sleep; we were just suddenly *there*."[10] This brief meditation on sleep by Henry Johnstone is a way of making sense of another event that eclipses us: that is, the experience of our own death. Although Johnstone is careful here to admit that "one cannot extrapolate from the *experience* of sleep to the experience of death," he nonetheless points out the "fact" of their shared attribute: "each is a loss of waking consciousness."[11] From this he infers that "if loss of waking consciousness is gateless in sleep" (something we cannot verify from the experience of sleep), "it must also be in death" (something which cannot be experienced as such and so, cannot be "verified"). Johnstone concludes: "The decedent experiences no transition to death; he is suddenly *there*. There is no 'crossing of the bar.'"[12] I would add that if the gatelessness of sleep has its counterpart in death, it is to their capacities to "save" one from the particular pull of consciousness—what Anne Carson in

her meditation on sleep calls "the analytic of the day"—that we owe
such an analogy.[13] John Keats, in his "Sonnet to Sleep," describes it
as "curious conscience, that still lords / Its strength for darkness."[14]
Sleep is said to seal the "hushed casket" of the soul and charm its
cares; and so, sleep here is not only understood as consolation but as
something that saves.

THE DAWN OF HAPPINESS

Violetta, symbol of Venice's innocence, is someone who is given over
to sleep without trouble to her conscience. She prepares for her day—
the dawn of her happiness—on the eve of the city's festival by going
to sleep. She says to her father, "I want, after a long sleep, to wake
up tomorrow at dawn for a whole day of joy" (VS 86). She then says
to Jaffier, unaware of the import of her own words, "If you knew,
Mr. Jaffier, what kind of day you will have tomorrow" (86). Sleep
is what allows her to rejuvenate, that is, to remake the day; both her
peace and happiness are at one with this new day. It seems that for
some, night can also be a passage, a going through and a prepara-
tion for day. Against the indifference that marks night, day is marked
by unicity. Day is the time of being together, of having time for the
other and passing those hours together. Again to her father, Violetta
says: "Tomorrow, at least, you must have some time for me. Tomorrow evening we'll spend a few hours riding a gondola under the stars,
won't we, Father? Tomorrow evening, after an entire day of celebration" (86). The fact that the new day—for the day, unlike the night, is
always new—is the day of the Venice festival underscores the notion
of its being an event to celebrate. Violetta says that one is "blessed"
by day; it is said in the manner of one who, through her innocence,
has earned this blessing, for day is the time of legitimate profit, significance, and merit. *Venise sauvée* ends with lines spoken by Violetta
that recognize precisely the blessing of the coming day.[15] From her
letters and notebooks we know that Weil returned to these closing
lines again and again, polishing each word. From her work on these
lines—the only "finished" lines of verse in the play—one can glean
their importance for Weil. Sweeter to one's eyes than sleep, the rays of
day alight upon the sea and the soul, making visible one's happiness.[16]

In her notes, Weil insists that Violetta be ignorant of the night's
proceedings. Upon waking she is to perceive nothing: "Violetta
knows nothing, she sleeps, and, fortunately, will certainly not

awake until everything is over. [Jaffier] knows that she wants to come see the sea and greet the day as soon as she awakes, but he hopes that she will not be aware of anything [that has happened during the night]" (102-103). All the efforts to ensure that Violetta know nothing of the night's disturbances put into relief all that Jaffier must witness. To be sure, her not seeing anything is an essential feature of Violetta's blank, untouched innocence, a perfect foil for Jaffier's wounded innocence, and against which his final words, spoken on the cusp of death, take on a particularly poignancy. "To my eyes soon without sight, how beautiful the city is," says Jaffier, affirming nothing more than the beauty of Venice, its transparent reality (146).

AND SLEEPLESS, AND AWAKE

Night is the time of repose, but its peace continually fingers the border of disruption. One cannot sleep; the others will not let you sleep. Just who these others are remains fundamentally unknown. In sleeplessness, consciousness is still captive to night in the form of a "curious conscience that still lords / Its strength for darkness." For Jaffier, the others are both the real and imaginary figures who keep him captive and sleepless. The other is precisely he who releases me so that I might sleep. I cannot give myself sleep; I can only be given over to sleep.

In "Ars somni," Nancy writes that the night is not simply that which replaces light. (It is true that one can sleep in day.) It is said to come from inside the sleeper, but curiously, most startlingly, if we look inside, if we could, it would be the fall of day inside the sleeper.

> He who sleeps, in a way, feeds himself. He who sleeps feeds on nothing that comes from without. Like hibernating animals, the sleeper feeds off his own reserves. He digests himself, so to speak. In addition to his own substance, his food is also made of the night. Not the night that surrounds him, and that can sometimes be replaced by light if the sleeper retires during the day, but the night that he first lowers upon himself, the night of drooping eyelids, indeed, in extreme circumstances, the night fallen upon eyes wide open. Fallen "upon," yet coming from within, coming from the fall of day within the sleeper.[17]

Day seems intact in this description. It is not so much fallen in the sense of its diminution but in the sense of its being held in reserve inside the sleeper. But it is unclear when this reserve—this day inside—is itself alimentary. Night is that which, in a certain manner, feeds the one before sleep (as in the one "felled" with sleep and not as one who is not yet asleep).

I would say that the time of sleep is not the time of before and after. For the one who cannot sleep, or who finally sleeps under extreme circumstances, night seems to reduce him to one with "eyes wide open." The time of sleep for the one with eyes wide open is the time of an incomprehensible simultaneity with a night that always seems nevertheless to surpass him since it cannot be counted as such and this would-be sleeper cannot be counted upon to catch up. That is why when one says, "I need to catch up on my sleep," it never rings true. One cannot catch up even if one sleeps. If one were to sleep and sleep for days, such as a hibernating animal, one would not catch up on one's sleep. Upon waking, the sleep is gone and so, too, is the night. One has spent one's resources (one's very body) to enter into a night that has no use for him and that can keep him at any moment without sleep. If night feeds the sleeper, and if the sleeper, additionally, uses his own reserves to feed sleep, for the one who cannot find sleep or whom sleep has not found, there is a suggestion that something comes to prohibit this assumption of sleep. But there is also the suggestion that the one without sleep is the one who cannot feed himself, who depends upon something outside himself to feed his sleep. The one with eyes wide open is an apt expression for the experience of one's exposure to an outside that is so troubling because that "outside" seems precisely to come from no place, from an externality external even to an outside. For the one without it, sleep seems effectively beyond his reach.

He cannot count on himself nor can he enter into a realm that is beyond his self. The one who desires sleep may long for it, but this longing is not what essentially defines his situation. He may miss sleep or he may want sleep, but it does not rigorously follow that his sleeplessness is thereby a lack or a want. Nonetheless, against the plenitude of sleep, the sleepless, with his psychic and somatic exhaustion, is shorn. And although one may think of being awake as presence and plenitude, being sleepless is not thereby an absence. Furthermore, being sleepless is not the opposite of being awake in day, and anyone can tell you that being awake in night is not the same thing as being awake in day. There are waking hours, but sleep does not have such hours. Sleep is more cunning, a forever prodigal son who does not cease to ask for more; the body gives in to its ceaseless demand.

It is foolish to say of the one without sleep that he is "free" to do, produce, etc. No time has been freed up, and the freedom of the one without sleep is not a difficult freedom; it is a useless freedom. It is a time without profit, although it is certainly true that he may be laboring for sleep. (His fatigue is always also literal). Shown—for night is the time of an exposure more awful than of daylight–and nothing to show for it. He has nothing to gain and nothing to lose. This is what is so terrible and so unthinkable about this time: it is not only without use, it is insignificant.

"IT IS DONE"

In Blanchot's *La Folie du jour*, the protagonist-narrator is a man with "eyes wide open."[18] His near-blindness is the metaphorical and literal condition for something that cannot be looked at directly, for something that passed or seems to have passed, is perhaps happening still, but that cannot be attested to, as such. The madness of day—its terrible measure and clarity, its happiness—after the world's madness; the resumption of an unthinkable equilibrium as the permanent and historical present of the day. In it is an interminable consciousness in time's reanimation and suspension: "Day that does not pass. At the heart of the time that passes, nothing goes on, nothing comes up," comments Levinas.[19] Or as Caroline Sheaffer-Jones puts it, "the madness of the day expands amorphously from one day to encompass all days, permeating everything."[20]

Everything returns to the same, infernally, in a mad repetition of near-sameness that is inscribed in a narrative structure that appears to end as it begins, in the question of a story. "A story? I began: I am not learned; I am not ignorant. I have known joys. That is saying too little" says the narrator, returning to the words with which the story begins (FJ 29). The narrator turns it into a question himself, oscillating in his final declaration between its not being one, no longer being one, and closing off the possibility of future stories: "A story? No. No stories, never again" (30; Non, pas de récit, plus jamais). So it is a story, if it can be called that, that questions itself from the outset, uncertain of what it can say and contesting what has been said by not exactly offering up anything. We know, moreover, that *La Folie du jour* was first published in 1949 as "Un récit" (A story) in *Empédocle* and listed in the table of contents as "Un récit?," further underscoring the instability of the narrative. The lingering trace inscribed in the

two titles suggests a kind of deferral or belatedness of knowing suggested by the not quite exact repetition of the title. In Sheaffer-Jones's
view, the question mark indicates "an interrogation that destabilizes
any unequivocal affirmation of a story."[21] Sheaffer-Jones's characterization of the not-exact repetition as an "interrogation" has a further
implication for our reading: recall that the repetition of the story ("I
am neither learned nor ignorant") begins as a response to the narrator
being interrogated about what happened, "Tell us 'just exactly' what
happened" (29)—precisely the question that I am suggesting cannot
be answered. Following Levinas's reading, we might say that it is the
fragile possibility of saying itself, known mostly through the elision
of its thematization as a "story." We know that *something* happened
but really only by way of the account demanded of the narrator-I
rather than the account itself, a version of "Tell us!" not so different
from what Jaffier's captors demand. Of what "it" is, we have only a
wounded clarity: the glass smashed into his eyes—what Levinas calls
a "transparency that wounds" and the story's central symbol.[22]

Immediately upon the removal of the broken glass from his eyes,
the protagonist is told that he slept for seven nights: "I was asleep! I
had to hold my own against the light of seven days—a fine conflagra-
tion!" (18). It becomes difficult in this dizzying world to know what
one has gained, what one has lost: "I have wandered; I have gone from
place to place. I have stayed in one place, lived in a single room. I have
been poor, then richer, then poorer than many people. . . . I see this
day, and outside it there is nothing. Who could take that away from
me? And when this day fades, I will fade along with it—a thought, a
certainty, that enraptures me" (9, 10). Nothing to gain and nothing to
lose, but we may say that he nonetheless owes something. The strangest thing about it is that it is a debt that was never contracted.[23] The
debt, furthermore, is unpayable, though there is the unfailing sense
that it must be paid. Awakeness at night is inseparable from this failure to pay up. One's awakeness only further increases the debt since
the one who does not sleep does not cease his expenditure. The debt
is as immemorial as night. The one who spends his night without
sleep is the paradox of the one who, in this expenditure, wastes night
(its repose) and who lives the last day (all last days) but without its
profitability, to be sure. It is a con, a way of pushing back tomorrow
by making yesterday last through the night. Without night how can
there be another day? For the next day is the day for one's accounts
to be in order. The conceit here is that if you do not sleep you do not

make room for such a day, for such an accounting. Or you might try to prolong sleep—indefinitely, as in a coma, or finally, as in death—as one of the patients in *La Folie du jour* attempts to do, swallowing poison *after* being given the prescribed sleeping medication. The narrator remarks: "The doctor called it a rotten trick. He revived him and 'brought suit' against him for this fraudulent sleep. Really! It seems to me this sick man deserved better" (20). What is the patient's ruse? Is it to evade sleep? But sleep is the reason the patient is there in the first place, so, no. Is it to evade day? That seems more likely, but the coma into which he slips and (forcefully) out of has not gone so far as death. "Fraudulent sleep," says the doctor in disgust; and he "makes a complaint" against it and the man who went along for the ride. Isn't this a way of forcing this man to pay up, to call him to account?

Upon waking up after being blinded, the narrator is immediately told that he slept for seven days and that he must tell what happened to him. "Yes, seven days at once, the seven deadly lights, became the spark of a single moment, were calling me to account. . . . I was asleep! When I woke up I had to listen to a man ask me, "Are you going to sue?" A curious question to ask someone who has just been directly dealing with the day" (18, 19). Again this notion of "making a complaint." Against what or whom? That is undoubtedly what those who question him would like to know.

The accounting does not fully strike the one still awake, although his distress and anxiety is perhaps the somatic and psychic response to his situation. The anxiety has its own permanence or inertia; the feeling one has is that nothing will change and nothing can change. "It is done," says the narrator of another "tale" of sleep and death, Marguerite Duras's *La Maladie de la mort*.[24] There, I think, the sickness of death moves between the one without sleep (the "you" to whom the words are addressed) and the woman who sleeps, via the unnamed third who narrates those words. Or perhaps "moves" is not quite right, since the malady of death has sleeplessness's inertia. It hangs in the air of the hotel room, and the constant waves of the sea outside are a metaphor for the distress and anxiety of the sleepless man who goes from one to the other, while stricken by both. But the sickness that is said to belong to him seems to emanate from the woman's nightly repose, or at least from his encounter with her and her sleep. The woman, remember, is under a paid contract; he pays for her (to) sleep, although he himself does not enjoy sleep. He enters her sometimes, but it is a false substitute for sleep. When she emits a cry of pleasure, he tells her to never speak her pleasure again. When the contract is up, she is gone. He, we can guess, remains suspended in night's malady. It is she who needs to tell him what he suffers from. He could never tell it (to) himself. There is a curious absence of introspection in sleeplessness; words and thoughts fall into a vortex of nonsense, sickness, disorder.

The circular trajectory of the "story"—and so, the reiteration of the narrative after the question of its being a story ("A story? I began: I am neither learned nor ignorant . . .") and the final declarative statement that only entrenches its ambiguous status ("A story? No, not a story. Never again.")—enacts this absence, and in so doing, points at once to the necessity of telling and the impossibility of testimony.[25] At the end, the narrator appears to be giving his interrogators the facts of his case (that is, the story of what happened), but we know that he cannot. This inability goes against the powers that others constantly ascribe to him throughout the narrative: "Look, you're an educated man; you know that silence attracts attention. Your dumbness is betraying you in the most foolish way" (28). And so when he claims silence for himself, those who interrogate him can only think he is conning them and betraying himself. When he begins to tell his "story," they say, *Now* we will finally uncover the facts. But the story, he tells us, is already over.[26] *It is done.*

MISSED DEATH

Betrayal is no small matter in these stories. There is no question that one has taken part in betrayal: the insistence upon a confession of what happened is not, as they say it is, to uncover anything new. The narrator of *La Folie du jour* tells us plainly, "They had pointed out to me that my answer would not reveal anything, because everything had long since been revealed" (28). What, then, is the point of the story?[27]

The protagonist of *La Folie du jour* works for the institution where he was once a patient. Actually, it is unclear whether he is still a patient there because the story he is telling us straddles the boundary between a therapeutic cure and one of many things he has already given the doctors, the police, the law. But what he gives up is precisely what cannot be captured in the narrative, a failure that becomes perceptible in the ever-increasing and paradoxical attempts by his interrogators to seize what they claim is already theirs: "Throwing open my rooms, they would say, 'Everything here belongs to us.' They would fall upon my scraps of thought: 'This is ours.' They would challenge my story: 'Talk,' and my story would put itself at their service. In haste, I would rid myself of myself. I distributed my blood, my innermost being among them, lent them the universe, gave them the day" (23). Taking possession of the objects, as with stripping the body of its "innermost being," is not only a way of reducing the subject to nothing, although that is just what it appears to be. The narrator tells us that he would "rid myself of myself." But it is precisely that in his radical dispossession, the subject exposes a limit to what can be seized and so, to what can be mastered (by the Law, the State, the day, etc.). A "perfect nothingness" (parfaite nullité) is what they get. For all that he gives—or *owes*—them, he is still accused of hiding something from them: "All right, where are you? Where are you hiding? Hiding is forbidden, it is an offense, etc." (23). What they say he is hiding from them is what happened to him. "Tell us *'just* exactly' what happened" is their unified cry (29; Racontez-nous comment les choses se sont passées au juste). He tells them, finally, but the story in the end is exactly how the narrative began: "I am not learned; I am not ignorant. I have known joys. That is saying too little . . ." (9, 29). At this repetition, the narrator tells us, is the end of the story: "A story? No. No stories, never again" (30).[28]

Here the words come to an abrupt stop, reflecting the structural impossibility of recounting what happened, since it is, notably, the story of what did not happen: it is the death that happened to the other, and that passed one by. The man in *La Folie du jour* was supposed to die; they put him against the wall. But it didn't happen to him. He missed his death, although it is certain that others (the others in the field, outside the castle) did not miss theirs. To know this one has to go to another book, *L'Instant de ma mort*.[29] More details of the "event" are in Derrida's commentary on that book, *Demeure*.[30] Yet, in *La Folie du jour*, this is all we get: "I was made to stand against the wall like many others. Why? For no reason. The guns did not go off" (11). Enough said: even if we were to know why (even if there were a reason), it would not give the secret of what it exposes.[31]

Jaffier, too, was supposed to die; or rather, his life was not supposed to be spared as it was. He missed the death he was supposed to have. But then in the last moments of the play, the opportunity arises for him to jump into an "anonymous" death—a solution that delights his captors since it means that Jaffier will die without Venice breaking its promise to spare his life. "If he joins these bandits," reasons one of the Venetians, "he'll be massacred along with them, and we'll be freed of him, without Venice having broken its word" (VS 144). But when this takes too long and the night's events come dangerously close to being known to Violetta, Jaffier's captors end up pushing him into the foray. And so, again, unwittingly and against what he can do, another one of Jaffier's resolutions is preempted, left unfulfilled—a kind of second "missed" death—except that this time, we suppose that it will end in his dying, even so.

"We don't have to ask why he betrayed his friends!" cries the apprentice, looking at Jaffier and his bag of gold. But what is this evidence? "He will go, loaded with gold, rich and content, engorged with his crimes!" (140). But what exactly is his crime? Jaffier does not need his captors to tell him he is guilty, since he is living it. And his innocence—"My whole crime was to have had pity," says Jaffier— still does not prevent him from the wish to hide in shame, nor from a despair that makes him cry out, "My God, I can neither die nor live" (133). After the unjustified privilege of escaping death, it seems that Jaffier can only emulate death in (the wish for) sleep. After receiving the bag of gold, Jaffier says submissively, "Thank you. I can now hide, eat and sleep." But the apprentice is mistaken when he claims that his friends "paid" for their crimes while Jaffier remains indemnified. He is compared to Judas, and the comparison is telling: like Judas, Jaffier is believed to have "given up" his friends and brought them to their deaths. Can we draw an analogy between betrayal and not keeping one's word? In one sense: they both turn upon "forgetting" the other—that is, upon not honoring the other. In these terms, Jaffier is not a traitor as his captors claim. But something seizes him nonetheless, and it must be that that is outside the terms set by his captors. To their question: "Must we leave that thing alive?" (135) is Jaffier's own grief-stricken question: "But how to stay alive?" (130).

Venise sauvée was never completed before Weil's death. The first two acts are only sketches, but the third and most important act is more fully drawn. In Weil's notes on the play, it seems that she was undecided on how to present Jaffier's response to the bag of gold: "In the 3rd Act, instead of his reply ('Where?—Thank you, I will drink and eat'), he might keep silent while others comment upon his gestures (he avidly clutches the gold). 'We don't need to ask why he betrayed his friends!' Stretch out this part of the act where he remains silent?" (24). We don't know what Weil would have ultimately chosen—whether Jaffier would have replied, "Thank you. I can now hide, eat and sleep," or whether he would have stayed silent, the act of clutching the gold the only sign of its acknowledgment. Whatever the final version would have been, I think that the two variants are not quite so different in the end. At the crux of both—the terrible "thank you" and the silent gestures—is the kind of unspeaking speech that might be said to describe the narrator in *La Folie du jour*. What can one say, after all? If the gold is outwardly the symbol of compensation for betrayal and is inwardly a sinister substitution for what one has to give, it is doubly and most strongly, the counterpoint to what cannot be bought and which gives itself weightlessly, regardless.[32] I think that it applies to Venice's beauty as well as to the secret of *La Folie du jour*. Without any dissimulation, the man blinded by the madness of day reveals this secret: "But this is the remarkable truth, and I am sure of it: I experience boundless pleasure in living, and I will take boundless satisfaction in dying" (FJ 9). A scandalous, extravagant secret that betrays nothing, that, finally, says nothing either. Like Venice's beauty, we might say, which sheds no light on either Jaffier's betrayal or his fidelity. And for which Jaffier's silence, like his awakeness—and finally, his death—is the tribute of an unlimited indebtedness and indemnity, both.

UNFINISHED

Weil's play takes place in Venice, and Venice, just as much as Jaffier, is its hero. It is curiously untouched by the violence of an event that never quite happened. And whereas Jaffier is to throw himself into death, Venice stands deathless. For all the city's precariousness, another day rises. And if we are to infer from Violetta's ignorance, it will carry no memory or knowledge of what happened that night. Weil goes against the tide of tragedy for most of the final act since the nexus of the play's movement is in Jaffier's stillness. Weil does not sustain this risk to the end of the play since she ultimately allows Jaffier to die fighting.[33] I do not know quite what to make of these two heroes, but I am inclined to think that Venice's preservation is not simply a postscript to the story. A strange energy emanates from the difference of these two heroes—and, really, from the indifference of Venice to the other. One possible solution might be that the city's innocence—its beauty—does, as Violetta insists in the second act of the play, save it from destruction. And if we accept this reading, we might say that Jaffier is the play's sacrificial lamb. "Only innocence expiates," writes Weil in her notebooks.[34] In good tragic fashion, Jaffier must die. But this is unlike the story of one of Weil's favorite tragic myths, the fall of Troy. It is also unlike the real story of the sacking of Carthage, a fact so grievous to Weil that it was almost a living memory for her. As I have said, the city is preserved; it would not be quite right to say that it is restored. Nothing is lost, really, and the bloodshed is unseen.[35] But I wonder, in the strange economy we have followed—in the unfinished obligation that sometimes speaks in the language of an unpayable debt, sometimes in the language of an unmet sleep—whether this new day has brought with it something new. Anne Carson writes something about Venice not unrelated to this vexing question, which I would like to intone here. That it is a "system of corridors where people follow one another but never meet, never find the way out. There is no way out, all corridors lead back into the system."[36] A puzzling economy, this gatelessness: all corridors and no way out.

CHAPTER 5

The Extravagant Demand
of Asking Nothing

*Destitution and Generosity in "Autobiographie
spirituelle" and* La Connaissance surnaturelle

. . . from the angle of inclination of his existence, and from the angle of
inclination in which the creature enunciates itself.

—Paul Celan, "The Meridian"

Ever since the posthumous publication of selected aphorisms from
her notebooks under the title, *Gravity and Grace (La Pesanteur et
la grâce)*, the name of Simone Weil has come to be identified with
her sudden mystical turn to God in her late twenties.[1] And yet, Weil
does not use the word "conversion" to describe a religious experience
that, although of singular importance to her, does not fundamentally
change anything in her thinking or in the way she lived her life.[2] After-
ward, as before, Weil would accommodate all the different registers
of her thinking in a syncretic whole that readers have variously found
fascinating or scandalous. Weil's approach, which Françoise Meltzer describes as a "rigorous inappropriateness," is concurrent with a
life that defies easy categorization. "She was, after all, of Jewish ori-
gin and Catholic faith; she was a Catholic who refused baptism and
scolded the church; a Communist troublemaker from bourgeois parents who refused to join the Party; an intellectual who hung out with
the working class," writes Meltzer.[3] Not surprisingly, Weil refused to
be baptized, explaining her reasons in what has come to be known
as her "Spiritual Autobiography" ("Autobiographie spirituelle"): "I
would betray the truth, that is to say the aspect of the truth that I see,
if I were to leave the point where I have found myself since birth, at
the intersection of Christianity and all that is not Christian."[4]

Concerning her position at "the intersection of Christianity and all
that is not Christian," Weil admits in a letter to Maurice Schumann,

a classmate from Henry-IV now working for the Free French, that "it is not an easy spiritual situation to define and make comprehensible."[5] Weil continues:

> I adhere totally to the mysteries of the Christian faith, with the only kind of adherence that seems to me appropriate for the mysteries: this adherence is love, not affirmation. Certainly I belong to Christ. At least I like to believe so. But I am kept outside the Church by philosophical difficulties which I fear are irreducible; they do not concern the mysteries themselves but the definition with which the Church has seen fit to clothe them in the course of centuries, and above all the use in this connection of the words *anathema sit*. Although outside the Church or, more precisely, on the threshold, I cannot resist the feeling that I am really within it nonetheless. Nothing is closer to me than those who are within it. (EL 198)

Weil's claim that her adherence to the Christian mysteries is bound by love rather than affirmation is key to understanding this "uneasy spiritual situation." It turns us to a deeper perplexity concerning what Weil means by love and returns us to some unfinished questions about unconditioned desire and its relationship to force and destitution raised at the outset of this book. Specifically, what is meant by love if God is love and if God, as Weil maintains, only loves himself? This has important implications for God's relationship to creaturely life, established first by his withdrawal from the world, so Weil claims, as an act of unconditional love. This withdrawal is a primary instance of destitution—a leave-taking that, although itself unmarked, leaves creaturely life in a wanting relationship not to what is no longer there (the "no longer" is precisely what cannot be known) but, rather, to *what is there*.[6]

The decreative aim of that relationship, first introduced in our discussion of beauty in *Venise sauvée*, is here discussed in view of Weil's account of leave-taking in her own life, wherein the "I" is impelled toward impersonal and depersonalized being. It offers us a terse picture of how, as Alexander Irwin puts it, one might write "in and with the substance of one's own life."[7] In the case of Weil, such writing paradoxically entails a reinscription of the self at the scene of its depersonalization. For Weil's creaturely existence is stubbornly intractable from its saying, even though that saying appears to demand exactly the opposite and that existence, exposed to physical and psychic destitution, appears to shut down the possibility of saying altogether. The problematic for us here is precisely the antinomy through which decreation unfolds, in this consent to not have or take, such as it is reflected in Weil's uneasy spiritual position at the threshold and the demand for nothing it assumes.

If we return to the idea of withdrawal as an act of unconditional love, we move between love for something that does not exist and love for something that can only be "had" under conditions of destitution. For Weil, unconditional love is love of the good (Weil says that love's object is the good), and yet, it is to desire without an object (the good is not an object). It is love for something that does not exist, as such (Weil says that the good belongs to the uncreated part of the soul), and so, for something that cannot be affirmed. On the other hand, human love would seem to be love for what does exist and so, for what is subject to continual degradation. How, then, might human love be transformed into an unconditional love which Weil calls "supernatural love" through decreation? The answer is surprising both for its sheer audacity (be like God) and for its total simplicity (do nothing, wait, withdraw)—an extravagance and surfeit of unused love! For the transformation is not a "progression" from human love to supernatural love: one does not exactly do anything, and decreation does not imply that one is no longer subject to force or necessity. It is rather this very force that, without ceasing to exert itself upon the human, is indispensable to that transformation. We are met here with another Weilian paradox: one needs this destitution, must allow it, even ask for it, until one has spent all one's resources. But being thus spent, one risks losing the capacity to love and so, to love what is wholly other than oneself. This last seems to be the case when Weil, alluding to Isaiah 40:30, writes that "those whom God loves are never tired," adding with horror that, "I am not one of them" (203).[8] This extravagance (doing everything, doing nothing) is the subject of the last part of this chapter, where Weil's "Projet d'une formation d'infirmières de première ligne" gives us our concrete example of doing nothing and everything out of love—a generosity, we might say, that is underwritten by the destitution of a self left behind.

EN HUPOMONE

Weil gives an account of her religious experiences in a letter to Father Joseph-Marie Perrin, shortly before her departure from France in May 1942.[9] The story itself can be summarized as follows. In 1936, after a year of factory work, exhausted and miserably ill—a work so brutal and dehumanizing Weil likened it to slavery—Weil spent some time in a small Portuguese village that was "very miserable also." Weil writes, "I was suddenly certain that Christianity is the religion of slaves par excellence, that slaves could not but belong to it, and I among others" (AD 43). The following year, Weil spent two days in Assisi: "There, alone in the little roman chapel . . . something stronger than myself obligated me for the first time in my life to kneel" (43). In 1938 Weil spent ten days in Solesme, following all the services of the Easter week. Despite being ravaged by the migraines that plagued her for her entire adult life, Weil recounts being able to listen attentively to the chants, "a pure and perfect joy" that enabled her to understand the possibility of loving God through affliction: "It goes without saying that during these services, the thought of the passion of Christ entered me once and for all" (43). The last moment of her conversion experience came upon reciting George Herbert's poem, "Love."[10] Weil recited the poem with all her attention whenever seized by debilitating headaches. It is during one of these recitations, Weil writes, that "Christ himself descended and took possession of me" (45). Of that encounter, Weil reflects in another letter, "I thought I was only reciting a beautiful poem but, unknown to me, it was a prayer."[11]

In Weil's description of her experiences there is a submission, beyond comprehension, beyond one's power. "Something stronger than myself obligated me for the first time in my life to kneel" and Christ "took possession of me," writes Weil in a language that closely resembles that of other Christian conversion narratives (43, 45).[12] Weil's encounter with Christ seems permeated by a certain violence, one that is as much constituted by a complete destitution as it is by being overtaken.[13] For although Weil sometimes uses the language of mystical union, that union is invariably disrupted. More than the initial union, it seems that the rupture and subsequent abandonment are what maintains her adherence to that love. If Weil is seized by the heights of love, it is surely in the "dark night" of abandonment that she finds her most compelling proof of God's love.[14]

Similarly, her experience in Solesme is articulated with physical and psychic suffering. Weil describes her attention to the beauty of the songs *through* the pain itself, concluding that "this experience allowed me, by analogy, to better understand the possibility of loving divine love through affliction" (43). The kind of attention Weil describes here is characterized by a stillness akin to the passivity and impersonality of fatigue in that one cannot withdraw from it once it enters. Such a being cannot be thought outside of its being enmeshed in the pain that does not cease to penetrate it. Unlike a form that would come to fill or fulfill it, it empties the self in the taking that is implied by its penetration.

Weil uses a Greek term found in the New Testament to describe such suffering: *en hupomone* (ὑπομονή), a term more beautiful and complex, says Weil, than its Latin translation as *in patientia*:[15] Weil explains: "But the Greek word, ὑπομονή, is infinitely more beautiful and charged with a different meaning. It designates a man who waits without moving, despite all the blows by which one tries to make him move" (PSO 145).[16] Taking its etymological roots into consideration, we might further guess its significance for Weil. The Greek suggests something more than a simple steadfastness or perseverance, such as is denoted by *in patientia*. Drawn from "hupo," meaning "under," and "meno," meaning "abide," *en hupomone* connotes a remaining under, a certain submission of the one undergoing difficulties. The term can also convey a kind of triumphalism or power in the face of adversity, but as Weil used it, *en hupomone* instead denotes an emptying or voiding of the self, of its bodily capacity and will. It exhausts, depletes, depersonalizes. It is a deeply anonymous suffering, the way that chronic fatigue seizes the body in an obscure and limitless way.

Importantly, the theme of suffering in Weil's religious experiences resonates with the physically demanding factory work she undertook during a teaching sabbatical in 1934–35, first detailed in *La Condition ouvrière* and further theorized in *Réflexions sur les causes de la liberté et de l'oppression sociale*.[17] Having long supported workers' rights in syndicalist movements, her intention in this "personal study" was to experience firsthand the conditions of unskilled work in modern factories.[18] More specifically, she hoped to test whether one of her theories concerning work held true: that it enables attention to flourish by uniting thought and action and, as such, is a singular locus of spiritual, moral, and cultural regeneration.[19] One of the prominent themes in the letters, essays, and journals that comprise *La Condition ouvrière* is the question of fatigue (understood and experienced by Weil as having physical, psychic, social, and spiritual dimensions) and its relationship to the structural conditions of factory work. Weil found the repetitive and physically numbing tasks demanded by the assembly line and piecework formation to be incapacitating, producing a stupor that made attention and thinking all but impossible. (On this score, the frequent mention of falling into a "reverie" during piecework in her factory journals begins to make sense. Outside of work hours, Weil relates the great temptation to sink into a "half-sleep" [CO 21].)[20] In one of her reflections near the end of her work experience at the Renault factory, Weil attests to the crushing effects of this mode of work: "I was all but broken. I almost was—my courage, the feeling of my dignity were more or less broken during that period, the memory of which would humiliate me if it weren't for the fact that, properly speaking, I did not keep a memory of it. I awoke with dread, I went to the factory in fear: I worked like a slave. . . . Time was an intolerable weight" (144).

But perhaps more insidious is the way fatigue enters unnamed into the endless lists (of tasks, of numbers, such as the number of parts made, the wages earned and deducted) that make up a substantial part of her factory journal. Nothing, Weil tells us, is simpler than a number. In her journal, Weil fixes upon the number as though by doing so she has also fixed upon the source of an exhaustion that will not end even after the work is done. Recalling her experience to Perrin six years later, Weil writes, "I had really forgotten my past and I did not look forward to any future, finding it difficult to imagine the possibility of surviving this fatigue" (AD 42). She writes: "Being in the factory, indistinguishable to all eyes, including my own, from the anonymous masses, the affliction of others entered my flesh and my soul. Nothing separated me from it" (42). If we follow Weil, suffering is indiscriminate and cannot be "owned," even as it does not leave you be. In a letter to Boris Souvarine, Weil tries to explain the particularity of a depersonalization born of suffering: "Even during those moments when truly I could do no more . . . I did not feel the suffering as though it were mine, I felt it as the suffering of the factory workers, and that whether or not I personally suffered seemed to me almost like an indifferent detail" (CO 41).[21]

"TO TELL IS A FUNCTION OF SELF"

We might consider this depersonalization further through a reading of "Le Prologue," a "parable of dispossession" written around the time of Weil's spiritual autobiography and the only finished piece of prose of a larger work intended to be developed from the wide-ranging and fragmentary notes that comprise her New York and London notebooks.[22] The prologue has been described as the "quintessence of her spiritual itinerary" and "the purest account by Simone Weil," but what I would like to suggest is that this seemingly autobiographical account shows how the "I" is put into question without, however, obviating the urge to reinstall that "I" into a biographical portrait of Weil.[23] Here is the prologue in its entirety:

> He entered my room and said: "Miserable creature who understands nothing, who knows nothing. Come with me and I will teach you things you do not know." I followed him.
>
> He led me into a church. It was new and ugly. He led me before the altar and said: "Kneel down." I told him: "I have not been baptized." He said, "Fall to your knees before this place, with love, as before the place where truth exists." I obeyed.
>
> He made me leave and climb to an attic from which one saw through the open window the whole city, some wooden scaffoldings, the river where boats were being unloaded. He bade me be seated.
>
> We were alone. He spoke. From time to time someone would enter, join the conversation, then leave.
>
> It was no longer winter. It was not yet spring. The branches of the trees were bare, without buds, in the cold air filled with sunshine.
>
> The light would rise, shine, fade, then the stars and the moon would enter through the window. Then dawn would rise again.
>
> Sometimes he would be silent, take bread from a cupboard, and we would share it. This bread truly had the taste of bread. I have never found this taste again.
>
> He would pour wine for me and for himself; this wine tasted of the sun and the earth upon which this city was built.
>
> Sometimes we would stretch out on the floor of the attic, and the sweetness of slumber would descend upon me. Then I would awake and drink in the light of the sun.
>
> He had promised to teach me, but he did not teach me anything. We discussed all sorts of things, in a desultory way, as old friends do.
>
> One day he told me: "Now go away." I fell to my knees, clasped his legs, I begged him not to drive me away. But he threw me out on the stairs. I descended them without knowing anything, my heart in pieces. I wandered through the streets. Then I realized that I did not know at all where this house was.
>
> I have never tried to find it again. I understood that he had come for me by mistake. My place is not in that attic. It is anywhere, in a prison cell, in a bourgeois salon full of knick-knacks and red plush, in a waiting room of a train station. Anywhere but in that attic.
>
> I cannot help myself from repeating sometimes, with fear and remorse, a little of what he told me. How am I to know if I remember it precisely? He is not there to tell me.
>
> I know very well that he does not love me. How could he love me? And yet, deep down within me, something, a single point of myself, cannot help from thinking, trembling with fear, that perhaps, in spite of everything, he does love me. (CS 9–10)

It is hard not to be shocked by the brutality in these lines and by the narrative arc that begins in plenitude and ends in deprivation. The violence of the separation excises the narrative of the intimacy and insularity of the I-you relationship. It forms the upsurge of the separation of the narrative "I" from the "he" of this scene. What remains is the trace of the divine, consigned ever after (and we only have it as such) as a "he." From the delicious complicity of its relationship to the other, the "I" is chased out like an intruder before being thrown out like an unwanted thing ("Now go away!"). She is thrown out across the threshold—indeed, to the stairs that are themselves a figure for this liminal space.[24] She makes her way to the streets neither knowing nor comprehending the import of her displacement.

It first appears that her exile is from an attic described as a shared space of nourishment, conversation, and sleep. The three things comingle and become so fluid in their happening that they themselves form the time of the world: the light that rises, descends, the stars and the moon that appear, the dawn that reawakens and continues this cycle are, along with the few others that come and go, witnesses to this happening. The time of the narrative, written after the narrator's experience and so, putting an additional scission between the "I" of the narrative and "I" of the narrator, contrasts with the time of the happening of the narrative, a time so perfectly cyclical that it seems immemorial. Weil roots the happenings to a daily routine and place that is banal, nondescript, and abstract (that is, it could happen any day; it does happen every day), just as it is the case in Weil's conversion narrative whereby, as Nicole Maroger notes, "These places are in reality perfectly anonymous and naturally integrated into the divine universe."[25] Indeed, the idea of the circle, which Weil takes from Greek philosophy (Weil cites Heraclitus and Plato's *Timaeus* specifically), is the image both of time and of eternity; it is the equilibrium of opposing terms.[26] In her notebooks Weil writes: "The circle makes one see the identity of the maximum and the minimum. Heraclitus. The same point is the end and the beginning of the circle."[27] This unity is juxtaposed with the terrible split between the temporal and the eternal that follows immediately upon the ejection of the "I" from that place of perfect harmony.

But on a second look, we see that the attic is not the first place from which she has been pulled. He first comes to her elsewhere, into the self-enclosed space of "her room." He tears into her seeming self-sufficiency and egoïc plenitude, calling it instead "miserable."

Destitution begins where we might not expect it. It is not first in the streets that the "I" experiences it but rather in the seemingly complete safety of one's own room, of one's own "I."[28] Put into doubt, released from the illusory fullness of its self-sufficiency, she goes with the other in order to "learn," having been told that she knows nothing. But what exactly has she learned?

She is not taught anything, and the little she tries to retrieve from memory is cast into extreme doubt, ushered back to the unknowingness that characterizes her state before the encounter. She chats with him about "all sorts of things" but about nothing that would appear to be the knowledge promised when he first took her from her room: "He had promised to teach me, but he did not teach me anything. We discussed all sorts of things, in a desultory way, as old friends do." She relates his absence to the absence of certitude and exactitude not only of knowledge but of the telling itself. She claims that it is for the other to tell her if what she is saying is exactly as it was. She is left in a present that has no such confirmation, with words lost in an uncertain memory of what has been left behind. What, indeed, happens remains obstinately opaque, suggesting the limits of the saying itself. But Weil, who is a writer by her own admission (and calling) and for whom language is communication (Anne Carson puts it succinctly in saying that Weil is engaged in a "writerly project . . . the project of telling the world about God, love and reality"),[29] cannot or does not say what "she" has been told. Whatever passes is nearly unmarked—not unlike what happens in Jaffier's soul—and fails to coalesce into an event or representation.[30]

"To tell is a function of self," writes Anne Carson in her comparative study of Weil, Sappho, and Marguerite Porete.[31] And Weil would agree: in this statement from her notebooks is the profound intractability of the self from saying, "We possess nothing in the world—for chance can take everything from us—except the power to say 'I.' That is what we have to give to God, that is to say, that is what we have to destroy" (PG 73). But here is where things become less assured: How is the self that gives up her "I" supposed to tell? What saying is left over? As Maroger writes of the prologue, "'He' and 'I' represent without doubt the most reduced form of language before reaching silence."[32] But in Carson's view, the language is driven by a certain compulsion toward speech; however uncertain the narrator claims to be, the "I" does not fail to tell and tell God.[33] The writerly self (Weil's writerly self, in Carson's reading) disappears into the project of telling to get out of the paradox of maintaining the writer's function ("telling is a function of self") while making that self disappear; it is "a dream of distance in which the self is displaced from the centre of the work and the teller disappears into the telling," writes Carson.[34] In this mode of reading, the "I" of the narrative bumps up against the "I" of Simone Weil, suspending what we might call, borrowing from Samuel Beckett, a "solution of continuity";[35] certainly, the anonymity of the "I" and the "he" in question and their subsequent figurative separation call attention to the seduction of this transposition even as it ultimately resists it. As the prologue suggests—as do nearly all of Weil's last letters and the "I" that occasionally and confoundingly dots her notebooks—the language that she would like to be as transparent as possible keeps the secret of what it says.

The language Weil uses to describe the encounter with divine silence, however unadorned and reduced, is not a straightforward moment of one's *bios*, then, even as nothing could be closer to the truth than to say that Weil did not live it.[36] We know that in May 1942, Weil made the anguished decision to leave France with her parents, frustrated by failed attempts to gather support in France for a plan she developed to help in the fight against Hitler's troops ("Projet d'une formation d'infirmières de première ligne") and hopeful that she might find support for it in New York and reenter France via London to implement it. She describes her efforts in this regard as one with her intellectual and spiritual vocation. In the final weeks before her departure, Weil tells Perrin:

> I have no wish to leave. I shall leave with anguish. . . . The thought guiding me, and which has lived in me for years, so that I dare not abandon it, though the chances of realizing it are weak, is pretty close to the project [the Frontline Nurses] for which you had the great generosity to help me a few months ago, and which did not succeed.
>
> Deep down, the principal reason that pushes me [to leave] is that, given the speed at which things are moving and the conjunction of circumstances, it seems to me that the decision to stay would be a personal act of will on my part. And my greatest desire is to not only lose all will but all personal being. (AD 31)[37]

Weil would only make it as far as London, never returning to France. For someone who lived the last years of her life in exile, sorrowfully uprooted from the country she never ceased regretting leaving, "Le Prologue" suggests that leave-taking (or more precisely, being compelled to go) is a difficult necessity. In this scene and, not unrelatedly, in Weil's own life, she would not have gone without the order to go. It is also hard to imagine that "she" would not have wanted to say, and to stay there forever, but the order comes one day to go. He had come for her by mistake. Her happiness, like her suffering, becomes "an almost indifferent detail" in view of this mistake.[38] But she suffers nonetheless—what difference does it make that it was not "hers" to suffer? As Ann Smock puts it, "it was this sign [of the Cross], of love, that passed her by. It was for someone else. . . . This branding pain was, we want to suggest, for someone who made, by eschewing it, the error she missed by cleaving to it."[39]

THE BODY'S USE

Weil left Paris with her parents in haste immediately following its surrender to German forces. The Weils eventually made their way to Marseille, with the hope of reuniting with André Weil, who had earlier emigrated to the United States; they would arrive in New York City in June 1942. During their two-year stay in Marseille (September 1940–May 1942), Weil befriended the poet Joë Bousquet, who had been severely injured during the First World War and who was paralyzed as a result, with a bullet lodged in his spine. In their brief but intense correspondence, Weil relates how bodily affliction figures in the love of God, of others, and of the order of the world. Weil cannot help express envy for Bousquet's paralysis: "That is why you are infinitely privileged, for you have the war lodged forever in your body, which for years has waited faithfully that you might be mature enough to know that" (PSO 75). She returns to Bousquet's condition almost obsessively but concludes that, although very near the point at which he might make the connection between his own suffering and that of others in war-torn Europe, he is not yet there.[40] Weil writes: "You, you are now ready to think of it. Or if you are not just yet—I believe that you are not—you have only a shell left to crack to get out of the darkness of the egg into the clarity of the truth, and you have already knocked against the shell" (74).

The redemptive function of affliction—that it not only parallels the order of the world, with all its necessity and force but also brings it home within the flesh itself—here echoes what Weil writes at greater length in her essay "L'Amour de Dieu et le malheur."[41] According to Weil, "the order of the world" (l'ordre du monde)—including the existence of suffering in the world—must be loved because it is the world

God created; to accept the latter is to accept unconditionally that God, who is love, created that world out of love for his creation. In her May 12, 1942, letter to Bousquet, Weil writes: "Happy are those whose bodily affliction is itself the affliction of the world of their time. They have the possibility and the task of knowing and contemplating the world's suffering in its truth and reality. That is the redemptive function itself" (76). To further illustrate the redemptive function of pain, Weil offers details of her own suffering in unblinking terms, reducing it to the most naked term possible: *biological mechanisms*.

> For twelve years I have been inhabited by a pain situated at the central point of the nervous system, at the juncture between the soul and the body, that lasts throughout sleep and that has not for a second been suspended. For ten years it was such, and accompanied by such a feeling of exhaustion, that most often my efforts of attention and intellectual work were almost equally as lacking in hope as those of someone condemned to death who is to be executed the following day. (79–80)

Death would come for Weil a little over a year later, but Weil gives us very little to doubt that it is already there, lodged somewhere "between the soul and the body."

Let us see how this can be called redemptive pain, despite the wretchedness and hopelessness described in the Bousquet letter. In Weil's view, bodily suffering figures as a lever for bridging the distance between God's presence (evident in his creation) and God's absence (evident in the destitution and force to which creation is subjected). Physical suffering by itself does not bridge the distance, but it does lay bare the enormity of the distance and one's finitude, and so, also, reveals the limits of what one can do against a greater force (here: the distance between God's presence and God's absence, but this would apply to any situation of unequal forces). The recognition of limits is critical and is a first step in bridging the distance between two uneven or otherwise incommensurable terms. The use of a lever, precisely because it submits to "natural laws" (which, for Weil, include both physical and moral registers), can effectively equalize or shift the relative "weight" of different forces—much the way that a kilogram could cede to a milligram depending on the length of the arms on a scale.

The body, Weil says elsewhere, is a "lever by which the soul acts upon the soul" (OC, vi/4 264). The "soul upon the soul" because, according to Weil's morphology, the soul is itself divided in two: there is the part that participates in creaturely life (and so, along with the body, is exposed to time and degradation), and there is the part that is "uncreated" and "eternal." The second part "feels nothing, unless by contagion" from the first part (258); not surprisingly, the first part of the soul is the one in contact with the body in this schema. The pain Weil describes undergoing is redemptive because in exhausting the body, pain also exhausts the "wandering" part of the soul, which Weil says—and in terms that bear more than a passing resemblance to Plato's model of the soul—must be tamed.[42]

> Through discipline imposed on the body, the wandering energy of the soul exhausts itself. If a goat is tethered, it pulls at the rope, turns round and round for hours and hours; but exhausted at last, it lies down. It is the same with the wandering part of the soul when the body is kept fixed. It agitates, but despite that it is always brought back to the body, and it is finally exhausted and vanishes.
>
> The soul needs to have been divided in two before one part of it can use the body against the other part in this way. (264)

Weil is unsparing. The body is to be used, exhausted, trained, "obedient to the eternal part of the soul."[43] She concludes this passage with something that oscillates between prayer and demand: "May my body be an instrument of torment and death for all that is mediocre in my soul" (265). And yet Weil can still write: "This happens without violence. The body consents to this domination" (264). Consent is said to transform domination from a state of violence to a state of obedient love; inversely, without love's consent there is only brute violence. Nonetheless, it cannot be said that the state of obedient love is without violence.

The training of the body and the lower part of the soul in service of the eternal part of the soul is not a simple reduction of the body and the soul's exposure to force. Nor is bodily suffering in and of itself is a sufficient condition to bridge the distance between God and creaturely life. It requires something more radical, a kind of subjection (what Weil calls "obedience") that becomes a gift to the other, a donation of self that makes of the very self something both gratuitous and necessary. "To make oneself completely into a sign" (Se fait entier signe), is how Levinas puts it, alluding to Weil and her "example of prayer."[44] Here is that prayer:

> Example of prayer.
> Say to God:
> Father, in the name of Christ, grant me this.

That I might be rendered unable to will any bodily movement, or even any attempt at movement, like a total paralytic. That I might be incapable of receiving any sensation, like someone completely blind, deaf, and deprived of the three other senses. That I might be beyond any condition [hors d'état] to make the slightest connection between thoughts, even the simplest ones, like one of those idiots who not only cannot count or read but have never even learned to speak. That I might be insensible to every kind of pain and joy, and incapable of any love for any being, for any thing, and not even for myself, like old people in the last stage of decrepitude.

Father, in the name of Christ, grant me all this in reality.

That this body might move or be still, with perfect suppleness or rigidity, in continuous conformity to your will. That this hearing, sight, taste, smell, and touch might receive the perfectly accurate impress of your creation. That this intelligence, in the fullest lucidity, might connect all ideas in perfect conformity with your truth. That this sensibility might experience, in their greatest possible intensity and in all their purity, all the nuances of pain and joy. That this love might be an absolutely devouring flame of love of God for God. That all this might be stripped away from me, devoured by God, transformed into the substance of Christ, and given to eat to the afflicted who lack every kind of nourishment in body and soul. And that I myself might be a paralytic—blind, deaf, witless, and utterly decrepit.

Father, effect this transformation now in the name of Christ; and although I ask it with imperfect faith, grant this demand *as if* it were pronounced with perfect faith.

Father, since you are the Good and I am mediocrity, tear this body and soul away from me to make them into things for your use, and let nothing remain of me, eternally, except this tearing itself, or else nothingness. (279–80)[45]

The prayer closes by asking for either nothing to remain of oneself or for nothingness. As for nothingness, it would seem we only "come to it" (on en arrive) through a total violence to the body and psyche: one is stripped and reduced, first of the senses, then of thought. Nothingness is not so much attained as it is forced. "Tearing away" (l'arrachement) is the word Weil uses here. What remains? If it is "nothing," how is that meant to be given as nourishment for others?

It is hard to imagine anyone reciting such a prayer—how could anyone willingly, sanely, ask for such things? Weil recognizes the enormity of the demand: "It is not voluntarily that one can ask for such things. *One comes to it in spite of oneself* [*c'est malgré soi qu'on en arrive là*]. In spite of oneself, yet one consents to it. One does not consent to it with abandon but with a violence exerted upon the entire soul by the entire soul. But the consent is total and without reservation, and given by a single movement of the whole being" (280).[46] The prayer puts one in the curious position of asking for something in spite of oneself. But perhaps the point here is first to think what it means to "come to" something in spite of oneself. We have been saying from the start that it entails the disappearance of the self. But putting it like that spares us too much, I think, from the terrible things Weil lists here: a dizzying collapse of the senses, one after the next. No sight, no hearing, no taste, no touch, no speech, too. No movement is possible, and no ability remains that would allow even two things to be put in relation to each other (this last, a critical hallmark of thinking for Weil). Furthermore, it would seem that each of those senses, each thing, becomes a discrete unit, of itself utterly useless.

But we have perhaps moved too quickly, plunged too readily into the prayer's stark images. Weil makes use of various strategies to try to get around the bind of consenting to something in spite of oneself, most obviously that it is an *example* of prayer and not itself a prayer. If we slow down the reading enough, we see that the paralysis of the first part of the prayer, at least, is an analogy, a way of thinking what it means to be still enough to be the receptacle of divine love—that is, "the love of God for God."[47] But it does not get us out of the difficulty of thinking that asking for divine love nonetheless requires "a violence exerted upon the entire soul by the entire soul." To say, as Weil does, that one gives one's consent in spite of oneself, and that it happens through a violent stripping and tearing away of all that one "has," beginning with one's perceptual faculties and body so that one is rendered *hors d'état*, is to first put into question what exactly it is that one has. To ask that all be taken away is a way of acknowledging that one has nothing, but to ask to be left with only this eternal tearing away is to keep that "nothing" ever present. When the body and all its perceptual and cognitive faculties can be annihilated, when the body has effectively disappeared, what can we say is left over?

THE DEMAND OF ASKING NOTHING

Weil begins the prayer thus: "Father, in the name of Christ, grant me this." What one would get is a wrenching, a tearing away of one's body and soul from oneself so that it lays open, in a nearly unbearable way, what one does not have. And asking for nothing, I would like to suggest, is how these words constitute a prayer. In her commentary on the "Our Father" prayer, Weil writes that we can only be absolutely, infallibly certain of God's will concerning the past.[48] Moreover, we cannot will the future, despite our desire otherwise (such as when desire for an object is premised upon the hope of its being one day possessed or fulfilled). Consequently, the object of our demand is necessarily subject to the same constraints. Since we can neither add nor subtract anything from the past, we must ask for what is, as such, for that which exists "really, infallibly, eternally" independently of our petition. That is "the perfect demand" (la demande parfaite), according to Weil (AD 216).

Periodically you find in the notebooks this small phrase, sometimes written in Greek: "Give that to me" (τοῦτο δὸς ἐμοί),[49] an allusion to a line from the "Our Father" prayer (Matthew 6:11) and that Weil translates as "Our bread, that which is supernatural, give it to us today" (220; Notre pain, celui qui est surnaturel, donne-le-nous aujourd'hui). The temptation here is to attribute this "me" to Weil's person, but as we have seen, Weil complicates the matter. Wherever you see it in her notebooks, you find it added to a passage describing the decreation of the "I." The content of the demand (cela) is the "nothing" of decreation. Here is one such instance: "And when it [the soul] has finally become something entirely belonging to him, he abandons it. He leaves it completely alone. And, in turn, the soul gropingly needs to cross the infinite thickness of time and space to go to what it loves. That is the Cross. . . . τοῦτο" (CTIII 26). And another: "Total humility is consent to death, which makes of us inert nothingness. The saints are those who while still alive have really consented to death. τοῦτο δὸς ἐμοί, κύριε [Father, give that to me]" (OC, vi/4 382).

That same formula is found in a different text altogether, Maurice Blanchot's L'Attente, l'oubli. There the narrator says, "'Give that to me.' An utterance that does not resemble a prayer, nor does it really seem like an order; a neutral, white utterance that (not without hope) he feels he will not always resist. 'Give that to me.'"[50] To ask to be given the nothing that is, is a demand that defies common sense. And yet, to return to Weil, this utterance that is not an order—the audacity of this speech is not of that kind—nonetheless asks. The asking presumes a "you" to whom the words are addressed but in a way that washes out the "I" and where the "me" exists solely as the receptacle for the nothing that is. The "you" remains but is unnamed, invisible, legible only in the address itself that does not enjoin "me" to "you," but rather, through this empty demand and the "me" emptied of its

self, enjoins God to God. Blanchot's narrator again: "'Give that to
me.' He listens to this injunction as if it came from him, addressing
itself to him."[51] For Weil, this empty speech, as if "it came from him,
addressing itself to him," is the very silence of God.

How might we situate the perfect demand with Weil's "uneasy"
position at the threshold, where she claims to be at once a part of the
anonymous masses and to belong to those on the other side? Whenever Weil speaks of the "anonymous masses" (a term we have seen
Weil use to describe both non-Catholics and the working class), she
pictures herself "among them," but only as one might use a parenthetical thought or comma that does little to change the picture. "I
did not feel the suffering as though it were mine, I felt it as the suffering of the factory workers, and that myself, whether or not I suffered,
that seemed to me almost like an indifferent detail," writes Weil of
her factory experience, terms she will repeat in her letters to Perrin
explaining her decision to not enter the Church. We have seen Weil's
recurrent use of this figure of the threshold, be it to talk about politics, philosophy, or religion. Whether viewed from the "inside" or the
"outside," it leaves her in the same place either way: divested of the
specificities of her ego, or what she calls "personal being," and asking only for more of the same. So Weil stays outside the door of the
Church, consenting to remain at the crossroads of all those who are
"given to God . . . and the immense and wretched mass of unbelievers" (AD 19). But she keeps on knocking, nonetheless.

Ann Smock points out that the door is a figure of which Weil likes
to make use.[52] She uses it to describe not only her position on the
threshold of the Church but more generally the posture of attention
(that which keeps you still) and desire (that which moves you). It is
a position that begins to make sense when we see that, for Weil, the
door is not the one you necessarily go through but the one you keep
knocking on regardless. "One must pause and knock, and knock
and knock, indefatigably, in an insistent and humble spirit of waiting," Weil reflects in her notebooks (OC, vi/4 317). The door shall be
opened, Weil states unequivocally. But what do you get on the other
side? Here is one answer, this one from Weil's poem, "La Porte":

> Open the door to us therefore and we will see the streams,
> We will drink its cold water where the moon has left its trace.
> The long road burns hostile to strangers.
> We wander unknowingly, not finding any place.
>
> We want to see flowers. Here thirst is upon us.

Waiting and suffering, here we are before the door.
If necessary we will break it down with our blows.
We press and push but the lock is too strong.

Languish, wait and look in vain.
We look at the door; it is shut, unbreachable.
We fix our eyes upon it; we cry under the torment;
We see it always; the weight of time crushes us.

The door is in front of us; what does it matter to wish?
It is better to go, abandoning hope
We will never enter. We are weary of ever seeing it.
The door, opening, lets pass so much silence

That no streams appeared, no flowers either,
Only the immense space of emptiness and light,
Was suddenly present through and through, filled the heart,
And washed the eyes, nearly blind from the dust.[53]

What the pilgrims see on the far side is not what they had anticipated, for everything appears to be the same as it is on the near side.
The "immense space of emptiness and light" here is nothing so much
like the luminous truth that Plato's philosopher sees at the end of his
struggles (and which Weil sometimes cannot help herself from repeating in the loftiest term), for Weil's pilgrims remain the destitute creatures they have always been, only now less dust-blind it seems. But
now that they apparently have their wish fulfilled (the door is finally
opened), it gives lie to what they had really expected to get on the
other side. If both sides of the door amount to the same, asks Smock,
what have Weil's pilgrims achieved in their ardent desire?[54]

We might begin to answer that question if we consider Weil's position at the threshold as a refusal to obtain or, put negatively, a consent
to not get. "And even if I believed in the possibility of obtaining from
God the repair of the mutilations of my nature," Weil writes, "I could
not bring myself to ask for it. *Even if I were sure to obtain it, I could
not.* Such a request would seem to me an offence against the infinitely
tender Love that has given me the gift of affliction" (AD 82).[55] This
same mode of refusal characterizes her decision not to be baptized.
This is not to say exactly that Weil did not wish to take the sacrament
but rather that she understood herself obligated not to do so. This
obligation, she tells us, is a vocation in the face of which she cannot
step aside. Furthermore, we learn that the obligation comes to her
from the other—"what God wants of me" and "what he commands
me," Weil explains in her spiritual autobiography. "I have never once

had, even for a moment, the feeling that God wants me to be in the Church. I have never even once had a feeling of uncertainty" (52). And in an earlier letter to Perrin, Weil writes, "If I had my eternal salvation placed in front of me on this table, and if I only had to stretch out my hand to take it, I would not put out my hand so long as I had not received the order to do so" (29). These words are nearly exactly those found in her notebooks:

> To not take one step, *even in the direction of the good*, beyond that to which one is irresistibly impelled by God, in action, word, and thought. But be willing to go anywhere under his impulsion to the farthest limit (the cross . . .) To be willing to go to the furthest limit is to pray to be impelled but without knowing where to.
>
> If my eternal salvation were on this table in the form of an object, and if I only had to stretch out my hand to grasp it, I would not put out my hand without having received the order to do so. (PG 98)[56]

It seems, then, that not taking the sacraments is determined by a strange relationality whereby the other surpasses me and whose transcendence or absence (for these two terms are interchangeable for Weil) leaves me outside myself, without the means to take in spiritual nourishment, without, then, the possibility of being inscribed into a community of believers. Whether or not her negative, "perfect," demand—the thing she never asks for, or the nothing that she does not cease asking for—constitutes a condition of her spiritual progress is beside the point for Weil.

IMITATO CHRISTI

We have seen that the disappearance of the "I" in Weil's writings is inseparable from its depersonalization at the site of physical and psychic pain. In my reading I have suggested that that pain is accompanied by a fissure, a tearing away of the "I" from an egoïc plenitude. Consenting to its disappearance is what Weil calls decreation. Decreating the "I" implies a deprivation or destitution that might be said to constitute one's relationship to God, a negative relationship that is, finally, God's relationship with himself, as "the perfect demand" suggests. The demand, such as it is operative in Weil's refusal to be baptized, is a way of refusing one's own existence. "As regards myself," Weil explains, "I ought to repeat in the opposite sense the abdication of God. I ought to refuse the existence that has been given me, and to refuse it because God is good. As regards other people, I ought to imitate God's abdication itself, to consent not to be in order that they may be" (OC, vi/4 246). Moreover, the consent to not take the sacraments, understood in its decreative aim, is to enjoin oneself to the Other (the divine and the trace of the divine in one's neighbor). However paradoxical it may seem, one is created through one's own destitution, and relationality is established through an open vulnerability to, and preference for, the other over oneself: "After that [after the destruction of the body and lower part of the soul], there is a new creation which the soul accepts, not for the sake of existing, since it desires not to exist, but solely for the love of creatures, in the same way that God consents to create. Accept being created, as God accepts creating, for love of other creatures" (258). The decreation of the "I," then, is an *imitato Christi*. The transformation is nothing less than a kind of Passion and Incarnation, for the uncreated part of the soul is said to be the equivalent of Christ himself. "But that in us which merits this is the uncreated part of the soul which is identical to the Son of God," writes Weil (332). One consents to one's own creaturely existence (that is, one's exposure to necessity) through one's decreation for sake of one's love of the other, just as, in Weil's reading, God renounced a part of himself in creating the world and in subjecting himself to creaturely existence through the figure of Christ.

Being subject to necessity, Christ is de facto abandoned by God—even before his cry of abandonment on the cross: "Already, as Creator, God empties himself of his divinity. He takes the form of a slave. He submits himself to necessity. He lowers himself. His love keeps beings other than himself in a free and autonomous existence, beings other than the good, mediocre beings. . . . My very existence is like a tearing of God, a tearing that is love. The more I am mediocre, the more the immensity of the love that keeps me in existence shines through" (PSO 35–36). Just as God is said to be love and to have created out of love (that is, to have given up a part of himself in doing so), divine love makes such a transformation of self possible and "real." The Passion as a metaphor for one's decreation is an example of what Weil calls a "real metaphor" (la métaphore réelle) in her late notebooks. And so, for instance, Christ having taken hold of Weil is a "real metaphor": while symbolic, it is also a real contact, the way that the transubstantiation of the Eucharist is understood to be a real contact with God. While Weil describes Christ's Passion as the decisive example of divine self-communication in which an otherwise absent God might be revealed to us, she also insists that that language is "the secret speech of God," conveyed through the poetic medium of metaphor.[57] That "secret speech" opens out onto the world, inscribed onto the visible, material world, through events, actions, and lives that then become examples of "real metaphors" in their own right. Reflecting on Weil's poetics, Alexander Irwin persuasively argues that the real metaphor engenders a mimetic process, "in which the original model generates ever-renewed forms of imitation": "Christians had to *become* real metaphors themselves. The point was not merely to grasp a discursive content, but to set forward a process of poetic communication, of writing, in and with the substance of one's own life."[58]

Weil's "example of prayer" offers a picture of how one might write "in and with the substance of one's own life." The prayer concludes with this petition: "That all this be stripped away from me, devoured by God, transformed into the subsistence of Christ, and given to be eaten to afflicted men whose body and soul lack every kind of nourishment." In the case of Weil's Christology, the bread that feeds the other is the very substance of one's own body. Nourishing the other through one's very body (another example of a "real metaphor") is, of course, to imitate Christ. But from someone who desired communion but consented not to take it, these words are particularly poignant, for it is a body that gives from nothing, having itself taken nothing. A hard pill to swallow, but perhaps the point here is that we aren't supposed to exactly, only contemplate the tension from a distance, the way that one might "occasionally stop and look for a time instead of eating" (OC, vi/4 335).[59] Again, the distance one takes from one's love object—even the one that would sustain or maintain one's very existence—is akin to the distance implied by the act of creation. In both instances, one's part in the world is known through this self-renunciation. Furthermore, claims Weil, one's love is proportional to this distance (PSO 36).

Whether or not we find this a compelling argument depends a lot on one's perspective. One passage from Weil's notebooks in particular situates the "I" from the place where it must not be, imagining its withdrawal out of love for God and for creaturely life:

> All the things that I see, hear, breathe, touch, eat, all the beings I meet, I deprive all that of contact with God, and I deprive God of contact with all that in so far as something in me says "I."
>
> I can do something for all that and for God: to know how to withdraw, to respect the tête-à-tête. . . .
>
> I cannot conceive the necessity for God to love me when I feel so clearly that even with human beings affection for me can only be a mistake. But I can easily imagine that he loves that perspective of

creation that can only be seen from the point where I am. But I act as
a screen.

I must withdraw so that he might see it.

I must withdraw so that God might enter into contact with the
beings whom chance places in my path and so that he might love me.
My presence is indiscreet, as though I found myself between two lovers or two friends. I am not the maiden who awaits her betrothed but
the unwelcome third who is with the two lovers and who ought to go
away so that they can really be together.

If I only knew how to disappear, there would be a perfect union of
love between God and the earth I tread, the sea I hear . . .

That I might disappear so that those things that I see may become
perfectly beautiful from the fact that they are no longer things that I
see.

I do not at all wish that this created world should no longer be perceptible, but that it should no longer be me to whom it is perceptible.
To me it cannot tell its secret which is too high. That I might leave,
then the creator and the creature will exchange their secrets.

To see a landscape as it is when I am not there . . .

When I am in any place, I blemish the silence of heaven and earth
by my breathing and the beating of my heart. (PG 93–95)

What do we make of the articulation of the "I" in this scene? And
how, in its leave-taking, does the "I" allow God to enter into contact
with other creatures? Carson reads in the passage above "the three-
cornered figure of jealousy."[60] Certainly, the image of lovers wherein
the "I" stands outside as an unwelcome third would seem to suggest as much. Actually, the "I" *would like to* stand outside the tête-
à-tête, tries to imagine it from the start, but as a meditation on how
one might get out of the way, it shows how difficult and surprising
that negotiation is. For Carson, "jealousy is a dance in which every-
body moves because one of them is always extra—three people trying
to sit on two chairs. . . . To catch sight of this fact [that I cannot go
toward God in love without bringing myself along] brings a wrench
in perception, forces the perceiver to a point where she has to disappear from herself in order to look. As Simone Weil says longingly: 'If
only I could see a landscape as it is when I am not there.'"[61] One of
the strangest sentences in the scenario of love, the one sure to cause
a "wrench in perception," is this: "I do not in the least wish that this
created world should no longer be perceptible, but that it should no
longer be perceptible to me." The landscape would be seen from the
point occupied by an "I" that has first vacated its place for that perception to take place. Only by relinquishing its centrality (becoming

an "unwelcome third" or disappearing altogether) might the self perceive the impartial "order of the world" (figured here as "a landscape
as it is"), free of the "screens" issuing from an egocentric perspective
that places the "I" at the center of time and space. The tête-à-tête
between the creator and the creature disposes (would need to dispose)
of the "I"; as a creature itself, its place-holding recalls us to the very
substitutability that makes such a union possible in the first place,
since this would be presumably be true of anyone's "I."

But doesn't it also implicate the notion of election? The withdrawal
of the "I" conceived of here sometimes works as a metaphor for
going away, sometimes as a metaphor for one's decreation whereby
one empties the self, undoes the creature in oneself to the point that
one then becomes, through this very emptying, the perfect imprint of
God's creation. And so it seems that the "I" is actually indispensable
as a mediator. God makes contact, then, with other creatures *through*
this decreated "I." And so, Weil can write: "We have the possibility of being mediators between God and the part of creation that is
entrusted to us. It requires our consent so that *through us* he might
perceive his own creation" (93).[62] In this dance that is surely more dizzying than that of jealousy, the unwelcome third is actually quite necessary, since it is the one through whom the two can meet. Again in
her notebooks, we find a passage that initially deepens the complexity: "The self, as it disappears, must become an empty space through
which God and the creation contemplate one another. Then the part
of the soul that has seen God must transform every relation with a
created being or thing into a relation between that being or thing and
God" (OC, vi/4 316). In the above passage, we encounter both election and substitution at once. The soul that has seen God is the soul
of the self that has disappeared. But the passage also suggests that the
creature that has benefited from that donation can also see God by
virtue of that donation. Whichever way you look at it, the disappearance makes possible both its seeing God and the process by which
God and other creatures might contemplate each other.

However, there is something in the passage that puts a kink in
reading it too theoretically, a place where the "I" disturbs the impersonality of the triangulation laid out above: "I must withdraw so that
God might enter into contact with the beings whom chance places in
my path *and so that he might love me*" (Je dois me retirer pour que
Dieu puisse entrer en contact avec les êtres que le hasard met sur ma
route *et qu'il m'aime*).[63] If you read it in the English translation by

Arthur Wills, you'll miss it since the problem it raises is effectively not there at all. This is how Wills translates the sentence: "I must withdraw so that God may make contact with the beings whom chance places in my path and whom he loves."[64] Indeed, Weil, speaking of herself, claims that she "cannot conceive the necessity for him to love me," citing a litany of her inadequacies and failures and echoing what she writes in her letters to Perrin and Schumann, sometimes sorrowfully, sometimes tenderly. The beating heart, the barely whispered breath of the last lines of "Le Prologue," attest as much to this: "I know very well that he does not love me. How could he love me? And yet, deep down within me something, a single point of myself, cannot help from thinking, trembling with fear, that perhaps, in spite of everything, he loves me." Despite everything, says Weil. Despite her horror and unrelenting regret over having left her beloved France suffering under German occupation. Despite her failures, which she tells Perrin are too many to list. And, finally, despite the growing and incapacitating fatigue to which we know, in the end, she would succumb. In wrenching terms, Weil describes the last of these in a letter to Schumann from London: "I have no right to speak of love, for it is not permitted me to ignore that love does not live in me. There where it lives, it operates with an uninterrupted gush of spiritual energy. There is in the book of Isaiah a sentence that is terrible for me: 'Those who love God are never tired.' Consequently, it is physically impossible for me to forget, even for an instant, that I am not of their number" (EL 203).[65]

Nevertheless, Weil found a way to translate this sorrow into proof of God's love—so long as it is merited. Grace (that which can only be given by God) and recompense (for what one has done, merited, or achieved) clash here in a profoundly tricky way:

> I cannot, of myself, make any use of these thoughts and all those that accompany them in my spirit. First of all, the considerable imperfection that I have the cowardice to let subsist in me puts me at too great a distance from where they are applicable. That is unforgivable on my part. Such a great distance, in the best of cases, can only be overcome with time. But by the time I would have overcome it, I will already be a rotten instrument. I am too exhausted. And even if I believed in the possibility of obtaining from God the repair of the mutilations of my nature, I could not bring myself to ask for it. *Even if I were sure to obtain it, I could not ask.* Such a request would seem to me to be an offense against the infinitely tender Love that has given me the gift of affliction. (AD 82)[66]

The "gift" of affliction must be merited. "We are subjected to a pressure from God, so long as we deserve to undergo it and to the exact extent we deserve it," she explains. "God rewards the soul that thinks of him with attention and love, and he rewards it by exerting on the soul a pressure that is rigorously, mathematically proportional to this attention and love" (15). And, as the following passage from her spiritual autobiography shows, it can be just as well merited by the lowliest (not surprisingly, Weil counts herself among them) as it can be by saints. The distinction here is worth pausing over because it is not entirely certain after reading this that Weil's mediocrity is not, well, quite exceptional:

> Adieu. I wish you all possible good, except the cross, for I do not love my neighbor as I love myself—you in particular, as you have seen. But Christ allowed his beloved friend, and undoubtedly all those of his spiritual line, to come to him, not through degradation, blemish, or distress but through ceaseless joy, purity, and sweetness. That is why I allow myself to wish that, even if one day you have the honor of dying a violent death for the Lord, that it be in joy and without any anguish; and that only three of the beatitudes (*mites, mundo corde, pacifici*) apply to you. All the others more or less entail suffering.
>
> This wish is not only due to the weakness of human friendship. For whichever human being in particular, I always find reasons to conclude that affliction does not suit him, be it that he seems too mediocre for such a great thing, or to the contrary too precious to be destroyed. We cannot more seriously fail the second of the two essential commandments. As for the first, I fail in an even more horrible way, for each time I think of the crucifixion of Christ I commit the sin of envy. (61–62)

If Carson is right in saying that Weil is dancing the three-cornered figure of jealousy, it is not so as to be the preferred beloved in a tête-à-tête with God, not even to be the thief who died "alongside" him (an envy expressed in her notebooks), but so as to die *as* Christ did.

WHAT YOU GET WHEN YOU'VE SPENT EVERYTHING

"Hunger looks like me but it is not original with me," sings Hephaistos in the first part of Carson's opera "Decreation."[67] That seems like a pretty good description of the hunger that was constant with Weil and that would ultimately consume her life; the coroner ruled her death a suicide, stating that "cardial failure due to myocardial degeneration of the heart muscles due to starvation and pulmonary tuberculosis" was the cause of death.[68] Weil is said to have hastened her death by refusing to eat more than what she imagined were French food rations under occupation—or by refusing to eat altogether, an account that is mitigated by Simone Pétrement's research into the circumstances surrounding Weil's death.[69]

If we are careful not to pathologize Weil's relationship to food and, more globally, to deprivation, such as I have tried to do throughout, we see that hunger is a "real metaphor" for one's relationship to love in both its creaturely and supernatural forms. Weil writes that if Eve had not eaten the fruit but had instead stopped and contemplated it, she would have had as real a relationship to the fruit as if she had eaten it. It is man's misery, she claims, that looking and eating are two different operations (AD 156). In order to preserve the good and so, also, one's desire for the good, one must not consume the object of one's desire.[70] While the good is, by definition, not an object and so, cannot be consumed, our desire—what Weil calls our "animal" or "supplemental" energy—is such that we confuse the need that desire first signals with its satisfaction. The problem begins not with our desire but with what we imagine we need. Weil says that we only have to imagine that our supposed needs have been met to know that our desire would still not be satisfied. Desire would grow anew for another object or, simply, for more than what we already have. Says Weil: "We always want something else. We want to live for something. It suffices to not lie to oneself to know that there is nothing here below for which we might live" (PSO 14).

Obviously, food is a real need of the body; it supplies us with the energy to serve our bare, biological needs—what Weil calls, loosely following terms found in Greek science, our "vegetative energy." The needs associated with vegetative energy are common to all created beings and are, as such, impersonal. They exist independently of the particularity of the person and his personality (or ego), although, to be sure, nothing works as efficiently as hunger to make bare one's own creaturely existence. That is how we might say that "hunger looks like me but is not original with me." In meeting these needs, Weil argues, one does not preserve the self but rather what is sacred in "man" (Weil's term), "as a creature" (en tant que créature) and as a "human being as such" (l'être humain comme tel).[71]

As for the needs of the soul, Weil argues, they are analogous to the needs of the body at its vegetative level.[72] Just as it is for the body, it is unlivable for the soul if its needs are not met. Once it reaches a certain level of degradation, the soul cries out its pain until one day, exhausted, it can no longer cry out and dies, just as the body does under similar circumstances. Conversely, if one reaches the vegetative level of existence, there is no more room for the soul. Everything outside the single thought of preserving one's life goes numb. And not even one's "life," for that is also too large a thought for someone in this condition. Weil says that under those circumstances, one no longer imagines the act of drinking (such as one who is not dying of thirst would do), since the capacity for representation disintegrates when one's life is reduced to "mere existence."[73] The image of water alone remains. One's obligation to the other in its physical and moral forms is strictly based upon this possibility, Weil argues. So the central image of feeding others in our earlier discussion takes on both its justification and its urgency in view of this fundamental obligation.[74]

The image of food for the body and the soul would seem to provide Weil with the clearest possible example of one's needs. Yet, as we have seen, the soul's ineluctable relationship to the body also provides it with its greatest illusions about need. That is because there exists, according to Weil's morphology (again mining Greek science), another kind of energy above the vegetative. Weil calls this our "animal" or "supplemental" energy. It entails everything that is outside strictly biological needs, such as thought, volition, and physical desire. It is the part of the self that says "I." The problem begins when one's vegetative energy is used to fulfill the apparent needs of one's supplemental energy should this last be exhausted. Then it is that "a quarter of an hour seems like endless duration. Then the cry: 'Enough!' invades the soul, and the soul is split in two if it does not endorse that cry" (OC, vi/4 254). Under these conditions, one is said to become "dead wood" while still alive. If the soul refuses to cry out against the loss of supplemental energy, Weil continues, it has pierced through time into the eternal. But that does not happen unless one is "rooted" in love and one has exhausted one's supplemental energy (254).

The refusal to heed the cry is said to produce a split in the self, and it aligns with our discussion in the first two chapters regarding the cry of radical subject dispossession under conditions of force. In our earlier discussion, where we were concerned with the cry that emerges from the depletion of one's fundamental vegetative energy, I argued that an ethical encounter issued from the recognition of the cry. This differs from the cry protesting the loss of supplemental energy, which, Weil insists, must not be heeded. We must distinguish, then, between these two levels of energy and the uses for which, in Weil's model, they are designed. But it does not get us away from our resistance to the depletion of supplemental energy, nor from the suspicion that the depletion of supplemental energy entails a terrible self-violence.[75] For Weil, the supplemental energy and the desires it feeds must be used up. To explain, she gives the example of the prodigal son.[76] Before he could find the object of true good, he had to use up all his father's resources—and so, what effectively does not "belong" to him, just as the objects of our desire do not belong to us. While Weil largely identifies these riches with our "supplemental energy," she argues that this depletion is required even of those passions that seem to belong to our "vegetative energy," passions that we feel are more necessary to ourselves than food itself. Weil gives the case of Phaedra, for whom "Hippolytus is really more necessary to Phaedra's life, in the most literal sense of the word, than food" (PG 87). Moreover, in "spending" one's supplemental energy, one must not invest it in other objects so as to recuperate one's energy. "What is essential," writes Weil concerning the prodigal son, "is that he should spend and not make money" (OC, vi/4 255). Weil goes further: the energy must not only be exhausted, but the objects of one's attachment must be taken away—indeed, torn from us. "And all this, we must not give up but lose—like Job," writes Weil (PG 86-87). Or like Niobe—another figure to whom Weil often turned, whose children were killed after a boast against Leto. For Weil, Niobe's loss gives an image of what one must represent to oneself even when one is not in danger of losing the objects of one's love. By such a representation, one trains oneself to endure the distance that is said to constitute a perfect love, such as the distance between creaturely life and its creator.

But how does one arrive at such a distance? How, in the face of losing one's object of love (so, in the extreme case, one's children), does one not cry out, "Enough!" How does one still find the energy to love when one's vegetative energy must serve the needs of one's entire being and only need remains? When desire itself has become "impotent" (OC, vi/4 254; le désir devenu impuissant)? If one has not died first (Weil admits that this is a real possibility), the desire comes from the very fact of its exhaustion. "When even the ability to cry is exhausted, one looks," writes Weil (256). It is in this state of utter destitution that desire, detached from its object and empty, "returns to itself" (revient sur lui-même) and, so, becomes pure desire rather than desire *for* something. It is when the soul is in this strange state of simultaneous emptiness and plenitude that the notion of the good, "pure, unconditional," is said to enter one's soul. It is not something that can be affirmed, since unconditional good is ineffable. But, following Weil, one can still adhere to this good that, in its ineffability, does not exist, as such, and that is said to produce "the certainty of an irrecusable reality" (PSO 43).

Let us consider this mystery of adhering to "what does not exist, as such." In a letter to Perrin, Weil included her translation of Sophocles's dialogue between Electra and Orestes. She tells Perrin, "In copying it down, each word resonated so profoundly and so secretly at the center of my very being that the interpretation of Electra as the human soul and Orestes as Christ is almost as certain for me as if I had written these verses myself" (AD 64). Weil finds a perfect instance of "en hupomone" in the example of Electra's still and abiding love amid circumstances that would seem to make such a love impossible. In Weil's reading, Electra's patient love for her brother does not depend upon his return, only upon his existence, which, however, she cannot know or affirm. In the face of such an unknown, Electra nonetheless remains in a state of perfect immobility, refusing all that is not her love for her brother. The refusal to find substitutions for her absent brother (such as her sister does, however reluctantly, in accepting his loss and their present situation) does not imply faith on Electra's part that Orestes will come back for her. For Weil, faith is beside the point: in waiting thus, Electra is not saying, "I know Orestes exists and I believe he will come back for me." That is not something Electra can state. Electra, in her undiluted and unconsoled pain (except for her tears, she refuses all consolations), hovers just this side of death. For Weil, the miracle of the play, its hard truth, is Electra's consent to this absence to her death if need be. It is a metaphor for our relationship to God, that is, for loving what does not exist. "If a man persists in this refusal," she writes, "one day or another God will come to him. Just like Elektra with Orestes, he will see, hear, embrace God; he will have the certainty of an irrecusable reality" (PSO 43).[77] The scene of recognition between Electra and Orestes, so moving for Weil, is the soul's recognition of supernatural love.

SURFEIT OF LOVE

In Weil's moral philosophy, light is ubiquitous, unowned; it shines without consideration for person or circumstance, upon both good and evil. Its meaning as it is applied to love, I have been suggesting, is a constellation of weightlessness and extravagance. Weil's favorite tragic heroines, Electra and Antigone have in common a certain "extravagant love." In her reading of a line from *Antigone* that Weil liked to quote, "I was born to share, not in hatred, but in love," Françoise Meltzer notes that Weil's Antigone suffers from an excess of love.[78] Surely this "share in love" exceeds whatever can be given, parceled out, or returned—an economy we have been following throughout this book. One spends everything one has and even what one does not have.

In her first letter to her parents from London describing some recent events in her life, Weil writes parenthetically, anticipating her mother's response to her predicament, "Always Antigone!"[79] It was a nickname that Weil evidently assumed, sometimes jokingly and sometimes in dead seriousness. Given what we know of Weil's life, it seems a pretty good fit.[80] Weil's compunction for love, like Antigone's, is not exactly a lawlessness but an adherence to the invisible and secret, but no less binding, laws of another world. Weil's commentary on the central scene of the play—the dialogue between Antigone and Creon after Antigone defies his order to leave her brother unburied—shows the madness and extravagance of Antigone's adherence:

> [Antigone:] "I was born to share, not in hatred, but in love". Creon, more and more reasonable, then says: "Go then to the other world, and since you must love, love those who dwell there." Indeed, that was really her rightful place. For the unwritten law that this young woman obeyed, far from having anything in common with rights or with what is natural, was nothing other than the extreme, absurd love that drove Christ to the Cross. Justice, the companion of the gods in the other world, dictates this excess of love. No right dictates it. Rights do not have a direct link to love.[81]

Such an adherence, of course, produces an ethical bind between two competing obligations that cannot both be satisfied, and so, in this way, can be said to produce failure.

But there is love—an audacious, absurd love—and the question we might pose here becomes, citing Carson on Sappho's "Fragment 31" and in the spirit of Antigone's taking her share of love, "What is it that love dares the self to do?" Here is Carson's translation of the poem:

> He seems to me equal to gods that man
> whoever he is who opposite you

sits and listens close
to your sweet speaking

and lovely laughing—oh it
puts the heart in my chest on wings
for when I look at you, even a moment, no speaking
is left in me

no: tongue breaks and thin
fire is racing under skin
and in eyes no sight and drumming
fills ears

and cold sweat holds me and shaking
grips me all, greener than grass
I am and dead—or almost
I seem to me.

But all is to be dared, because even a person of poverty . . .[82]

In Carson's reading of "Fragment 31"—that poem wherein the senses fail, one after the next, in love, and which reminds me of the dizzying plunge of the senses into total paralysis in Weil's example of prayer— daring love emerges from the most unexpected of places: in the destitution of a self left behind. Oddly enough, this poverty is another way of underwriting generosity, I think. *All* is to be dared, Carson points out. "Moreover she consents to it—or seems to be on the point of consenting when the poem breaks off." *Why does she consent?* Carson asks. We do not know: we do not have an explanation, and the self that remains is in a condition of absolute destitution and does so under that very condition. Weil, for her part, would tell us simply that one consents to the self left behind in spite of oneself.

This chapter began with the idea of destitution. To end, I would like to take up the gesture of generosity, elaborating it in the context of a project Weil hoped to realize through the Free French. It is a gesture that, if we follow the donation of the self implied in decreation, is also entailed in the destitution of leave-taking. Weil's seriousness combined with a recklessness is well known. From biographies (most especially that by her childhood friend Simone Pétrement), firsthand accounts (such as those by Father Perrin and Gustave Thibon), commentaries on her work (T. S. Eliot's preface to the English translation of *L'Enracinement* immediately comes to mind), and even from fictionalized portrayals of Weil (see the character Louise Lazare in

Bataille's *Le Bleu du ciel*), we get a picture of Weil that ranges from the saintly and selfless to the simply absurd.[83] Indeed, Weil draws a pathetic portrait when we think of her as a Colonna Durruti fighter during the Spanish Civil War, rescued by her parents two weeks into her mission after she stepped into a pot of cooking oil. But overwhelmingly, the image we get of Weil is not so silly, if still a bit mad. For it is the image of an abiding, if seemingly impossible, love for creaturely life (maybe not always for her own, true, but certainly for the life of the other).

This is nowhere more palpable than in her letters to Schumann, in which she begs his help in getting deployed on a sabotage mission for which she might usefully serve as a scapegoat. Weil assures him, "I would accept any degree of risk whatsoever (including certain death for a sufficiently important goal)" (EL 196). Her poor physical health not only made that an impossibility, but she was considered a liability for this type of resistance effort. Instead, the London-based resistance movement employed Weil as an editor in a London office to write responses to generic infrastructure proposals for a postoccupation France submitted by local leaders of the French Resistance. In this capacity Weil wrote *L'Enracinement*—her second "grand œuvre."[84] And all the while she was dying of a sorrow that, by not sacrificing her life for the resistance, she was "missing" her death.[85]

Weil's actions and plans did not always meet with favorable response, often because they were so wildly impractical. This is certainly true of Weil's "Projet d'une formation d'infirmières de première ligne," a project she first laid out in Marseille before her departure to the United States but for which she failed to garner the necessary support for implementation.[86] Upon reading Weil's proposal, General de Gaulle is supposed to have said, "But she's crazy!"[87] Those who knew Weil's intellectual acumen and her "saintly" life likewise did not heed her desperate requests that she be directly involved in the fight against Hitler's troops, something that is all too evident in the cold reception of Weil's final projects for the Free French.

Despite its impracticality, the project for frontline nurses still gives a particularly instructive image of one's "share in love."[88] The project called for a corps of unarmed nurses to be parachuted to the front lines to tend to wounded and dying soldiers. More significantly, Weil contended, their very presence would afford those soldiers a critically important moral support. While their practical contribution would lie in saving lives, the nurses would evoke a "spirit of sacrifice" by submitting their own lives to certain death on the battlefields (191–92). This, Weil argued, would provide a potent contrapuntal symbol to Hitler's forces and propaganda machine, "mak[ing], by their opposition, a tableau preferable to any slogan whatsoever. It would be the clearest representation possible of the two directions between which today humanity must choose" (193).

I would submit that behind the project, and even in its poor reception, is this: an offering of one's life when that life is superfluous, could be one life among others, a life that would be better served in removing itself from the path of others, and still the remaining obligation to give it for the sake of love of the other. That characterization of love that does not spare the self from risk, poverty, or even its own death, returns us again to what one owes but could never reasonably be paid in full.[89] Does the impossibility of full remittance relieve one's debt? If we follow Weil, it does not. The debt is not based upon what one has or does not have ("As for me, I do not have debts, I am a debt. My very being is a debt," writes Weil), but Weil still insists that we offer up the only thing we have, our "I" (OC, vi/4 322): "God can only forgive that debt by causing me to cease to exist—to cease while I am still alive in this world—and then by selling what remains, after my person has been annihilated, so as to provide food for his creatures" (322). To give one's life "solely for the love of other creatures" (258), we have said, is as premised on one's substitutability as it is upon the singularity of one's "debt" of existence. But it is also a way of saying that love is always other than you—something I think Weil says in one way or another throughout the whole of her writings. When Weil writes, "love doesn't live in me" (EL 203), it is not the failure of love that speaks, nor the failure of the one who loves. It is the love of the one who adheres to an impossible love—impossible because it cannot be affirmed or had, only exist in this very destitution.

CHAPTER 6

Empty Petitions

The Last Letters of Simone Weil

When one reads Simone Weil's notebooks, it is not the difficult coherence nor the refusal to think things all the way through that one might take as grounds for complaint. It is another regret one feels. She says that we can reach truth only in secret: *"truth is secret,"* love is this very secret itself. *"God is always absent from our love as he is from the world, but he is secretly present in pure love." "The heavenly father dwells only in secret." "Our Father which is in secret."* She nonetheless lacks this secrecy. No thought has more rigorously sought to maintain God's remoteness, the necessity of knowing that we know nothing of him and that he is truth and certitude only when he is hidden, the hidden God. But she does not cease to speak openly of this hidden God, with assurance and with indiscretion, forgetting that this indiscretion renders nearly all her words vain.

—Blanchot, "Affirmation (desire, affliction)"

So writes Maurice Blanchot of the dissonance between the agitated restlessness of Simone Weil's life and the perfect stillness of her thought. Blanchot continues: "Simone Weil gave in her thought the example of certitude and, in her works, the model of an even expression, almost calm and as though perfectly at rest in its movement. For attention, at times absent from the surface of her life, is present as much as possible in the depth of her language, for which she is, in her radiance, the uneven evenness."[1] Weil gives an arresting image of being at rest in movement in her notebooks, evoking at once the monotony of affliction and the eventless movement of grace: a squirrel turning in its cage and the rotation of the celestial sphere.[2] "[A] kind of empty perpetuity," writes Blanchot.[3]

Weil's last letters, dating from shortly before her departure from France in May 1942 to her death in England in August 1943, rigorously, resolutely, and perhaps failingly, seek to preserve that essential emptiness. The letters—their insistence, their open petitions—can leave the reader uneasy. We need only think of their length and an almost obsessive return to the topic of her vocation (itself "so obligatory that he who bypasses it misses the goal")[4] to guess that Weil surely exceeded the patience of her interlocutors. Each of Weil's letters to Father Perrin, for example, are followed by postscripts of sorts, whether in the margins of each letter or in the form of follow-up letters. In her letter dated January 19, 1942, Weil states, "I have decided to write you . . . in order to bring to a close—at least until further notice—our conversations concerning my case" (AD 13). That letter, which claims to be a closure on the subject of baptism—"a conclusion, which is the resolution, pure and simple, to no longer think of the question of eventually entering the Church at all" (same letter)—is nonetheless followed up by five more letters, the last of which was written from Casablanca en route to New York. Following her January 19, 1942, letter to Perrin, Weil writes: "This is a postscript to the letter that I told you was provisionally a conclusion. I hope for your sake that it will be the only one. I really fear that I am bothering you. But if that is so, you must blame yourself. It's not my fault if I feel that I owe you an account of my thoughts" (23). And in her May 15, 1942, letter to Perrin ("Autobiographie spirituelle"), Weil begins with this postscript, "to be read first": "This letter is horrifyingly long—but since there is no way to respond to it—even less so since I will already be gone—you have years ahead of you, if you wish, to read it. Read it, all the same, one day or another" (35). Similarly, in letters to her colleagues at the Free French, Maurice Schumann and Louis Closon, Weil acknowledges that she may be indisposing them with the sheer length of her letters, but she writes them anyway.

From what we know, Weil did not easily let go of things when she thought them vital to knowing the truth, often to the point where those to whom she addressed her questions would end up embarrassed or even harassed. The latter, it seems, was the case after her meetings with Benedict Dom Clément Jacob. His response to her questions concerning the possibility of being baptized given her refusal of the Church's doctrine of *anathema sit* was an unequivocal "no," stating furthermore that Weil's position was "heretical."[5] Their meeting, not surprisingly, is described as having been "harassing for the two interlocutors."[6] Be that as it may, it did not stop Weil from continuing to address her questions to as many priests as possible, notably, in a long letter to Father Marie-Alain Couturier in New York (published as

Lettre à un religieux) and reprised right up to her death in "Dernier texte."[7]

We might be tempted to consider Weil's search for the truth to be a kind of ceaseless chatter, especially when the replies she was given were remarkably similar each time. But I would like to instead suggest that these letters reflect the difficulty of contemplating the enigma of "secret speech"—a mystery that Weil says is expressed in the first line of the "Our Father,"[8] and that she paraphrases in a letter to Perrin thus: "Christ made promises to the Church, but none of these promises have the force of this expression: 'Your Father who is in secret.' The word of God is secret speech. He who has not heard this speech, even if he adheres to all the dogmas taught by the Church, is without contact with the truth" (58). Like the enigma of a secret speech that is heard, Weil's letters reveal a tension between an imperative to speak and preserving an essential emptiness through silence. We know from her epistolary exchanges, for instance, that Weil "jealously kept the secret" of her mystical experience.[9] If we consider Weil's "conversion" as involving a certain turning or address to the other, such a turn is surely complicated: despite "not ceas[ing] to speak openly about this hidden God," there remains at the heart of these letters a curious and incessant silence.[10] The letters keep the secret of what they say.

That tension extends beyond Weil's explicitly religious letters and mystical experiences. It reflects a larger problematic concerning the exigency to speak and expose oneself in speech against an imperative for stillness, such as we saw in the scenes of supplication (Priam to Achilles: "He spoke"), in self-justification (Jaffier to his captors), in self-accusation (Jaffier to himself), even in the absence of the other's response, both that of the human and the divine Other ("Le Prologue"), and finally, in what concerns us here: in the demand for nothing—"the perfect demand," the fundamentally empty petition of decreation[11]—that Weil does not cease to ask for in the last letters. That petition, which asks to be made use of in a Resistance mission— something she describes in one letter as an "inner necessity"[12]— complicates the notion of decreation since it would also entail the very real likelihood of one's physical death. In a blunt statement to Father Perrin (repeated in the same terms to Schumann), Weil expresses this as a fear of "missing" her death.[13] It surely puts anyone who would respond to Weil's final wish into an unspeakable bind, one that may not be ethically permissible according to the terms set by Weil herself, since one is obliged to preserve the other from harm.[14]

As a provisional conclusion to our question about the ethical bind and the possibility of decreating the self under conditions of force and unfulfilled desire, Weil's last letters tell us a lot about the extreme difficulty of honoring the perfect demand in practice. That is especially true of the demand that exceeds not only what the other can ethically give her but what she can ask for in the first place. For the difficulty of the demand, like the image of being at rest in movement, is that it is at once a form of emptiness and of plenitude. The perfect demand—that which asks for what "really, infallibly, eternally" exists independently of one's petition (216)—shows the outward incongruity of the completeness of the object of one's certitude (which exists independently of its being fulfilled or realized) and the narrative incompletion of positing such an object in the first place. To be sure, that Weil does not cease to ask for nothing in a body that is itself finally spent, lays open a failure to achieve the object of one's demand. But I would like to propose that such a failure is rather an exercise of articulation that, precisely in its exercise, brings into view the reality of existence.[15] To put it more simply, in Weilian terms, it is to honor that which really exists. So what do we finally make of Weil's own perfect demand in view of the decreative obligation to preserve the other from harm? What can we say about this responsibility to the other that is, after all, at the crux of her unheeded petitions—one that is in its articulation enacted without being fulfilled, as such? For Weil would die as she lived, exercising this "inner necessity." Is it here that we might locate her responsibility, even as it may finally be inconsequential?

AWAITING TRUTH

Martin Steffens writes that Weil "did not live according to norms other than those dictated by the exigency of living."[16] Weil's letters reflect a drive to tell, attesting to this "exigency of living" in all its imprudence and irrepressibility. It is a telling that does not cease to tell, that cannot tell enough, that says too much (or too little). Weil does not cease to tell the thing she was certain she needed to do (her "vocation")—with what insistence, with what indiscretion. She would tell it to anyone and everyone who might make possible for her to realize her final projects. This was true from the moment she first conceived her project for frontline nurses in 1939, through various changes to it after the fall of France to Germany. It was still true through her anguished decision to leave France and the hope to gather material support for this project in New York, and when that failed, to try to realize it via the Free French in London. The detours to get to that final point were understandably unbearable for Weil.[17]

Once in New York and failing to garner the necessary support for the project, Weil grew increasingly despondent that she had made a terrible mistake in leaving France. She desperately sought a way of returning via London to be used as a liaison or scapegoat for the French resistance in a clandestine mission, "preferably dangerous" (EL 186). Failing that, she wanted to be used by the English army—naturally as one of the fearless nurses described in her project for frontline nurses, a proposal she includes in her first letter (July 30, 1942) to Maurice Schumann, a classmate from Henri-IV, now working for the Free French in London under the direction of André Philip, minister of the interior for the Free French. Weil asks Schumann to make it possible for her to come to London to realize her projects, "to bring me out of the painful moral situation I find myself in" (187), as she puts it, unable to directly help the French under German occupation.

In a follow-up letter (also dated July 30, 1942), Weil elaborates how she might be used as a liaison for a sabotage operation in France, arguing that "a woman is just as capable as a man of being sent in this way, even more so, so long as she has a sufficient amount of resolution, self-possession and spirit of sacrifice" (196). That woman in question, of course, is herself. In her letter she states very simply that she has already had occasion to prove her composure under the threat of imminent death. Weil closes the letter with the plea: "I beg you, make it possible for me to come to London. Do not leave me to waste away here from sorrow. I call upon you as a comrade" (197). That plea is repeated in her next letter from New York: "Just make it possible for me to come." In that letter Weil writes: "I cannot help myself from having the shamelessness, indiscretion, and insistence of beggars. Like beggars, in lieu of arguments, I can only cry out my needs. To this there is Talleyrand's horrible reply: 'I don't see the necessity.' But you, at least, will not give me this reply" (214). Schumann makes Weil's passage to London possible but indicates the unlikelihood of realizing the project. Nonetheless, Weil left New York still hopeful that her projects might be realized. Once in London, given a desk job rather than the fieldwork she so desperately wanted, Weil continued to advance her proposals under increasingly diminished chances while writing L'Enracinement. During this time, Weil grew increasingly despondent over her halted vocation, while her fragile health—described by Weil as her "growing fatigue" (212)—put her projects at further risk of not being realized.

Understanding herself to be at the brink of what she could reasonably give, Weil made a final plea to Schumann to facilitate her contact with sabotage organizations in France "for the case where they might need one day to gain an advantage at the price of a life" (212). That life in question is Weil's, a life that she deems at once expendable ("like a usable product" [212]) and necessary to the life of others through its very death.[18] Echoing something she tells Perrin in her "Autobiographie spirituelle," Weil tells Schumann, "I have always had in me the fear of missing, not my life, but my death" (213). Realizing such a death would be the same thing as the "exigency of living" discussed earlier. Weil describes it as "awaiting truth": "Putting to the side what can be granted me to do for the good of other human beings, for me, personally, life does not have another meaning and has never, in the end, had any other meaning than awaiting truth" (213).

Let us consider this "awaiting truth" in view of what we have discussed in earlier chapters concerning need and objectless desire.[19] In its double meaning of awaiting and expectation, "l'attente" invokes the perfect demand which both asks for the nothing that is and which does not ask for anything, as such. Understood in this sense, expectation becomes the certitude of one's need, not of what one will get in the end. That need, so evident in the irrepressible urgency of Weil's demand, is not unlike desire that has been extinguished of its supplemental energy, where the only energy left is to cry one's hunger.[20] "A child does not stop crying if we suggest to him that perhaps there is no bread. He cries even so," writes Weil elsewhere in this vein (AD 209). But in the anxiety that she will "miss" her death is something that seems at a first look to put a kink into the perfect demand and the consent to its asking for nothing, as it does into the notion of self-dispossession at the center of decreation. It is the fear that, in being unable to directly participate in the Resistance, the truth (in relation to which one can only be the vessel of its transmission, according to Weil) will never be given to her, straining the notion of unrealized desire at the heart of "l'attente" (specifically, "awaiting truth") as we have been discussing it. As Weil explains to Schumann: "I am experiencing a wrench—both intellectually and at the center of my heart—that does not stop worsening, by my inability to understand in its truth the affliction of men, the perfection of God, and the relation between the two things. I have the inner certitude that this truth, if it is ever given to me, will only be at the moment when I am myself in physical affliction, and in one of the extreme forms of the present affliction" (EL 213). Yet despite the force of her demand, Weil would never be given the chance to renounce the very "I" that wrote these words, her speech too weak, it seems, to be heard by anyone.

THE QUESTION OF PERSONAL MATTERS

Weil writes at the top of the first page of an undated letter to Schumann: "I am horrified to see how many pages I've written you without noticing. It is but a question of personal matters. That is without any interest. Only read this when and if you really have time to waste."[21] Weil often prefaces what she says to her interlocutors by simply saying that since she has thought them she must say them. Her justification for taking up their time is that the truth compels her to write them thus. Here the "question of personal matters" (which Weil claims to be of "no interest") is sublated with the impersonal truth that obliges her to write nonetheless. Later in the same letter, Weil writes, "there is the obligation to trample everything in oneself rather than allow an obstacle to block the passage, through oneself, of the truth. It is this obligation which forces me to write things that I know I have no right, personally, to write" (EL 202).

There, as elsewhere, Weil describes that truth as having fallen upon her, lodged there by grace, chance, or error, and understands herself to be the simple vessel or instrument of that truth. In reply to her mother's belief that she has something to offer the world, Weil writes: "Darling M., you believe that I have something to give. That's poorly expressed. But I also have a kind of growing inner certitude that there is a deposit of pure gold in me that is to be passed on" (250). Driving this telling, then, is the exigency of a truth that is not one's own but that makes use of oneself and in the face of which one has no rights, only obligations "to be passed on" (à transmettre). That dispossession—situated somewhere between giving and passing on— is nowhere clearer than when Weil literally gives away those words. Before her departure from Marseille, she entrusts her notebooks to Gustave Thibon, telling him that the thoughts therein now "belong" to him to be transformed under his pen. She adds that he is to consider them his property if he does not hear from her after three or four years. In her letter to Thibon from Casablanca in May 1942, Weil explains: "You say that you have found in my notebooks, in addition to things you have already thought, others which you had not yet thought but which you had waited for; these thoughts belong to you, then, and I hope that having undergone a transmutation under your hands they will come out one day in one of your works."[22] Weil would like the hand that writes to count for very little in this. For the writer is meant to be but an instrument through which the greater operation of truth might be expressed.

The letter continues: "For those who love truth, the hand that writes and the body and soul attached to this operation—with all its social envelope—are things of infinitesimal importance. Infinitely small, to the nth degree. That is at least the measure of importance that I attach, in relation to writing, not only my person but also your person and that of every writer I esteem" (PSW). We can liken the writing hand to the blind-man's stick, a Cartesian analogy to which Weil often referred: a means of knowing the world outside one's self, an intermediary (metaxu) between thought and action. According to Françoise Meltzer, "for Weil, the hand is supposed to be the very organ of elision her writings require" for this operation from the one to the other.[23] But as Meltzer also points out, as a *metaxu*, Weil's own hands pose an unwanted problem: neither fast enough nor "useful" enough (Meltzer's words), they are at once a bridge and an obstacle to the movement from thought to action. Meltzer points out that the awkwardness of her hands is "the site of struggle for Weil": "She could keep the beat neither in her writing (which she believed, with Alain, should be beautifully penned in a manner that eluded her) nor in her manual tasks. The hand, then, remains the place in Weil where the smoothness of thought is interrupted, where the erasure of the I fails because it constantly draws attention to itself."[24] Reading this, I am reminded of something the painter Francis Bacon once said in an interview: "We nearly always live through screens—a screened existence. And I sometimes think when people say my work is violent that from time to time I have been able to clear away one or two of the screens."[25] Bacon's search for the "facts" of reality (Bacon's term) seems to align with Weil's own for that which "really, infallibly, eternally exists" behind screens. Anne Carson characterizes Bacon's "screens" this way: "They are part of our normal way of looking at the world, or rather our normal way of seeing the world without looking at it."[26] Bacon goes further, I think: it is said to be a *screened existence*. If both Bacon and Weil would agree that these screens form the way we look at things, the question for Weil is how to effect a total shift in perspective, such that the things we see might be free of the perspectival intrusion of our own screened existence onto the scene. She calls it looking at a landscape when one is not there (PG 93–95). But how exactly do we remove our own screened existence from the scene of looking and writing, as it were? In the landscape passage, Weil says most simply: "I must withdraw." However, as Meltzer points out, withdrawing the "I" is not only complicated by the inscription of that "I" at the site of its deinscription—in the case of the letters, a possible "block[age] of the passage, through oneself, of the truth"—through a necessary textual elaboration of the impersonal "I" that effectively shores it up. Meltzer's stronger point here, I think, is regarding the *site* itself: for the site of erasure constantly, unwillingly, draws attention to itself, haunting the scene of its intended elision. For those hands do not convey a weakness or maladroitness without also conveying the intrusion of physicality into the relationship between the hand that writes and the truth that it is said, impersonally, to transmit.

"THE FORCE OF THIS SPEECH IS IN ITS WEAKNESS"

Recognizing her physical limitations, Weil asks to make use of this weakness.[27] Weil argues that it would actually be an advantage to any mission entrusted to her insofar as it would allow her to guard "the obligation of the secret"—to her death, if necessary: "The purpose being to die without giving up information, one must reach as quickly as possible a state whereby one is, in fact, incapable of giving it up. Precisely because of my physical weakness, that would come about rather quickly for me. A moderate amount of ill treatment would put me definitively into a state where thought is void" (EL 207). And so, Weil asks to be made use of, but finally, she understands herself simply to be useless, limited to what the Free French would have her do instead. In her last letter to Schumann she warns that she is near a triple limit—morally, intellectually, physically. And "the limit reached, I'll say that I can no longer give anything" (213). By the time she writes to Louis Closon, another of her colleagues at the Free French, on July 25, 1943, Weil has reached that limit: the possibility of accomplishing her vocation, along with Weil herself, are exhausted. There is no hope left in this letter. In addition to effectively resigning from her post (by this point Weil was in the hospital with tuberculosis, unable to work), Weil writes in the starkest possible terms that she has totally given up her efforts for the French Resistance.

The penmanship of that letter, written only days before her death, shows the signs of her incredibly weakened state. Weil's impeccably neat and uniform handwriting has given way to her illness, and Weil admits: "Such a letter, in my state, is madness. But it must be written. I hope it will not trouble your rest" (PSW). Weil was surely aware that such a letter troubled the "rest" of her reader. All her readers in the end, it seems, were exhausted by Weil. And all these letters addressed to the other, for the other—what we have been saying all along that one has to give—received by no one. But she writes nonetheless, as she writes all her last letters, because she must.

The force of this weak speech is also at play in Weil's last letters from England to her parents. The letters evince a total intellectual lucidity even as they do not disclose anything about the real state of her health. (Weil was discovered unconscious on the floor of her room; she would die a few weeks later at a sanatorium in Kent from cardiac failure brought on by tuberculosis and self-induced starvation.) Carson describes this disjunction rather quixotically: "Certain aspects of disappearance had to be concealed from the parents and so her many letters to them are repetitions of the one same glowingly factitious postcard that every good daughter sends home—Dear people what splendid weather thanks for the chocolate I'm making lots of friends here kisses to all—meanwhile she was dying. And when she did die the cable astonished them: her last letter from London had said everything was fine."[28] I think this characterization bears some claim to truth—at least as Weil might concede to it: as Weil tells Closon, it is madness to write such a letter given the circumstances.

In her August 4, 1943, letter to her parents, written only a few days before her death, Weil writes:

> When I saw *Lear* here, I asked myself how the intolerably tragic character of these fools was not, for a long time, blindingly obvious (including to myself). Their tragic character does not consist of sentimental things, such as we sometimes say, but in this:
>
> In this world, only those beings fallen to the final degree of humiliation, far below that of begging, not only without social consideration but seen by all as devoid [dépourvus] of reason, the foundation of human dignity—only they have, in fact, the possibility of saying the truth. All others lie.
>
> In *Lear* this is striking. Even Kent and Cordelia attenuate, mitigate, soften, and veil the truth, manipulate the truth, so long as they are not forced either to say the truth or to straight out lie. . . .

The extreme end of tragedy is that these fools, having neither the
title of teacher nor bishop, and with no one anticipating that some
attention should be paid to what they say—being already certain of
the opposite, since they are fools—their expression of the truth is
not even heard. No one, including all the readers and spectators of
Shakespeare of the last four centuries, knows that the fools are telling
the truth. Not satirical or humoristic truth but just the truth. Pure,
unmixed, luminous, profound, essential truths.

Is that also the secret of Velasquez's fools? Is the sadness in their
eyes the bitterness of possessing the truth, of having, at the cost of
an unnamable degradation, the possibility of saying the truth, and of
not being heard by anyone? (except Velasquez). It is worth the trouble
of considering them [fools] again with this question in mind. (EL
255–56)

Let us ask this question, then, about the secret of unheard fools. What
is it to possess the truth, to have, at the cost of degradation without
name, the possibility of saying (it), and of not being heard by anyone?
This is a question about truth, surely. But it is a truth lodged in the
saying that is, nonetheless, not heard. For who would understand or
hear the words of a fool? Who, indeed, would want to?

Here and elsewhere Weil writes that she feels certain that there
is truth in her, and that it is only the fact of its residing in her that
makes it unbelievable to others. More than a year before her death
Weil anticipates the dismissal of her projects, stating in her last letter
to Perrin (May 26, 1942):

If no one consents to pay attention to those thoughts that, though I
don't know how, have been placed in a being as insufficient as myself,
they will be buried with me. If, as I believe, they contain truth, that
will be unfortunate. I am prejudicial to them. The fact that they are
found in me prevents others from paying attention to them. . . . But
who knows whether those thoughts I bear are not at least partially
destined for you to make some use of them? They can only be destined for someone who has a little bit of friendship for me, a true
friendship. Because for others, in a way, I don't exist. I am the color
of dead leaves, like certain insects. (AD 83–84)

Weil expresses a certainty of the truth (she goes so far as to say to
her mother that it can even be possessed) in unfaltering terms. But
the certainty of truth is not equivalent to its expression, to what Weil
calls in the earlier passage, "the possibility of saying it." (In Weil's
example, it is from the mouth of a fool who cannot say it such that it
is heard by others.) Thus, the saying-truth departs from the truth; it
concatenates, splinters off from itself, multiplies ("*des* vérités," writes

Weil), even though it is also said to remain "pure, unmixed, luminous, profound, essential." One says the truth, but the saying implicates a degradation of the possibility of (saying) the truth; one does not speak (the truth) without that truth already absenting itself from what is said. In any case, we may recall from chapter 4 that secret speech "may be obliged to unsay itself in order to avoid disfiguring the secret it exposes."[29]

To ask, as Weil does, about the secret of the unheard is already to ask an unwanted question. Weil uses a term to describe its messenger that is more precise than "unwanted" and that has no exact equivalent in English: "dépourvu"—that is, to be lacking or wanting in, without; to be devoid of, without; to be bare of, without. But it also suggests a certain poverty, or subpoverty, as in to be penniless, destitute, without money or even to be without interest. (In this regard, recall what Weil writes about her person, that she is without interest.) One can also use "dépourvu" to say that one is caught off guard (prendre quelqu'un au dépourvu). Indeed, Weil herself seems to be caught off guard by what has passed her by in all her years of reading tragedy, and which now, at that moment, so close to her death, in a body *dépourvu* of its corpulence and usefulness, she understands.

To return to the letter: "When I saw *Lear* here, I asked myself how the intolerably tragic character of these fools was not, for a long time, blindingly obvious (including to myself)." It would seem that the idea is gotten only after a long time (we know that it is after years of meditation on the tragic). "For a long time," she writes, and it seems, moreover, that in this "for" is a necessity to give in turn—in the form of the letter, in the form of this address, itself without guarantee—to another who might also return to this secret by seeing it again. To speak of giving is unlike the notion of reciprocity; there is no guarantee of return or reception. The unfulfilled demand of Weil's last letters leaves nothing to doubt here on that score. Moreover, one gives, is given over to giving, but without the means of doing so. For what does Weil give here? She does not exactly give the secret of the tragic character of fools, of what, at the outset of this chapter, we called "secret speech." What she does is ask the other to see—and, indeed, to see again as if for the first time. Let us remain in the apparent paradox of this logic, of what is secret and at the same time what is most obvious. What is to be seen, even if it is the most unseen and unheard, unspeakable and secret.

Here is Weil's last letter, of August 16, 1943, received by her parents after having already learned of her death:

Darlings,
      Very little time and inspiration available for letters now.
      They will be short, spaced out, irregular. But you have another source of solace.
      When you will have this letter (if it is not quick), you will also perhaps have the cable you are expecting. (Nothing is certain! . . .)
      More and more, Closon is someone really good, with an authentic value that grows unceasingly. More and more he is a true friend. (Our André did not understand him at all, of course.) More and more, Zette is a friend.
      Their friendship for me is an infinitely precious support.
      It is the only one, for Schumann is kind but not at all serious.
      Good-bye [au revoir], darlings. All my affection [mille et mille tendresses],
      Simone[30]

What is in question here is neither the "possession of truth" nor the "truth of being." Her parents do not know what has happened; the messenger will come, and it will be too late. The letter will be received after they have already been notified of Weil's death. What is the message here? Her last words attest to lived time (it is finite), to friendship (it is infinitely precious), and to filial love (it is tender). But still, in the final salutation, banal, everyday, nonspecific, is perhaps the unspoken wish to see again. The open secret of those last words, their weightless extravagance when there is nothing left to give, like those of Jaffier on the cusp of his death: "To my eyes soon without sight, how beautiful the city is."

"THE LIMIT REACHED . . ."

We know that Weil's demands to be sent on a mission were refused her.[31] We might think, as her interlocutors surely did, that fulfilling her demand was simply out of the question—impractical and dangerous not only for Weil but for others as well. Or we might, as Weil herself wrote despairingly at the end, attribute the refusal to her weakness. Both the weakness of this speech and the inadequacy of the other's response seem to imply the failure of one's obligation to the other. But as I think Weil's last letters suggest instead, it may tell us more profoundly that the measure of one's responsibility is neither forfeited nor held by any guarantee. And the address is not constituted by an exchange so much as it is by the demand in the first place. If we consider the question of how one is bound to the other, as we have throughout, it seems that the demand brings one outside oneself, decreated, as Weil would insist.

Blanchot offers a way to correlate the two aspects of Simone Weil's work that has troubled Weil scholarship from the start: the "uneven evenness" of Weil's life and the perfect stillness of her thought. Without reducing the one to the other, such a formulation lets the two strands stand, neither in opposition nor in complementarity. For the exigency that would impel Weil's life and thought is predicated upon both, even as it is nearly undone by the one or by the other at times. The binding and relentless force of the claims to which they respond—ultimately, to preserve the other's "human's presence"—may exceed one's resources, without that obviating the obligation to give nonetheless and leaving open the question of what constitutes the fulfillment of the obligation in the first place. In the competing claims here—between what one has and what one has to give; between the other's subject affirmation and one's own dislocation; between forced dispossession resulting from the exercise of power and consented dispossession of the "I" from its egological centrality—is all the difficulty of a decreative ethics that does not offer a prescriptive answer. I have sought to show that decreative ethics offers instead a mode of self-dispossession that, by relinquishing the power to say "I," opens up a fragile passage to the other that is also, however strangely, the fragile possibility of saying itself. That is "the angle of inclination of one's existence"; that is "the silent thing that must be expressed."[32] And it is the perfect demand: *To see a landscape as it is when I am not there.*[33]

ACKNOWLEDGMENTS

I wish to thank Ann Smock, Anne-Lise François, Ramona Naddaff, and Judith Butler, for their gentle and inestimable guidance in writing the original manuscript. They showed me, in the luminosity of their thinking and writing, a way to read Simone Weil differently.

At Fordham University Press, the late Helen Tartar offered her unstinting support, and when an injury and long recovery sidelined this project for years, gave me still more. I wish that she could read its finished form. I wish that I could thank her. Tom Lay deftly picked up the pieces of the unfinished book and encouraged me to return to them. I am grateful for his editorial patience. I wish to also thank Susan Murray for her careful copy editing; Eric Newman and Tim Roberts for their work in making the book a tangible object; and the Modern Language Initiative for funding that made that possible in the first place. My sincere thanks to readers at the Press for their generous and engaged readings of the manuscript. I hope the final iteration bears at least the imprint of their fine suggestions.

I also thank Catherine Flynn and Rashida Braggs for their thoughtful comments to parts of the manuscript in process; Bulbul Tiwari for the fineness of her friendship, care, and encouragement, particularly when physical pain made writing all but impossible; Michael Allan for his enthusiastic and graceful help throughout; Karen Wong and Natalya Sukhonos for pulling me from too hermetic an existence while revising; Jared Sexton, Laila Malik, and Jami Xu for conversations that have changed my thinking and words that have enthralled me; Jae Carey with whom I first read Simone Weil and because of whom I loved to read those words; and Jin K. Lee, whose inimitable gifts of friendship include the cover art for this book.

I am grateful to my family for their loving encouragement: Yong Rang Cha, Soon Bun Yoo, Jinny Ahn, James Ahn, Megan Perrett,

Joshua Ahn, Josiah Ahn, John Cha, Lauryn Cha, and Madelyn Cha. This book would have been unthinkable without them. And for my little family, my deepest thank you: Hugh Holmes, my true love and support; Beckett, my spirited and loyal companion; and Laila Grace Holmes, my sweetness, my wildest dream come true.

And again: for Judith Butler, my interlocutor at every stage of this book and to whom these words were first addressed, my profound thank you, always.

NOTES

PREFACE

1. Maurice Blanchot, "L'Affirmation (le désir, le malheur)," *L'Entretien infini* (Paris: Gallimard, 1969) 153, trans. Susan Hanson, "Affirmation (desire, affliction)," *The Infinite Conversation* (Minneapolis: U of Minnesota P, 1993) 106.

2. Françoise Meltzer, "The Hands of Simone Weil," *Critical Inquiry* 27.4 (2001): 623.

3. Blanchot, "Affirmation (desire, affliction)" 106.

4. I am defaulting to masculine pronouns throughout wherever the gender-neutral term "one" does not fit. This is partly for the sake of expediency and partly to follow Weil's own pronoun usage. The notable exception is in my discussion of "Le Prologue" in chapter 5 (see chap. 5, note 24).

5. See *Sophocles I: Antigone, Oedipus the King, Oedipus at Colonus*, trans. Mark Griffith (Chicago: U of Chicago P, 1991).

6. Simone Weil, "Autobiographie spirituelle," *Attente de Dieu* (Paris: Fayard, 1966); hereafter cited as AD; translations are mine, with page numbers referring to the original.

7. While I address the notion of chronic fatigue in Weil's factory journals, I do not explicitly address Weil's theory of labor in this study (see chap. 5). For this, I refer readers to two excellent studies: Robert Chevanier's *Simone Weil: Une Philosophie du travail* (Paris: Cerf, 2001); and Nadia Taïbi's *La Philosophie au travail: L'Expérience ouvrière de Simone Weil* (Paris: L'Harmattan, 2009).

8. A point I take from Jeff Fort, *The Imperative to Write: Destitutions of the Sublime in Kafka, Blanchot, and Beckett* (New York: Fordham UP, 2014) 165.

9. Gilbert Kahn, an otherwise careful reader of Weil, is representative of those who uncritically (and unwittingly) iterate Weil's position. See his "Limites et raisons du refus de l'ancien testament par Simone Weil," *Cahiers Simone Weil* 3.2 (1980). I refer readers to Daniel Boitier's essay "L'Impossible conversion," *Cahiers Simone Weil* 17.4 (1994) for a discussion of Weil's troubling position and the negation of her own status as a Jew in occupied France. Emmanuel Levinas offers a sober account of Weil's relationship to

Judaism and her highly selective reading of the Bible (see Levinas, "Simone Weil contre le Bible," *La Liberté difficile: Essais sur le judaïsme* [Paris: Albin Michel, 1976], trans. Sean Hand, "Simone Weil Against the Bible," *Difficult Freedom: Essays on Judaism* [Baltimore: Johns Hopkins UP, 1990]). Thomas Nevin's *Simone Weil: A Portrait of a Self-Exiled Jew* does an especially good job at situating Weil's relationship to Judaism and her own Jewishness within a historical context (see Nevin, "A Stranger unto Her People: Weil on Judaism," *Simone Weil: Portrait of a Self-Exiled Jew* [Chapel Hill: U of North Carolina P, 1991]).

10. A word about the context of the initial posthumous publication of her work is helpful here. A disproportionate amount of what has been written—particularly in the years immediately following her death—has been problematically entrenched in Christian and sometimes hagiographical expositions of her thought. The name of Simone Weil has come to be synonymous with saint; the counterpoint to this, also problematic, is the portrait of Weil as a self-hating Jew (see Paul Giniewski, *Simone Weil, ou la haine de soi* [Paris: Berg International, 1978], for an example of the latter). The polarized characterizations of Weil borrow from the same lexicon that reflexively affirms or invalidates her (thought) out of hand; and whether it is the one or the other, her thought is inevitably obscured in this operation. There is a historical impetus for this particular kind of reception (both poles of it), outside of what the actual content of her writings might proffer. The first wave of secondary literature responded to her first posthumously published and still most widely known work, *La Pesanteur et la grâce* (*Gravity and Grace*). This slim volume culled from notebooks is emblematic of the kind of Christian-leaning extraction done to Weil's thought. First, by forcibly and neatly thematizing her writing (section titles include "Void and Compensation," "Detachment," "The Impossible,") where no such groupings are to be found in her notebooks. Second, by poeticizing and mystifying her writing to the possible occlusion of her thinking—a process that is more easily rendered given the aphoristic and necessarily fragmentary nature of the notebooks and reinforced by the unsurpassed pellucidity of Weil's prose. Third, the initial publication of her notebooks in this form, especially with the original preface by Thibon, which reads like an apologia, tacitly Christianizes Weil's thought. This is also reflected in T. S. Eliot's preface to the publication of *L'Enracinement* in English, which presumes that Weil emerged, foremost, out of the context of a Christian Europe (see T. S. Eliot's preface to Weil, *The Need for Roots: Prelude to a Declaration of Duties Toward Mankind* [New York: Harper and Row, 1971]). And yet, as Nevin has persuasively argued, her conceptions of social justice, universalism, and labor as obedience to God might be better said to belong to distinctly Jewish traditions of thought. Read in isolation, apart from her many nontheological essays and outside of the historical context of trauma and displacement of Vichy France in which Weil wrote some of her most important work (including those writings on harm and injurability that are of especial interest to this book), *La Pesanteur et la grâce* goes far in attempts to exculpate Weil from a certain

responsibility to which her troubled relationship to Judaism attested and, more critically, refused.

And yet, what are we to make of her refusal to enter the Church, remaining on the threshold so as to not be cut off from "the immense and wretched mass of unbelievers"? (AD 19). Who are these so-called unbelievers of her time and place with whom that she aligned herself with, *despite herself* (for she desperately wanted to partake in the church sacraments), so as to *belong to them* (Weil's words), if not the Jews of Catholic Vichy France? For as Nevin notes: "It is instructive that she stated this concern to Perrin in a letter of January 19, 1942, the month she was distributing the *Cahiers du Témoignage chrétienne*'s denunciation of anti-Semitism. In a nation ostensibly Catholic, who more than Jews could be called "a wretched mass of nonbelievers"? If the Judaic roots of Christendom kept Weil from entering the church, could it be that the suffering of Jews worked on her as well?" (Nevin, *Simone Weil: Portrait of a Self-Exiled Jew* 267). Weil's position vibrates against her claim, "I was born, raised and always stayed in the Christian inspiration" (AD 37). That statement surely cannot be divorced from the anti-Semitic political, social, and religious (Catholic) milieu of the time and, not incidentally, from her turn to Christianity when the assimilationist strategies of her parents' and grandparents' generations likewise adopted by Weil held no currency. Nevin notes the strength of that link: Weil's sudden mystical experiences of a Christian nature happened when Weil was most at threat for being a Jew. None of this exculpates Weil, of course, although it may go some way to mitigating our own difficult response to Weil's anti-Judaism. And that our own response might be, as Blanchot so ably puts it, "to expose oneself to the even greater difficulty of undergoing the ordeal of history to which Simone Weil was obliged (by what necessity of thought, what pain in thinking of it?) to close her eyes" (Blanchot, "L'Indestructible," *L'Entretien infini* [Paris: Gallimard, 1969] 180, trans. Susan Hanson, "The Indestructible," *The Infinite Conversation* [Minneapolis: U of Minnesota P, 1993] 123).

11. Levinas, "Simone Weil contre le Bible."

12. Weil, AD 65; and "Dernier texte," *Pensées sans ordre concernant l'amour de Dieu* (Paris: Gallimard, 1962) 149, my translation.

INTRODUCTION

1. Simone Weil, *La Pesanteur et la grâce* (Paris, Plon: 1988) 57; hereafter cited as PG; translations are mine, with page numbers referring to the original.

2. See Weil, "La Personne et le sacré," *Écrits de Londres et dernières lettres* (Paris: Gallimard, 1957); hereafter cited as PS; translations are mine, with page numbers referring to the original.

3. Weil writes, "We possess nothing in the world—for chance can take everything from us—except the power to say 'I.' . . . [T]here is absolutely no other free act that is permitted us. . . . One cannot offer anything other than the 'I'" (PG 73).

4. I am borrowing here from Judith Butler's characterization of the Levinasian subject's responsibility for the other: "In others, I cannot disavow my relation to the Other, regardless of what the other does, regardless of what I might will. Indeed, responsibility is not a matter of cultivating a will . . . but of recognizing an *unwilled susceptibility* as a resource for becoming responsive to the Other . . . It is, of course, something of an outrage to be ethically responsible for those to whom one never chose to be responsible, but here is where Levinas draws attention to those modes of being implicated in the lives of others that precede and subtend any possible conditions of choice" (Butler, *Parting Ways: Jewishness and the Critique of Zionism* [New York: Columbia UP, 2012] 43, emphasis added).

5. Butler, *Precarious Life: The Powers of Mourning and Violence* (New York: Verso, 2004) 43.

6. Diane Perpich's critical engagement with Levinasian ethics has been especially helpful in my own framing of Weil's ethics (see Perpich, *The Ethics of Emmanuel Levinas* [Stanford: Stanford UP, 2008]).

7. Let me note that Weil vacillated between an imprescriptible understanding of the obligation issuing from decreation and a more constructivist approach in *L'Enracinement*, a work written for the Free French with proposals for the cultural and spiritual regeneration of postwar France (see *L'Enracinement: Prélude à une déclaration des devoirs envers l'être humain* (Paris: Gallimard, 1949). I would argue that Weil's attempt to formulate a practical, normative application of her idea of obligation in *L'Enracinement* is a rendition of obligation that is at odds with her conceptualization of it everywhere else. In arguing that Weil does not offer a normative ethics, I am, in a sense, reading Weil against herself but with a view to retaining what I understand to be essential to the ethical force and decreative aim of obligation.

8. See Maurice Blanchot, "Traces," *La Nouvelle Revue française* 129 (September 1963): 472–80.

9. See Miklos Vetö, *The Religious Metaphysics of Simone Weil* (Albany: State U of New York P, 1994); and Anne Carson, *Decreation: Poetry, Essays, Opera* (New York: Knopf, 2005).

10. Although there has been some recent interest in Weil's ethics (see, for example, A. Rebecca Rozelle-Stone and Lucian Stone's excellent collection, *The Relevance of the Radical*), there are not yet any book-length treatments of it, as such, or on a decreative ethics emerging out of self-dispossession and vulnerability, specifically (see A. Rozelle-Stone and Stone, *The Relevance of the Radical: Simone Weil 100 Years Later* [London: Continuum, 2010]).

Of course, many themes readily associated with Weil—her political and philosophical thought rooted in Platonism, her theory of labor, her mysticism, her refusal of normative constructions and prescriptive models of gender, race, and religion—all of which are no doubt fundamental to an integral consideration of Weil's writings, lie outside the scope of the present study and are not expressly treated. I refer readers interested in Weil's political thought to Mary G. Dietz, *Between the Human and the Divine: The Political Thought of Simone Weil* (Totowa, NJ: Rowman and Littlefield, 1988); in

Weil's theories of labor, to Robert Chevanier, *Simone Weil: Une Philosophie du travail* (Paris: Cerf, 2001) and Nadia Taïbi's *La Philosophie au travail: L'Expérience ouvrière de Simone Weil* (Paris: L'Harmattan, 2009); in Weil's Platonism, to Eric O. Springsted, *Christus Mediator: Platonic Mediation in the Thought of Simone Weil* (Chico, CA: Scholars Press, 1983) and Springsted and E. Jane Doering, eds., *The Christian Platonism of Simone Weil* (Notre Dame: U of Notre Dame P, 2004); in Weil's religious and gender identification, to Rachel Feldhay Brenner, *Writing as Resistance: Four Women Confronting the Holocaust* (University Park: Pennsylvania State UP, 1997).

11. E. Jane Doering, *Simone Weil and the Specter of Self-Perpetuating Force* (Notre Dame: U of Notre Dame P, 2010) 63.

12. Joan Dargan, *Simone Weil: Thinking Poetically* (Albany: State U of New York P, 1999).

13. Weil, *Œuvres complètes*, Tome 6, Vol. 1: *Cahiers (1933–septembre 1941)* (Paris: Gallimard, 1994) 302.

14. Emmanuel Levinas, "Exercises on 'The Madness of Day,'" *Proper Names*, trans. Michael B. Smith (Stanford: Stanford UP, 1996) 157.

15. See Butler, *Precarious Life*; Butler, "Bodily Vulnerability, Coalitions, and Street Politics," *Notes toward a Performative Theory of Assembly* (Cambridge: Harvard UP, 2015); Butler, "Vulnerability and Resistance," *Profession* (March 2014), http://profession.commons.mla.org/2014/03/19/vulnerability-and-resistance/; and Butler and Athena Athanasiou, *Dispossession: The Performative in the Political* (Cambridge: Polity, 2013).

16. Butler, "Vulnerability and Resistance" 4.

17. See also Butler, *Parting Ways* 9: "Once ethics is no longer understood exclusively as a disposition or action grounded in a ready-made subject, but rather as a relational practice that responds to an obligation that originates outside the subject, then ethics contests sovereign notions of the subject and ontological claims of self-identity. Indeed, ethics comes to signify the act by which place is established for those who are 'not-me,' comporting me beyond a sovereign claim in the direction of a challenge to selfhood that I receive from elsewhere. The question of how, whether and in what way to 'give ground' to the other becomes an essential part of ethical reflection; in other words, reflection does not return the subject to him or herself, but is to be understood as an ec-static relationality, a way of being comported beyond oneself, a way of being dispossessed from sovereignty and nation in response to the claims made by those one does not fully know and did not fully choose."

18. See Butler and Athanasiou, *Dispossession* 3–5, for a discussion of forcible or privative dispossession versus dispossession by virtue of contact with another.

19. "It may seem like something of a leap, but I want to suggest that this very brief account of what is unchosen in the force of the image articulates something about ethical obligations that impose themselves upon us without our consent. So if we are open to this point, though we have reason enough not to accept it fully it would seem to suggest that consent is not a sufficient ground for delimiting the global obligations that form our responsibility. In

fact, responsibility may well be implicated in a vast domain of the noncon-sensual" (Butler, *Notes toward a Performative Theory of Assembly* 103).

20. "Already undone, or undone from the start, we are formed, and as formed, we come to be always partially undone by what we come to sense and know. What follows is that form of relationality that we might call "ethical": a certain demand or obligation impinges upon me, and the response relies on my capacity to affirm this having been acted on, formed into one who can respond to this or that call. . . . I am only moved or unmoved by something outside that impinges upon me in a more or less involuntary way. . . . I would say that we must affirm the way we are already and still acted on in order to affirm ourselves, but self-affirmation means affirming the world without which the self would not be and that means affirming what I could never choose, that is, what happens to me without my willing that precipitates my sensing and knowing the world as I do" (Butler, *Senses of the Subject* [New York: Fordham UP, 2015] 11–12).

21. Ibid. 11.

22. Maurice Blanchot, *L'Attente l'oubli* (Paris: Gallimard, 1962) 12, my translation.

23. For another discussion of a prayer that asks for something already undergone in any case, see my essay "Necessary Repetition/Répétition: Rehearsing Loss in the Theatre of Samuel Beckett," *Journal of Dramatic Theory and Criticism* 27.2 (2013): 7–30.

24. Blanchot, "L'Affirmation (le désir, le malheur)," *L'Entretien infini* (Paris: Gallimard, 1969) 178–79, trans. Susan Hanson, "Affirmation (desire, affliction)," *The Infinite Conversation* (Minneapolis: U of Minnesota P, 1993) 122.

25. "When one reads Simone Weil's notebooks, it is not the difficult coher-ence nor the refusal to think things all the way through that one might take as grounds for complaint. It is another regret one feels. . . . No thought has more rigorously sought to maintain God's remoteness, the necessity of know-ing that we know nothing of him and that he is truth and certitude only when he is hidden, the hidden God. But she does not cease to speak openly of this hidden God, with assurance and with indiscretion, forgetting that this indis-cretion renders nearly all her words vain" (Blanchot, "Affirmation [desire, affliction]" 118–19).

26. Ann Smock, "Translator's Introduction," *Rue Ordener, Rue Labat*, by Sarah Kofman (Lincoln: U of Nebraska P, 1996) xii.

27. Ibid. x.

28. I am widely indebted to Anne-Lise François's work on recessive action for the idea of a reading that does without narrative fruition (see François, *Open Secrets: The Literature of Uncounted Experience* [Stanford: Stanford UP, 2008]).

29. Weil, *The* Iliad *or the Poem of Force*, trans. James Holoka (New York: Peter Lang, 2005) 31; hereafter cited as PF.

30. This is a quote attributed to the Athenians in response to the plea by the people of Melos to be spared, in Thucydides's *History of the Peloponnesian*

War. As quoted in Weil, "Luttons-nous pour la justice?" *Écrits de Londres et dernières lettres* (Paris: Gallimard, 1957) 45, my translation.

31. Blanchot, "La Mesure, le suppliant," *L'Entretien infini* (Paris: Gallimard, 1969), trans. Susan Hanson, "Measure, the Suppliant," *Infinite Conversation* (Minneapolis: U of Minnesota P, 1993).

32. Weil, *Venise sauvée: Tragédie en trois actes* (Paris: Gallimard, 1955).

33. Blanchot, *La Folie du jour* (Paris: Gallimard, 2002); trans. Lydia Davis, *The Madness of Day* (Barrytown, NY: Station Hill, 1981).

34. See Weil, "Autobiographie spirituelle," *Attente de Dieu* (Paris: Fayard, 1966); hereafter cited as AD; translations are mine, with page numbers referring to the original.

35. It falls outside the scope of this book to situate the concept of decreation within Weil's larger religious metaphysics, an idiosyncratic syncretism of neo-Platonic mysticism, Pythagorean geometry, selective Christian theology, Hinduism, and ancient Egyptian religious traditions. While there are many excellent studies that examine her religious metaphysics within a single religious tradition (Miklos Vetö, *The Religious Metaphysics of Simone Weil*, is seminal in this regard; while A. Rebecca Rozelle-Stone and Lucian Stone's recent and carefully articulated *Simone Weil and Theology*, despite a chapter devoted to Weil's religious pluralism, still situates Weil's religious writings within a Christological framework), a comprehensive panreligious study of Weil's metaphysics would be a welcome addition to Weil studies (see Vetö, *The Religious Metaphysics of Simone Weil*; and Rozelle-Stone and Stone, *Simone Weil and Theology* [London: Bloomsbury T&T Clark, 2013]).

36. See Weil, "À Propos du 'Pater,'" AD 215–28.

37. Weil, *Œuvres complètes,* Tome 6, Vol. 4: *Cahiers (juillet 1942–juillet 1943): La Connaissance surnaturelle (cahiers de New York et de Londres)* (Paris: Gallimard, 2006) 279–80.

38. See Weil, *Écrits de Londres et dernières lettres*; Papiers Simone Weil, Boîte XI: Lettres de Simone Weil à ses parents, Bibliothèque Nationale Française, Paris; Papiers Simone Weil, Boîte I(I): Correspondance générale, Bibliothèque Nationale Française, Paris; and Papiers Simone Weil Carton VIII: Documents Maurice Schumann, Bibliothèque Nationale Française, Paris.

39. Levinas, *Paul Celan: De l'être à l'autre* (Saint Clément de rivière: Fata Morgana, 2004) 25, trans. Michael B. Smith, "Paul Celan: From Being to the Other," *Proper Names* (Stanford: Stanford UP, 1996) 43.

40. Weil, *Écrits de Londres et dernières lettres* 213.

CHAPTER 1: THE VULNERABILITY OF PRECIOUS THINGS: "LA PERSONNE ET LE SACRÉ"

1. Simone Weil, "La Personne et le sacré," *Écrits de Londres et dernières lettres* (Paris: Gallimard, 1957); hereafter cited as PS; translations are mine, with page numbers referring to the original.

For her work as a *rédactrice* for the Free French organization in London from November 1942 to shortly before her death in August 1943, Weil wrote prodigiously—some six hundred pages on subjects largely responding to projects developed by Resistance committees concerning the reorganization of France after the war. The most expansive work Weil wrote in this regard was the posthumously titled *L'Enracinement*, of which its principle themes are treated *in nuce* in "La Personne et le sacré" (see Springsted, "Beyond the Personal: Weil's Critique of Maritain," *Harvard Theological Review* 98.2 [2005]: 209–18; Simone Fraisse, "Simone Weil, la personne et les droits de l'homme," *Cahiers Simone Weil* 7.2 [1984]: 120–32; and Christopher Hamilton, "Simone Weil's 'Human Personality': Between the Personal and the Impersonal," *Harvard Theological Review* 98.2 [2005]: 187–207). See also Weil, *L'Enracinement: Prélude à une déclaration des devoirs envers l'être humain* (Paris: Gallimard, 1949); hereafter cited as EN; translations are mine, with page numbers referring to the original.

2. Weil, *La Pesanteur et la grâce* (Paris: Plon, 1988) 94; hereafter cited as PG; translations are mine, with page numbers referring to the original.

3. The word Weil uses is "le mal," which connotes suffering, harm, and, in a classically philosophical sense, evil—a wide range of meanings for which we do not have an exact equivalent in English. Depending upon the context of its use, it can mean one or more of the things stated above. I have chosen to translate it as "harm." What is unequivocally true regardless of context is that "le mal" is for Weil always the opposite of the good (le bien), which Weil understands in its Platonic sense. That "le mal" cannot be so easily condensed into a single word in English may pose problems for English-language readers, but Weil uses both "le mal" and "le bien" in a simple and straightforward manner that reflects her understanding of each term as an evident truth. According to Weil, at issue is intellectual honesty rather than intellectual acumen: the task is to think through their operation (not to question whether they exist) as clearly and unblinkingly as possible. Considering the political state of affairs in the time of her writing, Weil argued that what were needed were not intellectuals, specialists, or so-called "men of genius." In a sweeping statement, Weil dismisses them as "men of talent" at best. Far superior, writes Weil, is the factory worker who lives and works in miserable conditions, or the village idiot who could not expound upon the good but who knows it nonetheless. For Weil, they are those who can perceive "le mal" and "le bien" as nakedly as possible, with an attention or practical bearing that dispenses with eloquence and qualification. To know good is to desire only the good; to know suffering and sorrow, it suffices to undergo it. The problem, practically and politically, of course, is precisely in their incapacity to speak these.

4. Weil says that to hear this cry is harder that it would be for a happy child to commit suicide, underscoring both the absurdity and seriousness of an obligation that must be met even under unimaginable conditions (PS 36).

5. Judith Butler, *Precarious Life: The Powers of Mourning and Violence* (New York: Verso, 2004) 43.

6. See, for example, Judith Butler and Athena Athanasiou, *Dispossession: The Performative in the Political* (Cambridge: Polity, 2013) 95: "But perhaps most importantly, this sensibility is neither mine nor yours. It is not a possession, but a way of being comported toward another, already in the hands

of the other, and so a mode of dispossession. To refer to 'sensibility' in this sense is to refer to a constitutive relation to a sensuous outside, one without which none of us can survive." See also Butler, *Parting Ways: Jewishness and the Critique of Zionism* (New York: Columbia UP, 2012) 9: "Once ethics is no longer understood exclusively as a disposition or action grounded in a ready-made subject, but rather as a relational practice that responds to an obligation that originates outside the subject, then ethics contests sovereign notions of the subject and ontological claims of self-identity. Indeed, ethics comes to signify the act by which place is established for those who are 'not-me,' comporting me beyond a sovereign claim in the direction of a challenge to selfhood that I receive from elsewhere. The question of how, whether and in what way to 'give ground' to the other becomes an essential part of ethical reflection; in other words, reflection does not return the subject to him or herself, but is to be understood as an ec-static relationality, a way of being comported beyond oneself, a way of being dispossessed from sovereignty and nation in response to the claims made by those one does not fully know and did not fully choose."

7. Ann Pirruccello, "Making the World My Body: Simone Weil and Somatic Practice," *Philosophy East & West* 52.4 (2002): 482.

8. The limitations issuing from material existence are examined more comprehensively in the second chapter through a reading of "*L'Iliade* ou le poème de la force," while the third chapter on *Venise sauvée* treats the idea of others as a limitation of one's volition (see *The* Iliad *or the Poem of Force*, trans. James P. Holoka [New York: Peter Lang, 2005]; hereafter cited as PF. See also *Venise sauvée: Tragédie en trois actes* [Paris: Gallimard, 1955]; hereafter cited as VS; translations are mine, with page numbers referring to the original.).

9. "La Personne et le sacré" was written as part of a larger project for the Free French envisioning the spiritual and political renewal and reorganization of a postwar France, particularly its conception of justice. The essay is in part a critical reaction to the latest iteration of personalist philosophies in 1920s and 1930s France led by Weil's contemporaries Emmanuel Mounier (and the journal he founded, *Esprit*) and Jacques Maritain. Weil's example of the unintelligible cry illustrates the limitations of personalism to respond to the claim of injury inasmuch as it is based upon the notion of a stable and indelible personhood, one that is conditioned upon the presumption that human beings cannot be destroyed and upon the ability of an individual to ultimately overcome circumstances, however dire (see Eric O. Springsted, "Rootedness: Culture and Value," in *Simone Weil's Philosophy of Culture*, ed. Richard H. Bell [Cambridge: Cambridge UP, 1993] 170–71).

In Weil's view, personalism fails to understand the "human being as such" (l'être humain comme tel) at a very basic level, for Weil maintains that human beings can indeed be destroyed. Moreover, Weil argues that the presumption of the individual's capacity (to meet suffering or have that suffering be addressed) in personalism erroneously puts the onus for suffering on the one who undergoes it. In contrast, obligation, as Weil understands it, does not stem from what one can or cannot do; indeed, Weil argues that one's responsibility for the other is anterior to and sometimes exceeds what one can do, leaving both oneself and the other vulnerable to suffering and under a shared sense of precariousness.

10. See esp. Butler, *Precarious Life*; and Butler, *Parting Ways*. See also Butler, "Bodily Vulnerability, Coalitions, and Street Politics," *Notes toward a Performative Theory of Assembly* (Cambridge: Harvard UP, 2015); and Butler, "Vulnerability and Resistance," *Profession* (March 2014), http://profession.commons.mla.org/2014/03/19/vulnerability-and-resistance/.)

11. Plato, *Republic*, bk. VI, 439a–494a.

12. Ibid., bk. VII, 514a–517c.

13. Weil, *Attente de Dieu* (Paris: Fayard, 1966) 24; hereafter cited as AD; translations are mine, with page numbers referring to the original.

14. See Weil, VS.

15. This is most evident in the character Renaud, who spearheads the plot, but the principle is no less true for the most minor and displaced of the conspirators.

16. *The Rights of Man and Natural Law* was published in French in New York in 1942. Maritain was an influential voice in the postwar reorganization debate, an "intellectual hero," writes Springsted ("Beyond the Personal" 210). "La personne" has also been translated into English as "personality" (see "Human Personality," trans. Richard Rees, *Simone Weil: Selected Essays, 1934–1943* [Oxford: Oxford UP, 1962]).

17. See Jacques Maritain, *Humanisme intégral: Problèmes temporels et spirituels d'une nouvelle chrétienté* (Paris: Fernand Aubier, 1936). For a clear account of European personalism in the early twentieth century, see Johan De Tavernier, "The Historical Roots of Personalism: From Renouvier's *Le Personnalisme*, Mounier's *Manifeste au service du personnalisme* and Maritain's *Humanisme intégral* to Jansens' *Personne et Société*," *Ethical Perspectives* 16.3 (2009): 361–92.

18. "The notion of rights is even more profound than that of moral obligation, for God has sovereign rights over his creatures and doesn't have any moral obligations toward them (even as he owes it to himself to give them what is required by their nature")" (Jacques Maritain, *Les Droits de l'homme et la loi naturelle* [Paris: P. Hartmann, 1945] 37, my translation. Also quoted by Weil in EN 349).

19. Considering what counts in the "human being as such" would first require recognition of the other's life—of his "existence as such," as Weil puts it (PG 122). While such recognition is true for any time or circumstance, it becomes especially strained under prolonged or chronic exposure to degradation, such as they are under conditions of war. In her essay on the *Iliad*, Weil writes that war has "the power to change a human being into a thing by making him die"; recognition of life might only issue from loss of that life. And so, I think we must read in Weil's claim that only the impersonal in human beings counts the inadequacy of the "person" to account for human life, without exclusion and under all conditions, especially those that would put that life most at risk of perishing (see Weil, PF 46).

20. Hamilton, "Simone Weil's 'Human Personality'" 193.

21. Emphasis in original. Similarly Weil writes in a letter to Father Perrin: "It is that I long to know them so as to love them just as they are. For if I do not love them as they are, it is not them I love, and my love is unreal" (AD 19).

22. "One feels justified in concluding that a loss of the kind has been experienced, but one cannot see clearly what has been lost, and may the more readily suppose that the patient too cannot consciously perceive what it is he has lost. . . . That is, when he knows whom he has lost but not what it is he has lost in them" (Sigmund Freud, "Mourning and Melancholia," *General Psychological Theory* [New York: Touchstone, 1997] 166, emphasis in original).

23. "Each single one of the memories and hopes which bound the libido to the object is brought up and hyper-cathected, and the detachment of the libido from it accomplished. . . . [W]hen the work of mourning is completed the ego becomes free and uninhibited again" (Freud, "Mourning and Melancholia" 166). For another discussion of the refusal to substitute the lost object of love, see my essay "Necessary Repetition/*Répétition*: Rehearsing Loss in the Theatre of Samuel Beckett" *Journal of Dramatic Theory and Criticism* 27.2 (2013): 7–30.

24. Monique Broc-Lapeyre, "Le Passage de la personne à l'impersonnel," *Simone Weil: Le grand passage* (Paris: Albin Michel, 2006) 106–8, my translation.

25. Weil, *La Connaissance surnaturelle* (Paris: Gallimard, 1950) 249, 250; hereafter cited as CS; translations are mine, with page numbers referring to the original.

26. See chapter 5 for a reprisal of this question, where I treat the ethical dimension and spiritual impetus for existing as "one thing among many others."

27. Emmanuel Levinas and Richard Kearney, "Dialogue with Emmanuel Levinas," *Face to Face with Levinas* (Albany: State U of New York P, 1986) 24.

28. See Hamilton, "Simone Weil's 'Human Personality'" 192.

29. Levinas and Kearney, "Dialogue" 24.

30. See Matthew 5:45.

31. See chapter 2 for a fuller discussion of force.

32. I owe the term "the field of audibility" to Judith Butler.

33. This is the term used by Weil (rather than the historical appellation "Jesus") and will be the one used throughout this chapter.

34. Butler, *Precarious Life* 133.

35. Ibid., 134, 134.

36. Levinas, *Is it Righteous to Be? Interviews with Emmanuel Levinas*, ed. Jill Robbins (Stanford: Stanford UP, 2001) 48, emphasis in original. See chapter 3 of this book for more on the Levinas's notion of the face and its unrepresentability.

37. Butler, *Parting Ways* 10.

38. Ibid., emphasis in original.

39. Ibid. 10.

40. Ibid. 12.

41. Levinas, "Paix et proximité," Altérité et transcendance (Saint Clément de rivière: Fata Morgana, 1995) 145, my translation.

42. Levinas, "Sans identité," L'Humanisme de l'autre homme (Saint Clément de rivière: Fata Morgana, 1972) 104, my translation.

43. Weil writes: "Creation, the Passion, the Eucharist—always this same movement of withdrawal. This movement is love" (CS 26). Not surprisingly, Weil did not consider the Resurrection of Christ to be critical in the Passion. For her it sufficed that God took human form and suffered death. It seems, as I have been suggesting in my reading of Weil with Levinas, that there is no "showing" at all, unless it is in the form of a "baring" (dénudation) or exposure.

44. Weil writes: "There are only two moments of nudity and perfect purity in human life: birth and death. We can only adore God in human form without blemishing His divinity when newly born or on our deathbed" (PG 88).

45. Rowan Williams, "Simone Weil and the Necessary Non-existence of God," Wrestling with Angels: Conversations in Modern Theology (Grand Rapids, MI: Eerdmans, 2007) 217.

46. As quoted in Butler, "Bracha's Eurydice," The Matrixial Borderspace by Bracha Ettinger (Minneapolis: U of Minnesota P, 2006) ix.

47. "On ne peut pas offrir autre chose que le je" (PG 73).

CHAPTER 2: UNCOMMON MEASURE: "L'ILIADE OU LE POÈME DE LA FORCE"

1. Simone Weil's essay was first drafted in 1937 and completed in 1939. It was first accepted for publication in La Nouvelle Revue Française on the condition that Weil heavily redact its final pages, which she refused to do. It was eventually published in two parts in Les Cahiers du Sud in December 1940 and January 1941, following the German occupation of Paris. Despite its being a commentary on political circumstances in Europe of that time—in the opening paragraph Weil calls the Iliad a "document," "the most beautiful and flawless of mirrors" (PF 19)—Weil eschews a historical reading of the wars and they are never explicitly named nor analyzed, as such. Weil considered the Iliad to be the most perfect instance of literary achievement, illuminating the exposure to force and its effects on human livability. See Weil, The Iliad or the Poem of Force, trans. James Holoka (New York: Peter Lang, 2005); hereafter cited as PF, with page numbers referring to the original. Where indicated, I have also used Richmond Lattimore's translation, The Iliad (Chicago: U of Chicago P, 1961). All citations from the Iliad in French are Simone Weil's translations; I have used James Holoka's translations of these into English.

2. Weil, "Réflexions sur la barbarie," Œuvres Simone Weil (Paris: Gallimard, 1999) 506.

3. "La Personne et le sacré," Écrits de Londres et dernières lettres (Paris: Gallimard, 1957) 14.

4. Plato, *Republic*, esp. bk. VII, 514a–515c.

5. E. Jane Doering notes the importance of this story for Weil: "Weil referred to the incident five times in her notes, always from a different perspective, seeing in its poignant message an application to themes that she was also pursuing in sacred Indian texts. She transcribed the full incident in the notebook that she took with her on the voyage to America. . . . The formula reappears in two later essays: "Are We Struggling for Justice?" and "Forms of the Implicit love of God" (Doering, *Simone Weil and the Specter of Self-Perpetuating Force* [Notre Dame: U of Notre Dame P, 2010] 62–63).

6. Weil, "Luttons-nous pour la justice?" *Écrits de Londres et dernières lettres* (Paris: Gallimard, 1957) 45; hereafter cited as LJ; translations are mine, with page numbers referring to the original.

7. See Weil, *Intimations of Christianity among the Ancient Greeks*, trans. E. Chase Geissbuhler (London: Routledge and Kegan Paul, 1957); Weil, *On Science, Necessity, and the Love of God*, trans. Richard Rees (London: Oxford UP, 1968); and Weil, "Formes de l'amour implicite de Dieu," *Attente de Dieu* (Paris: Fayard, 1966).

For an excellent and thorough introduction to the idea of gravity, necessity, and equilibrium in Weil's writings, see Ann Pirruccello, "'Gravity' in the Thought of Simone Weil," *Philosophy and Phenomenological Research* 57.1 (1997): 73–93. For a brief historical discussion of force in philosophy, see Françoise Meltzer, "The Hands of Simone Weil," *Critical Inquiry* 27.4 (2001): 611–28. For a fuller discussion of "necessity" and "equilibrium," see Peter Winch, *Simone Weil: "The Just Balance"* (Cambridge: Cambridge UP, 1989) 60–89.

8. Translation modified.

9. E. Jane Doering, *Simone Weil and the Specter of Self-Perpetuating Force* 2.

10. Ibid. 1.

11. The fallen are "dearer" to vultures as food than they are to their wives from whom they are far away. Weil notes the bitter truth of this transformation and estrangement, writing elsewhere that it expresses "with incomparable power the wretched limitation of human love." There she continues: "It is not true that human love is stronger than death. Death is much stronger. Love is subdued to death" (Weil, *La Connaissance surnaturelle* [Paris: Gallimard, 1950] 292; hereafter cited as CS; translations are mine, with page numbers referring to the original). The superior strength of death is everywhere apparent in Weil's reading of the *Iliad*; those who fight against it, insisting upon the greater power and protection of their love, lend the poem much of its pathos.

12. This may be a privileged episode in the *Iliad*, but Weil reminds us that it is not really different from the other deaths that fill the pages of the epic. "No single man is found in it who is not, at some time, forced to bow beneath might" (PF 25, my translation).

13. Lattimore translation.

14. "In both of his feet at the back [Achilles] made holes by the tendons in the space between ankle and heel, and drew thongs of ox-hide through them,

and fastened them to the chariot so as to let the head drag" (22.396–99, trans. Lattimore). The Achaians delight in stabbing the inert corpse, joking that at last Hektor is "softer to handle" (22.373, trans. Lattimore). Meanwhile, Hector's body is preserved from physical mutilation and rotting only through the intercession of the gods.

15. A point I take from Ann Pirruccello's excellent articulation of Weil's concept of gravity (see Pirruccello, "'Gravity' in the Thought of Simone Weil").

16. Weil, *La Pesanteur et la grâce* (Paris: Plon, 1988) 41; hereafter cited as PG; translations are mine, with page numbers referring to the original.

17. Emphasis in original.

18. The concept of gravity is especially persuasive and accessible as an explicative model for the soul (or more generally, for human behavior) subjected to force because, as Pirruccello notes, it is immediately confirmed in everyday ordinary experience.

19. Pirruccello, "'Gravity' in the Thought of Simone Weil" 82.

20. Emphasis added.

21. LJ 46–47. I have used Peter Winch's translation (see Winch, *Simone Weil* 109).

22. Winch comments: "This hesitation is primitive in that it is not based on any prior reflection. One direction in which this primitive hesitation may develop in the course of our dealing with each other is towards the various kinds of restraints on our will which we (sometimes) observe, and also in the application of various kinds of criticism (both of others and ourselves) when those restraints are not observed. So, the concept of a fellow human being thus formed *is* the one to whom a certain concept of consideration, or respect, is *due*" (ibid. 115, emphasis in original).

23. Maurice Blanchot, "La Mesure, le suppliant," *L'Entretien infini* (Paris: Gallimard, 1969) 134, trans. Susan Hanson, "Measure, the Suppliant," *Infinite Conversation* (Minneapolis: U of Minnesota P, 1993) 95; hereafter page numbers will refer to the original.

24. "Suffering [le Mal] is without place. When we say that its place is in us, we mean that we give pain a provisional place, for suffering is not exclusive to us; but suffering, for its part, would not exist if there wasn't man who suffers, man seized with his own pain, to experience it, to testify to it, in sum, to justify its reality—and for which his tears and his cries are but the devastating manifestations of his suffering" (Edmond Jabès, *L'Enfer de Dante* [Saint Clément de rivière: Fata Morgana, 1981] 10–11, my translation).

25. Weil, *Intimations of Christianity among the Ancient Greeks*, trans. E. Chase Geissbuhler (London: Routledge, 1957) 185.

26. "Force is what is called today a force field, where, philosophically, the universe is seen as a vast system ruled by the interaction of energies (as it was for the Stoics, who abandoned Aristotle's model of contiguity)" (Meltzer, "The Hands of Simone Weil" 615).

27. Pirruccello, "'Gravity' in the Thought of Simone Weil" 74.

28. Aeschylus, *The Eumenides*, as quoted in Blanchot, "La Mesure, le suppliant" 133–34.

29. Lattimore translation. Here is Weil's translation of the passage:

À ce moment Zeus le père déploya sa balance en or.
Il y plaça deux sorts de la mort qui fauche tout,
Un pour les Troyens dompteurs de chevaux, un pour les Grec bardés
    d'airain.
Il la prit au milieu, ce fut le jour fatal des Grecs qui s'abaissa. (PF 26–27)

30. Blanchot, "La Mesure, le suppliant" 134.
31. PF 25.
32. Blanchot, "La Mesure, le suppliant" 134.
33. Ibid.
34. Lattimore translation.
35. In an exchange with Hekabe, Priam asks: "Come then, tell me. What does it seem best to your own mind for me to do? My heart, my strength are terribly urgent that I go there to the ships within the wide army of the Achaians" (24.197–99). Priam's words are expressed simultaneously as a question ("Come, then, tell me") and a demand (a call from the radically other, that is, Zeus and Hector [dead but unburied]). Both the question and the demand are underpinned by an obligation that cannot be refused. They show how the demand and question are held together by the exigency to go outside oneself. Being told to, what can the "I" not do? The heart, the strength is "terribly urgent"; it demands an affirmation of that strength from the one who has also been dispossessed.
36. Hector's corpse is preserved only through divine intercession.
37. Here is the "missing" passage. Although Weil did translate this scene, it is not included in her final draft of the essay.

But now Priam spoke to him in the words of a suppliant:
"Achilleus like the gods, remember your father, one who
is of years like mine, and on the door-sill of sorrowful old age.
And they who dwell nearby encompass him and afflict him,
nor is there any to defend him against the wrath, the destruction.
Yet surely he, when he hears of you and that you are still living,
is gladdened within his heart and all his days he is hopeful
that he will see his beloved son come home from the road.
But for me, my destiny was evil. I have had the noblest
of sons in Troy, but I say not one of them is left to me. . . .
. . . I come now to the ships of the Achaians
to win him [Hektor] back from you, and I bring you gifts beyond num-
    ber.
Honour then the gods, Achilleus, and take pity upon me
remembering your father, yet I am still more pitiful:
I have gone through what no other mortal on earth has gone through;
I put my lips to the hands of the man who has killed my children."
(24.485–506; trans. Lattimore)

38. Blanchot, "La Mesure, le suppliant" 134, 134–35, 134.
39. Ibid. 133.

40. Ibid. 132.

41. Ibid.

42. He "can," but he is not permitted to. Blanchot argues that the suppliant, although outside of all power, is subject to another "power," a different "law." That law is divine or sacred (see ibid.).

43. Winch, *Simone Weil* 109.

44. Blanchot, "La Mesure, le suppliant" 134.

45. Joseph Slugia, "The Communication of the Impossible," *Diacritics* 31.2 (2001): 53.

46. Maurice Blanchot, *La Communauté inavouable* (Paris: Éditions de Minuit, 1983) 21, trans. Pierre Joris, *The Unavowable Community* (Barrytown, NY: Station Hill, 1988); page numbers refer to the original.

47. Lattimore translation.

48. Lattimore translation.

49. Weil, *The Notebooks of Simone Weil*, trans. Arthur Wills (London: Routledge, 1956) 546.

50. James Holoka, "Commentary," *The* Iliad *or the Poem of Force*, by Simone Weil (New York: Peter Lang, 2005) 78.

51. Holoka notes that Weil adopts the story of Niobe as it is recounted by Homer (other versions of the myth do not incorporate the story of eating); it is the only version to which Weil refers (see Holoka's "Commentary," PF 78).

52. Blanchot, "La Mesure, le suppliant" 134.

53. Blanchot, "The Song of the Sirens," trans. Lydia Davis, *The Station Hill Blanchot Reader* (Barrytown, NY: Station Hill, 1999) 448.

54. See Weil's notes to her play *Venise sauvée: Tragédie en trois actes* (Paris: Gallimard, 1955). See chapter 3 for a fuller discussion on stillness.

55. Weil says that love is the other moment where, through a certain kind of dispossession, one finds one's soul. In the context of the passage, Weil suggests that love cuts through the anonymity and blindness of force. This is certainly the case with Achilles's love for Patrocles.

56. Translation modified. "Les voilà exposés nus au malheur, sans l'armure de puissance qui protégeait leur âme, sans plus rien désormais qui les sépare des larmes" (PF 28).

57. The passages concerning tears translated by Weil call attention to an apparently irrecusable distance—sometimes signaled by a push, other times by ridicule or by the privacy of anguish—that marks the one in tears and separates him from those who do not share or recognize his pain.

58. Emmanuel Levinas, "Sans identité," *L'Humanisme de l'autre homme* (Saint Clément de rivière: Fata Morgana, 1972) 104, my translation.

CHAPTER 3: STILLNESS AND THE BOND OF LOVE:
VENISE SAUVÉE

This essay is indebted to Ann Smock and to Anne-Lise François for their beautiful meditations on *Venise sauvée* (see Ann Smock, "Speaking-Not Speaking in a Single Movement," *What Is There to Say?* [Lincoln: U of

Nebraska P, 2003]; and Anne-Lise François, "Toward a Theory of Recessive Action," *Open Secrets: The Literature of Uncounted Experience* [Stanford: Stanford UP, 2008]).

1. The notes, drawn from Weil's notebooks and published as a preface to the 1955 Gallimard publication of *Venise sauvée*, offer critical cues to a play that would never be completed due to Weil's untimely death. From the editor's note: "In order to illuminate her intentions and to complete as much as possible the text of this unfinished tragedy, we are publishing as a preface the notes scattered in Simone Weil's notebooks which refer to *Venise sauvée*" (*Venise sauvée: Tragédie en trois actes* [Paris: Gallimard, 1955] 7; hereafter cited as VS; translations are mine, with page numbers referring to the original).

2. Weil based her play, an allegory for the Second World War, upon historical events as recounted by Abbé de Saint-Réal in his *Conjuration des Espagnols contre la République de Venise* (Paris: Editions Bossard, 1922). Here is Weil's synopsis, written in her notebooks and published as supplementary notes to the play:

> *Venise sauvée.* Nota.—In 1618, the Marquis of Bedmar, Spanish ambassador to Venice, conceived a conspiracy to bring Venice under the power of the king of Spain, which was then the master of almost all of Italy. Wishing to remain in the shadows because of his post as ambassador, he entrusted the execution of his plans to Renaud, a French lord of advanced years, and to Pierre, a renowned Provençal pirate, captain, and marine. Renaud was in charge of the preparation, Pierre of the military operations. A large part of the mercenary troops stationed in Venice and many of the officers, the majority of them foreigners in the service of Venice, were won over to their side. The plan was a surprise attack in the middle of the night, simultaneously occupying the important positions in the city and setting fire to all the neighborhoods at the same time to spread confusion, killing all those who try to resist. The night chosen for the attack was the night before the Pentecost. Jaffier, one of its leaders, made the conspiracy fail by revealing the plans to the Council of Ten out of pity for the city. Historians, especially Spanish ones, have denied the authenticity of this conspiracy but with very weak arguments. It is certain, in any case, that the Council of Ten executed several hundred men and that Bedmar had to leave Venice. (VS 26–27)

3. Aristotle, *Poetics* 1452a29–32. Anne-Lise François notes that *Venise sauvée* lacks the reversal characteristic of Aristotelian notion of tragedy. While that is certainly true of the plot (of course, central to Aristotle's definition), there is, nonetheless, recognition—albeit, not at the level of plot. Whether or not this makes *Venise sauvée* a "failed" tragedy is another question (see François, *Open Secrets: The Literature of Uncounted Experience* [Stanford: Stanford UP, 2007]).

4. Weil, *The* Iliad *or the Poem of Force*, trans. James Holoka (New York: Peter Lang, 2005) 37; hereafter cited as PF.

5. See *Attente de Dieu* (Paris: Fayard, 1966), 130; hereafter cited as AD; translations are mine, with page numbers referring to the original.

6. The "self-perpetuation of force" is a term I borrow from E. Jane Doering, discussed in chapter 2 (see Doering, *Simone Weil and the Specter of Self-Perpetuating Force* [Notre Dame: U of Notre Dame P, 2010]).

7. Weil, *Œuvres complètes*, Tome 6, Vol. 1: *Cahiers (1933-septembre 1941)* (Paris: Gallimard, 1994) 302, my translation.

8. See Maurice Blanchot, *L'Entretien infini* (Paris: Gallimard, 1969). See also Sarah Kofman's reworking of Maurice Blanchot's formulation in her *Paroles suffoquées* (Paris: Éditions Galilée, 1987).

9. In her most extensive and sustained writing on belonging—or what she calls *l'enracinement* (rootedness)—Weil goes further, claiming that it is one of the needs of the soul, "perhaps the most important and most misunderstood need of the human soul" (Weil, *L'Enracinement: Prélude à une déclaration des devoirs envers l'être humain* [Paris: Gallimard, 1949] 62, emphasis added; hereafter cited as EN; translations are mine, with page numbers referring to the original).

10. Even Jaffier's "natural" (but not entitled) nobility cannot make him rise above his outsider status. We need look no further than the Council's decision to banish him from Venice instead of putting him to death, and this despite the Secretary's earlier suggestion that he would gladly accept Jaffier as his son-in-law. Here we see the more subtle operation of the exclusionary politics of "déracinement" in designating the exceptional (i.e., being "like us") by way of underscoring that one is not, "in fact," "one of us."

11. Weil, *La Pesanteur et la grâce* (Paris: Plon, 1988) 254; hereafter cited as PG; translations are mine, with page numbers referring to the original.

12. J. P. Little, "Society as Mediator in Simone Weil's *Venise sauvée*," *Modern Language Review* 65.2 (1970): 301, 298.

13. "En 1940, Simone Weil commença d'écrire une tragédie, *Venise sauvée*. Ce projet lui tenait au cœur, ses confidences et plusieurs cahiers de brouillons en témoignent. (On a pu réunir, par exemple, une cinquantaine de versions du grand monologue de Jaffier.) Pour éclairer ses intentions et compléter, dans la mesure du possible, le texte de cette tragédie restée inachevée, nous publions en préface les notes éparses dans les cahiers de Simone Weil et qui se réfèrent à *Venise sauvée*. C'est du reste sur sa demande que ces notes furent réunies, et lui furent envoyées à Londres en même temps qu'une copie du texte de la tragédie. L'intention du Simone Weil était à ce moment d'achever *Venise sauvée*. La mort, seule, l'en empêcha" (VS 7).

14. When the play is read as an allegory for World War II, Renaud additionally represents those who rationalized that Paris must be saved at all costs—even if it meant killing or destroying the city in order to do so. I thank Anne-Lise François for first pointing this out to me.

15. I am reminded of Marguerite Duras's unblinking account of her experience (as "Thérèse") torturing a French traitor as part of her resistance activities and thus, as one of the "good guys." Duras conveys the pleasure Thérèse has in directing the torture: "The more they hit, the more he bleeds, the clearer it is that we have to hit, that it is true, it is just. These images emerge

from the blows. Thérèse is transparent, enchanted by the images" ("Albert des Capitales," *La Douleur* [Paris: P.O.L, 1985] 154, my translation).

16. Weil writes in her January 14, 1942, letter to Father Perrin that "one of the most dangerous forms of sin, or perhaps the most dangerous, consists in putting the unlimited in an essentially finite domain" (AD 15). See chapter 2 for a discussion of equilibrium and limits.

17. To submit others to your will as the "only reality" is Renaud's blueprint for a successful government after the overthrow. The people of Venice must feel themselves "foreigners in their own homeland." As he explains, "Uprooting conquered peoples has always been, will always be the politics of conquerors." In another sense, it is the remaking of the world according to which there is no "sharing." The example Renaud gives of having the nobles wait in line to obtain authorization to do anything is an image of the dream of power as the exercise over time itself (how standing in line, etc. makes a standstill of time; how time is drawn into units of activity or nonactivity akin to factory work or other monotonous work that makes time enter the body in the mode of fatigue, boredom, and stupor in a manner that is not unlike how the "aversion to a monotonous existence" acts upon the conspirators [14]). As such, time at once derealizes and imprints itself (evoked by the necessity of entering the endless waiting rooms of the Spanish conquerors; the bureaucratization of time and the degradation of the one who must, of necessity, submit to its machinations). Again Renaud:

> Look at them, proud, free, and happy. Tomorrow, none of them must dare raise their eyes to the least of your mercenaries. Afterwards it will be easy for you to govern the city peaceably and with glory for yourselves, so long as you take care to humiliate the nobility, which will alarm the people. . . . The nobility should no longer have any place; they who were too proud to speak to foreigners must no longer be able to do anything, neither commerce, marriage, nor moving, without first having to wait for hours in the waiting rooms of the Spanish for authorization permits. Tonight and tomorrow the people of Venice must feel that they are nothing but our playthings; they must feel lost. The ground beneath their feet must be suddenly and forever lost to them so that they can only find their equilibrium in obeying you. . . . It is this stupor that makes one submit. Starting tomorrow, they must believe themselves to have always been subjected to Spain, to have never been free. (VS 64–66)

There is something horrific in this scene of derealization precisely because of the abasement of those who must submit to it in order to live. Ever replayed and parlayed to an imaginary start, there can be, in point of fact, no sense of "result" or even beginning; rather, it is accumulation as a manner of living. The extraordinary paradox is that one must "show up" for these authorizations in order to state that one is there precisely at the site of one's slow degradation.

18. Jean Améry's unflinching argument regarding what he calls "resentments" is a succinct picture of the transmission and transference of violence in *Venise sauvée*—one that requires brutalizing the body in order to stop

speech altogether. That is the case even when torture is supposedly "justi-fied," and the torturer is on the side of the just (see Améry, *At the Mind's Limits: Contemplations by a Survivor of Auschwitz and Its Realities*, trans. Sidney Rosenfeld and Stella P. Rosenfeld [Bloomington: Indiana UP, 1980]).

19. There is, of course, the question of what communication would be adequate to one's suffering.

20. Weil, "L'Amour de Dieu et le malheur," *Pensées sans ordre concernant l'amour de Dieu* (Paris: Gallimard, 1962).

21. See Weil, "La Personne et le sacré," *Écrits de Londres et dernières lettres* (Paris: Gallimard, 1957).

22. "The Venetian governor of the Greek Island where she was born (of the most noble family there), seduced her after a formal promise of marriage. He had her father assassinated for demanding that he keep his promise. She came to Venice seeking justice; instead, she was ruined by the cost of the pro-cess. Finding herself alone and without resources in Venice, she was forced to become a courtesan. She has all the resentment against Venice that a once noble woman has for her fallen status" (VS 74–75).

23. Weil, "Réflexions sur le bon usage des études scolaires en vue de l'Amour de Dieu," AD.

24. Weil, *Cahiers, Tome III* (Paris: Plon, 1956) 40, my translation.

25. Emphasis in original.

26. Cathy Caruth, *Unclaimed Experience: Trauma, Narrative, and History* (Baltimore: Johns Hopkins UP, 1996) 37.

27. My reading of the elision of sight and its capture into language and a history that can be mastered through narrative is heavily influenced by Cathy Caruth's reading of *Hiroshima mon amour*. She writes, "the act of seeing, in the very establishing of a bodily referent, erases, like an empty grammar, the reality of the event" (29) (see her "Literature and the Enactment of Memory," *Unclaimed Experience* 25–56).

28. See also chapter 1 for a discussion of the Levinasian "face."

29. Emmanuel Levinas, "Paix et Proximité," *Altérité et Transcendance* (Saint Clément de rivière: Fata Morgana, 1995) 144, my translation.

30. Weil, "Formes de l'amour implicite de Dieu," AD 157.

31. The subheading is from Maurice Blanchot, "Battle with the Angel," *Friendship*, trans. Elizabeth Rottenberg (Stanford: Stanford UP, 1997) 133.

32. Walter Benjamin, "Oedipus, or Rational Myth," *Selected Writings*, vol. 2 (Cambridge: Belknap Press of Harvard UP, 1999) 579, 570, 579.

33. Blanchot, "Battle with the Angel" 133.

34. "No, do not hide him from me; I still want to look at him. Move aside a bit, let me look at him, I ask of you" (VS 136). The apprentice seems to be transfixed: looking at "the thing" he is disgusted, but the disgust only seems to fuel his desire to see "more" of him. When the apprentice says, "I would volun-tarily strangle him" (135), we move from the desire to kill to a strangled desire: I want to see him still though he disgusts me. In seeing him I want to strangle him; I want to strangle him at the same time that I want to hear him speak. The equivocation of speaking and crying shows emphatically where violence intrudes upon speech and the seamless movement from the face to the voice.

35. Weil notes: "Mercy implies an infinite distance. One doesn't have compassion for what is near. Jaffier" (VS 20).

CHAPTER 4: UNFINISHED OBLIGATION: *VENISE SAUVÉE* AND *LA FOLIE DU JOUR*

1. Simone Weil, *Venise sauvée: Tragédie en trois actes* (Paris: Gallimard, 1955); hereafter cited as VS; translations are mine, with page numbers referring to the original.

2. See Weil's notes to VS 18.

3. Emmanuel Levinas, "Exercices sur 'La Folie du jour,'" *Sur Maurice Blanchot* (Saint Clément de rivière: Fata Morgana, 2004) 59, trans. Michael B. Smith, "Exercises on 'The Madness of Day,'" *Proper Names* (Stanford: Stanford UP, 1996) 159.

4. Maurice Blanchot, *La Folie du jour* (Paris: Gallimard, 2002) 18, trans. Lydia Davis, *The Madness of the Day* (Barrytown, NY: Station Hill, 1981); hereafter cited as FJ; page numbers refer to the original.

5. Sarah Kofman, *Paroles suffoquées* (Paris: Galilée, 1987) 81–82. Kofman draws upon Robert Antelme's firsthand account of the camps in *L'Espèce humaine* (Paris: Gallimard, 1957), along with what she knows of her father's death there, and Blanchot's *L'Écriture du désastre* (Paris: Gallimard, 1980).

6. "If, in my turn, I do harm to another I receive something from him: what? What has one gained (and which will have to be repaid) when one has done harm? One has enlarged, spread oneself—One has filled part of the void in oneself by creating a new element of void in another person" (Weil, *The Notebooks of Simone Weil*, vol. 1, trans. Arthur Wills [New York: Routledge, 1976] 181).

7. See also chapter 3 for a discussion of the double valence of the term "has to."

8. This is a play on the title of a book by Ann Smock, *What Is There to Say?* (Lincoln: U of Nebraska P, 2003).

9. Jean-Luc Nancy, "Ars Somni," *Dormir, rêver . . . et autres nuits* (Lyon: Fage éditions, 2006) 106, my translation.

10. Henry W. Johnstone Jr., "Toward a Phenomenology of Death," *Philosophy and Phenomenological Research* 35.3 (1975): 396.

11. Ibid., emphasis added.

12. Ibid. 397, emphasis in original.

13. See Anne Carson, "Every Exit is an Entrance (A Praise of Sleep)," *Decreation: Poetry, Essays, Opera* (New York: Knopf, 2005) 19.

14. John Keats, "Sonnet to Sleep," *Complete Poems*, ed. J. Stillinger (Cambridge: Belknap Press of Harvard UP, 1978).

O soft embalmer of the still midnight!
Shutting with careful fingers and benign
Our gloom-pleas'd eyes, embower'd from the light,
Enshaded in forgetfulness divine:

O soothest Sleep! if so it please thee, close,
In midst of this thine hymn, my willing eyes,
Or wait the Amen ere thy poppy throws
Around my bed its lulling charities.
Then save me, or the passed day will shine
Upon my pillow, breeding many woes;
Save me from curious conscience, that still lords
Its strength for darkness, burrowing like a mole;
Turn the key deftly in the oiled wards,
And seal the hushed casket of my soul.

15. Beautiful dawn that appears suddenly like a smile
Hovering in the air over my city and its thousand canals.
Those who dwell in your peace
See how sweet the day is.
This night has satisfied my thirsty heart
More than sleep ever had before.
Yet the gentle day has come and filled my eyes
Even more than sleep.
And so, the dawning of this day so anticipated
Caresses the stone and water of the city.
In the air still mute everywhere,
A quivering has surged forth.
Your happiness is there my city, come and see.
Spouse of the seas, see far, see near
So many waves swelled with happy murmurs
Blessing your wakening.
The limpid light spreads slowly on the sea.
The celebration will soon fulfill our desires.
The calm sea waits. Oh! Beautiful the rays of daylight
Shimmering on the sea. (trans. E. Jane Doering, *Simone Weil and the
    Specter of Self-Perpetuating Force* [Notre Dame: U of Notre P, 2010]
    148)

Jours qui viens si beau, sourire suspendu
Soudain sur ma ville et ses mille canaux,
Combien aux humains qui reçoivent ta paix
Voir le jour est doux!
Le sommeil encor jamais n'avait comblé
Tant que cette nuit mon cœur qui le buvait.
Mais il est venu, le jour doux à mes yeux
Plus que le sommeil.
Voici que l'appel du jour tant attendu
Touche la cité parmi la pierre et l'eau.
Un frémissement dans l'air encor muet
A surgi partout.
Ton bonheur, est là, viens et vois ma cité.

Epouse des mers, vois bien loin, vois tout près
Tant de flots gonflés de murmures heureux
Bénir ton éveil.
Sur la mer s'étend lentement la clarté.
La fête bientôt va combler nos désirs.
La mer calme attend. Qu'ils sont beaux sur la mer,
Les rayons du jour! (VS 146–47)

16. For Weil, seeing is a special kind of work; not quite an abstaining, it is nonetheless a kind of negative or recessive action. Seeing is paying attention, an entrancing of the world against one's movement proper in that world. It is a letting come. That is how Violetta welcomes the day. Actually, paying attention is not exactly a "seeing," if by that we mean that we must always see something. But that is still not nothing; Weil insists it is real: "Certain realities are more or less transparent; others are opaque; but behind each, indistinctly, is God. Our only concern is to look in the direction of the point where it is found, *whether or not we can see it*" ("Réflexions sans ordre sur l'amour de Dieu," *Pensées sans ordre concernant l'amour de Dieu* [Paris: Gallimard, 1962] 37, my emphasis and translation). However real it may be, Weil makes it clear that it is not founded upon one's *ability* to see it.

17. Nancy, "Ars Somni" 101.

18. The heading "It Is Done" is from Marguerite Duras, *La Maladie de la mort* (Paris: Éditions de Minuit, 1982) 53, my translation.

19. Levinas, "Exercices sur 'La Folie du jour'" 59.

20. Caroline Sheaffer-Jones, "The Point of the Story: Levinas, Blanchot and 'The Madness of the Day,'" *Modern Fiction Studies* 54.1 (2008): 173.

21. Ibid. 162.

22. Levinas, "Exercices sur 'La Folie du jour'" 64–65.

23. That is an idea I take from Levinas; he is writing about ethics as a noncontracted debt to which one is nonetheless bound—*before* any freedom, before any consciousness: "Ethics would be the reminder of that famous debt I have never contracted" (Levinas, "L'Autre, Utopie et Justice," *Entre nous: Essais sur le penser-à-l'autre* [Paris: Grasset Fasquelle, 1991] 261, my translation). See also *Otherwise Than Being or Beyond Essence* for a discussion of debt characterized as a responsibility animated by the face of the other: "This response answers, before any understanding, for a debt contracted before any freedom and before any consciousness and any present, but it does answer, as though the invisible that bypasses the present left a trace by the very fact of bypassing the present" (trans. Alphonso Lingis [Dordrecht: Kluwer Academic, 1991] 12).

24. Duras, *La Maladie de la mort* 53.

25. Of this double urgency—of knowing, of not being able to know—Blanchot writes in *L'Écriture du désastre*: "And how, in fact, can one accept not to know? We read books on Auschwitz. The wish of all, there, in the camps, the last wish: know what has happened, do not forget, and at the same time never will you know" (*The Writing of the Disaster*, trans. Ann Smock [Lincoln: U of Nebraska P, 1995] 82; Maurice Blanchot, *L'Écriture du désastre* [Paris: Gallimard, 1980] 131).

26. "I had been asked: Tell us "*just* exactly" what happened. A story? I began: I am not learned; I am not ignorant. I have known joys. That is saying too little. I told them the whole story and they listened, it seems to me, with interest, at least in the beginning. But the end was a surprise to all of us. "That was the beginning," they said. "Now get to the facts." How so? The story was over!" (FJ 29).

27. This is also the title of Caroline Sheaffer-Jones's essay on Levinas's reading of Blanchot's *La Folie du jour* ("The Point of the Story: Levinas, Blanchot and the 'The Madness of the Day'").

28. For a discussion of the end of the "récit" post-Shoah, see Sarah Kofman, *Paroles suffoquées* (Paris: Galilée, 1987).

29. Blanchot, *L'Instant de ma mort* (Paris: Gallimard, 2004).

30. Jacques Derrida, *Demeure: Maurice Blanchot* (Paris: Galilée, 1998).

31. See Levinas, "Exercices sur 'La Folie du jour.'" Concerning the deciphering of the text and how to preserve the saying from thematization, he writes, "It may be obliged to unsay itself in order to avoid disfiguring the secret it exposes" (56).

32. I am indebted to Anne-Lise François for this phrase (see François, *Open Secrets: The Literature of Uncounted Experience* [Stanford: Stanford UP, 2007]).

33. Or rather, Jaffier is ultimately pushed into the fight by his captors in which, we are to presume, he will die.

34. Weil, *La Connaissance surnaturelle* (Paris: Gallimard, 1950) 62.

35. As a good republic, the cleanup must happen before anything can be detected to upset its citizens, which also raises the question of what it is that Violetta, in those final verses, sees.

36. Anne Carson, *Grief Lessons: Four Plays by Euripides* (New York: New York Review of Books, 2006) 163.

CHAPTER 5: THE EXTRAVAGANT DEMAND OF ASKING NOTHING: DESTITUTION AND GENEROSITY IN "AUTOBIOGRAPHIE SPIRITUELLE" AND *LA CONNAISSANCE SURNATURELLE*

1. Simone Weil, *La Pesanteur et la grâce* (Paris: Plon, 1988); hereafter cited as PG; translations are mine, with page numbers referring to the original.

2. The continuity of Simone Weil's thinking before and after her mystical experiences is evident from her earliest political writings on syndicalism, factory work, through to her last complete writing, *L'Enracinement: Prélude à une déclaration des devoirs envers l'être humain* ([Paris: Gallimard, 1949]; hereafter cited as EN; translations are mine, with page numbers referring to the original). Likewise, the notebooks and letters do not mark a rupture in the most important strands in her thinking—force and necessity, relations of power, the place of the individual vis-à-vis the collectivity, the importance of intellectual freedom and probity, the importance of Platonic notions of the good and truth, etc., continue to figure prominently. As Maurice Blanchot notes, "she was then no less turned toward the same light than she is

now that she has (dangerously) at her disposition a religious vocabulary that is more precise" ("L'Affirmation [le désir, le malheur]," *L'Entretien infini* [Paris: Gallimard, 1969] 154, trans. Susan Hanson, "Affirmation [desire, affliction]," *The Infinite Conversation* [Minneapolis: U of Minnesota P, 1993] 107).

As many commentators have noted, Weil's Christology looks more like a mystical or neo-Platonism than it does anything strictly Catholic. Blanchot writes: "And the word conversion is not a word she uses willingly, except in the sense of this word that she finds in the texts of Plato. . . . If it is true that she is a Christian, she owes it to Plato, for it is first of all in Plato that she found the Good, and it is through the beauty of the Greek texts that the name of the Good revealed itself to her as the sole reality, the unique response capable of illuminating the true reality of her desire and the unreality of all the rest" ("L'Affirmation" 154, 158). Weil went so far as to say that Plato was a mystic and an incarnation of Christ, stating as much in her letters to Father Couturier (*Lettre à un religieux* [Paris: Gallimard, 1951]) and in an undated letter to her brother, André Weil, from Marseille in Spring 1941: "That reminds me that I never replied . . . to the letter you sent me in Rouen in which you asked me whether I thought mysticism existed in classical Greece. It seems probable to me and almost certain as it concerns the Elysian mysteries, the Pythagoreans and Plato; and they must have been mystical exercises in the school of Plato for which mathematics served as the matter or the exterior envelope. Obviously, that is not easy to understand" (Papiers Simone Weil: Boîte I, Correspondance Simone Weil André Weil, Bibliothèque Nationale Française, Paris; my translation). It is developed at greater length in *La Source grecque* (Paris: Gallimard, 1953) and *Intuitions pré-chretiennes dans les grecs* (Paris: La colombe, 1951). It might even be argued that Christ was an incarnation of Plato rather than the other way around for Weil. In a quixotic aside that reflects her stubborn and unequivocal love of the ancient Greeks, Weil muses that the Lord's Prayer must have been recited originally in Greek to explain its perfect beauty.

3. Françoise Meltzer, "The Hands of Simone Weil," *Critical Inquiry* 27.4 (2001): 622.

4. Weil, "Autobiographie spirituelle," *Attente de Dieu* (Paris: Fayard, 1966) 54; hereafter cited as AD; translations are mine, with page numbers referring to the original.

This chapter does not examine the theological roots of her refusal, nor the possible connection to Judaism. For two very different discussions on this, see Robert Chenavier, "Simone Weil, 'La haine juive de soi'?" *Cahiers Simone Weil: De Simone Weil à la question juive* 14.4 (1991); and Daniel Boitier, "L'Impossible conversion," *Cahiers Simone Weil: Rencontres avec Oscar* 17.4 (1994).

As far as we know, Weil remained convinced that this position was the only possible one for her, despite her confessed desire for the Eucharist. From their correspondence, it seems that Father Perrin urged Weil to reconsider her position, including those beliefs contrary to the dogmas of the Catholic faith. Perrin states that the subject of Weil's baptism was the central topic of their interviews and correspondence (see Joseph-Marie Perrin and Gustave Thibon, *Simone Weil telle que nous l'avons connue* [Paris: Fayard, 1967] 36). The rift between her desire to take communion and her conclusion that she could not appears to have been painful for Weil right up to her untimely death at the age of thirty-four. In one of her last writings, Weil still professes "the need, not abstract, but practical, real, urgent, to know" whether a formal request for baptism would be granted (should she ask) given her unwavering position against certain Church doctrines. The point, I would submit, is that she does not ask (see Weil, "Dernier texte," *Pensées sans ordre concernant l'amour de Dieu* [Paris: Gallimard, 1962] 152; hereafter cited as PSO; translations are mine, with page numbers referring to the original). Weil states her opposition to *anathema sit*, the history of the Church's crimes against unbelievers, and her belief in the implicit forms of God's love (i.e., outside the Church and Christianity) in her essay "Formes de l'amour implicite de Dieu" (AD 122–214). Her position is also detailed in a letter she wrote to the Franciscan priest Father Couturier, during her time in New York. It is published as *Lettre à un religieux* (see also AD and her letter to Gustave Thibon, a fragment of which is also published in AD).

5. Undated letter from New York (see *Écrits de Londres et dernières lettres* [Paris: Gallimard, 1957] 198; hereafter cited as EL; translations are mine, with pages referring to the original). Weil writes about adherence and affirmation in similar terms in "Dernier texte," a profession of faith of sorts:

I believe in God, the Trinity, the Incarnation, the Redemption, the Eucharist, and in the Gospels.

I believe, that is to say, that I do not consider what the Church says on these points in order to affirm them as one affirms facts of experience or of geometry theorems, but that I adhere to the perfect truth—elusive and enclosed inside these mysteries—through love, and that I try to open my soul to them so as to allow the light to penetrate me. . . . For me, in the effort of reflection, an apparent or real disagreement with the teachings of the Church is simply a reason to suspend thought for a long time, to push away examination, attention, and scruple as far as possible before daring to affirm anything. (PSO 149–50)

6. We are met here with one of Weil's contradictions: the "event" of conversion is, except for these few letters, unmarked and unremarked upon, as is God's "withdrawal" from his creation. However, Weil does not cease to say—and sometimes in reference to herself and in explicit reference to her mystical experiences—that the suffering resulting from blind force (directly a result of God's leave-taking) marks the body and soul. She likens those who suffer from affliction to branded slaves; of her time in the factories, Weil says that it had "killed my youth" and "I received the mark of slavery" (AD 41, 42).

7. Alexander Irwin, *Saints of the Impossible: Bataille, Weil, and the Politics of the Sacred* (Minneapolis: U of Minnesota P, 2002) 198.

8. Undated letter to Maurice Schumann from London, 1943. See Isaiah 40:28–31: "He does not faint or grow weary; his understanding is unsearchable. He gives power to the faint, and strengthens the powerless. Even youths will faint and be weary, and the young will fall exhausted; but those who

wait for the Lord shall renew their strength, they shall mount up with wings like eagles, they shall run and not be weary, they shall walk and not faint" (*The New Oxford Annotated Bible, New Revised Standard Version* [Oxford: Oxford UP, 2007] 1032–33).

9. The date of the letter reads, "From Marseille, around May 15," a date that is, as Nicole Maroger puts it, "strangely imprecise" given that the letter will go on to give a precise chronological and geographical account of her religious experience. As Maroger notes: "It is only seemingly precise here. These places are actually perfectly anonymous and, as such, naturally integrated into the divine universe." Weil's most intensely personal biographical account is divested from the start of its self-referentiality—an impersonal autobiography, as it were (see Maroger, "Simone Weil ou le voyage immobile," *Cahiers Simone Weil: Chemins de Simone Weil* 17.3 [1994]: 273, my translation).

10. Love bade me welcome: yet my soul drew back,
Guilty of dust and sin.
But quick-eyed Love, observing me grow slack
From my first entrance in,
Drew nearer to me, sweetly questioning
If I lacked anything.
"A guest," I answered, "worthy to be here":
Love said, "You shall be he."
"I, the unkind, ungrateful? Ah, my dear,
I cannot look on thee."
Love took my hand, and smiling did reply,
"Who made the eyes but I?"
"Truth, Lord; but I have marred them; let my shame
Go where it doth deserve."
"And know you not," says Love, "who bore the blame?"
"My dear, then I will serve."
"You must sit down," says Love, "and taste my meat."
So I did sit and eat.

11. See Weil's postscript to her May 12, 1942, letter to Joë Bousquet: "I enclose the English poem, *Love*, that I'd recited to you. It played a big role in my life because I was repeating it to myself at the moment when Christ came to take possession of me for the first time. I thought I was only reciting a beautiful poem but, unknown to me, it was a prayer" (PSO 84).

12. If Weil appears to adopt the kind of language and themes of mystical literature to later describe her experiences, she claims that, at the time she underwent them, she had never read any and to have had only "vaguely heard about this sort of thing but without ever having believed in it" (AD 45).

13. This is the term used by Weil (rather than the historical appellation "Jesus") and will be the one used throughout this chapter.

14. See "The Dark Night of the Soul" by St. John of the Cross, which Weil often quoted or alluded to in her last writings.

15. See "Autobiographie spirituelle" (AD 35–62) and "Théorie des sacrements" (PSO 135–45).

16. Similarly, in a letter to Joë Bousquet, Weil writes: "We translate it as *in patientia*, but ὑπομένειν, is altogether different. It is to stay in place, immobile, in waiting, without being weakened or moved by any shock from the outside" (PSO 76).

17. She goes further: in *La Condition ouvrière*, Weil makes explicit the connection between the worker's condition—calling it a form of a slavery—and Christianity, which she calls in a letter to Perrin "the religion of slaves par excellence" (AD 43) (see *La Condition ouvrière* [Paris: Gallimard, 1951]; hereafter cited as CO; translations are mine, with page numbers referring to the original. See also *Réflexions sur les causes de la liberté et de l'oppression sociale* [Paris: Gallimard, 1955]).

18. "Nowadays, it's almost impossible to enter a factory without a work certificate [Weil was able to gain employment in the factories through connections]—especially when one is, like I am, slow, clumsy, and not very tough. . . . I simply took a year's leave [from teaching] for 'personal studies'" (see Weil, "Letter to a Student," CO 32).

19. See Meltzer's essay "The Hands of Simone Weil" for a discussion of Weil's metaphysics of work, specifically the union of thought and action in work and its relationship to attention. This relationship is also discussed in Nadia Taïbi's study of Weil's philosophy of work, *La Philosophie au travail: L'Expérience ouvrière de Simone Weil* (Paris: L'Harmattan, 2009).

20. Weil, "Three Letters to Madame Albertine Thévenon," CO 21.

21. Weil, "Letter to Boris Souvarine," CO 41.

22. The quotation used in the heading is from Joan Dargan, *Simone Weil: Thinking Poetically* (Albany: State U of New York P, 1999) 65. At the head of "Le Prologue," Weil indicates, "The beginning of the book (the book which will contain these and many other thoughts)" (CS 9). The notebooks are published as *La Connaissance surnaturelle* (Paris: Gallimard, 1950; hereafter cited as CS; translations are mine, with page numbers referring to the original) and as *Œuvres complètes*, Tome 6, Vol. 4: *Cahiers (juillet 1942–juillet 1943): La Connaissance surnaturelle (Cahiers de New York et de Londres)* (Paris: Gallimard, 2006); hereafter cited as OC vi/4; translations are mine, with page numbers referring to the original.

23. Nicole Maroger, "Simone Weil ou le voyage immobile," *Cahiers Simone Weil* 17.3 (1994): 282, my translation; Gilbert Kahn, "Le Style narratif," *Cahiers Simone Weil* 10.4 (1987): 381, my translation.

24. Of course, there is no gender assigned to the narrator; all we are given is an "I." For the sake of expediency, I have assigned one here: a "she," so as to not be confused with the "he" of the narrative. My reading resists a simple transposition of the "I" of Simone Weil with the "I" of the narrative, even as it draws attention to how Weil's life troubles any reading that would strictly separate the life from the work. Joan Dargan offers an interesting argument concerning the gender of the narrator (for Dargan, it is a male narrator): "A notion of universality that tends to exclude rather than embrace appears to be at work. But whereas, in this symbolic universe oriented to Christian values, an attitude of love is shown to triumph over the unadministered sacrament, the feminine simply disappears. Access to higher knowledge is represented

as a male province" (55). This reasoning, in my view, is unsupported by the conclusion of the parable, however: the narrator is either denied access to higher knowledge or cannot retain what that might have been, regardless of the narrator's gender (see Dargan, *Simone Weil: Thinking Poetically* 51–66.)

25. Maroger, "Simone Weil ou le voyage immobile" 273.

26. The cyclical character of time in the prologue aligns more generally with Weil's view that the self's fullest realization in time and space is symbolized by the circle. In her essay on the role of somatic practices in Weil's philosophy, Ann Pirruccello writes: "She sees the need for a set of practices that would link people to the rhythms of nature, rhythms whose cyclical character would transform one's relationship to time. . . . Identifying the body with the cyclical rhythms . . . would allow moments and what they bring to be experienced as equal realities and annul our egocentric perspective in time" (Pirruccello, "Making the World My Body: Simone Weil and Somatic Practice," *Philosophy East & West* 52.4 [2002]: 488).

27. Weil, *Cahiers, Tome III* (Paris: Plon, 1956) 351; hereafter cited as CTIII; translations are mine, with page numbers referring to the original.

28. This is strikingly similar to Emmanuel Levinas's early writings on the plenitude of the egoïc "I" in his self-enclosure (see *Totalité et infini: essai sur l'extériorité* [La Haye: Nijhoff, 1968]).

29. Anne Carson, *Decreation: Poetry, Essays, Opera* (New York: Knopf, 2005) 171. Writing is ineluctably tied to Weil's intellectual and spiritual vocation. From biographical accounts, we know that Weil wrote unceasingly, and often despite unfavorable circumstances—writing nonstop on her journey to New York, seated on one of the few available chairs on the ship (her parents would take turns occupying it whenever Weil would briefly rest so as to not lose the precious chair) and writing deep into the night after work hours in London under increasing ill health are but two instances. In one of her last letters, Weil imagines what she will do after recovering from her bout of illness (Weil had tuberculosis by this point and would never recover): she will write but not for the Free French (see her July 25, 1943, letter to Louis Closon [Papiers Simone Weil, Boîte I[I]): Correspondance générale, Bibliothèque Nationale Française, Paris). That letter, along with her intellectual and spiritual vocation, will be discussed at greater length in chapter 6.

Language is communication for Weil, but as I have been suggesting throughout, that communication is not necessarily straightforward or transparent. For example, poetic communication—one way she characterizes God's "secret speech"—can be "read" (in the sense of "lecture"), but a good reading is in no way guaranteed. Weil also relates language to action in her notes to *Venise sauvée*: "Action would be like language. Like works of art, etc. We communicate something by an action" (*Venise sauvée: Tragédie en trois actes* [Paris: Gallimard, 1955] 16).

30. See chapter 3 for a discussion of what passes unmarked in Jaffier's soul in Weil's play *Venise sauvée*.

31. Carson, *Decreation* 172.

32. Maroger, "Simone Weil ou le voyage immobile" 287.

33. Carson is not describing "Le Prologue" specifically, but, more generally, how Weil, Sappho, and Marguerite Porete "talk about their own telling" (173). "Telling God" is a phrase I borrow from Carson.

34. Carson, *Decreation* 173.

35. Samuel Beckett, "Note" to *That Time, Samuel Beckett: The Grove Centenary Edition*, ed. Paul Auster, vol. 3 (New York: Grove, 2006) 417.

36. As Meltzer states from the outset of her essay "The Hands of Simone Weil," "we must be careful not to confuse her life with her philosophy (a difficult task, as any work on Weil will attest)" (611). Meltzer's meticulous approach to the work, one that keeps within a decidedly philosophical register, cannot help from supporting her reading of two strains in Weil's thinking (Marxism and Catholicism) with biographical-historical details of that very life. She explains in a parenthetical aside: "I speak again here of her life only because the political activity is for her to be seen as a natural extension of her thought, and vice versa" (622). Pirruccello, on the other hand, takes the approach that "Weil's philosophy grew directly from her personal experiences," particularly those that emphasized certain bodily practices (479). Alexander Irwin's approach goes ones step further, reading Weil's life as a performance and inscription of her writing, "how the practice of writing and the work (or *désœuvrement*) of life flowed together, as both authors [Simone Weil and Georges Bataille] sought to transform themselves into sacred symbols" (xviii) (see Meltzer, "The Hands of Simone Weil"; Pirruccello, "Making the World My Body: Simone Weil and Somatic Practice," *Philosophy East & West* 52.4 [2002]: 479–97; and Irwin, *Saints of the Impossible: Bataille, Weil, and the Politics of the Sacred*).

37. The postscript to the April 16, 1942, letter bears repeating here also: "You know that for me [my departure] concerns something altogether different than escaping suffering and danger. My anguish comes precisely from the fear that in leaving, despite myself and unwittingly, I shall be doing what I want above all not to do: that is to say, running away. Until now we have lived here very peacefully. If this peace should disappear precisely after my departure, it would be awful for me. If I was certain it would be like that, I believe I would stay. If you know anything to forecast how things might go, I count on you to communicate it to me" (AD 33).

38. Recall Weil's letter to Boris Souvarine regarding her factory experience: "I did not feel the suffering as though it were mine, I felt it as the suffering of the factory workers, and that whether or not I personally suffered seemed to me almost like an indifferent detail" (CO 41).

39. Ann Smock, "Doors: Simone Weil with Kafka," *Modern Language Notes* 95.4 (1980): 859.

40. Note that it is the same war that Weil thought about ceaselessly, grievously for years; "since 1914 the war has never left my thinking," claims Weil in an undated letter to Schumann from London in 1943 (Papiers Simone Weil Carton VIII: Documents Maurice Schumann, Bibliothèque Nationale Française, Paris; my translation).

41. AD 98–121.

42. See Plato, *Phaedrus*, trans. Alexander Nehemas and Paul Woodruff (Indianapolis: Hackett, 1995).

43. See Irwin for another discussion of Weil's model for spiritual transformation. He argues that the discipline, control, and training in her model shifts in her New York and London notebooks to a religious purification that employs receptivity and waiting (l'attente). See also Pirruccello's excellent study of somatic practices in Weil's thought, which also considers the role of training in spiritual transformation.

44. Emmanuel Levinas, *Paul Celan: De l'être à l'autre* (Saint Clément de rivière: Fata Morgana, 2004) 25, trans. Michael B. Smith, "Paul Celan: From Being to the Other," *Proper Names* (Stanford: Stanford UP, 1996) 43. In the footnote that accompanies this passage, Levinas quotes from the example of prayer: "Simone Weil is able to write: Father, tear this body and this soul away from me to make of them your things, and let nothing remain of me eternally except that tearing-away itself" (176) (42, emphasis in original; "Simone Weil peut dire: *Père, arrache de moi ce corps et cette âme pour en faire des choses à toi et ne laisse subsister de moi éternellement que cet arrachement lui-même*") (see Weil, OC vi/4, 280).

45. Emphasis added.

46. Emphasis added.

47. In the end, there is the constant worry that one has said too much. Blanchot, who notes the worry in his essay "L'Affirmation," says that Weil "seems to be constantly unfaithful to it" (161). At the end of the "example of prayer" Weil adds parenthetically: "But all these spiritual phenomena are absolutely beyond my competence. I know nothing about them. They are reserved for those who possess, to begin with, the elementary moral virtues. I can only speak of them haphazardly. And I cannot even sincerely tell myself that I am speaking haphazardly" (OC, vi/4 280).

48. "À Propos du 'Pater,'" AD 215–28.

49. "Donne-moi cela."

50. Blanchot, *L'Attente l'oubli* (Paris: Gallimard, 1962) 12, trans. John Gregg, *Awaiting Oblivion* (Lincoln: U of Nebraska P, 1997); page number refers to the original; translation slightly modified.

51. Ibid.

52. See Smock, "Doors: Simone Weil with Kafka."

53. Simone Weil, *Poèmes, suivis de Venise sauvée* (Paris: Gallimard, 1968) 9, my translation.

54. Smock writes: "But this near side, this outside—suffused in the pure light of no other side, in the radiance that pours from the closed door in Kafka: it is not the place we are and have been always and would in any event necessarily have found ourselves. It is not a place where any abide (though to be sure there is no place else)—but the place with no entrance except the exit, from which all depart before arriving. It has no access except no step, which all the while not taken is not even that step, and which when at last it is taken is one step too many. . . . You cannot make one mistake except by making the other. To die is unavoidable and this false step which guarantees: no other side, is the one all take in any case. But no one ever manages not to avoid it—not, in taking the required false step, to overstep it, thus falling fatally short. No one is immortal. This side of the door, Simone Weil's side,

where we die, is like the error which is necessarily always missed. This side is the other, the near side the far, only in the sense that one error is always only the other, and all mistakes come to the same" (859–60).

55. Emphasis added.

56. Emphasis in original.

57. See CS 150.

58. Irwin, *Saints of the Impossible* 199, 198.

59. "Here below, to look and to eat are two different things. We have to choose one or the other. They are both called loving. The only people who have any hope of salvation are those who occasionally stop and look for a time instead of eating. 'One eats the fruit, the other looks at it.' The eternal part of the soul feeds on hunger. When we do not eat, our organism consumes its own flesh and transforms it into energy. It is the same with the soul. The soul that does not eat consumes itself. The eternal part consumes the mortal part of the soul and transforms it. The hunger of the soul is hard to bear, but there is no other remedy for our disease. To make the perishable part of the soul die of hunger while the body is still alive. In this way a body of flesh passes directly into God's service" (OC, vi/4 335).

60. Carson, *Decreation* 168.

61. Ibid. 168–69.

62. Emphasis added.

63. Emphasis added.

64. Weil, *Gravity and Grace*, trans. Arthur Wills (Lincoln: U of Nebraska P, 1997) 88.

65. This is an allusion to Hebrews 10:1.

66. Emphasis added.

67. Carson, *Decreation* 189.

68. As quoted in Simone Pétrement, *Simone Weil: A Life* (New York: Random House, 1976) 537.

69. See Simone Pétrement, *Simone Weil: A Life* (New York: Random House, 1976) 517–39. Weil's relationship to food and to hunger has been the subject of many studies. The readings cover an entire spectrum, ranging from it being evidence of Weil's pathological and self-destructive tendencies, to more sympathetic but fixed accounts of Weil's "anorexia," to approaches that see Weil's relationship to food as an extreme practice of attention and refusal to consume the object of one's desire (which, Weil argues, feeds the ego), so central to decreating the self. My own approach follows this last while noting the very real way in which her "refusal to consume" resulted in her physical death and not only in the loss of her "personal being" (AD 31).

70. See also chapter 1 for a discussion of not consuming the object of one's love.

71. See chapter 1 for a discussion of Weil's notion of "the sacred" and "the human being as such."

72. See Weil, "Les Besoins de l'âme," EN.

73. "As when one is at the limit of thirst, when one is sick with thirst, one no longer thinks of the act of drinking in relation to oneself, nor even of the act of drinking, generally speaking. One only thinks of water, water alone,

but this image of water is like a cry of one's whole being" (AD 217). Robert Antelme puts one's relationship to food under conditions of extreme deprivation in remarkably similar terms in his personal account of the concentration camps (see Antelme, *L'Espèce humaine* [Paris: Gallimard, 1957]).

74. See Weil, EN.

75. The idea of depleting one's supplemental energy has given rise to commentaries that Weil's notion of decreation is invested in pathological forms of transformation, one that is tantamount to self-hatred.

76. The figure of the prodigal son, used to illustrate the decreative process, is extensively explored in Weil's New York notebooks (see Weil, *La Connaissance surnaturelle*). Irwin identifies the loss of will and control in the decreative expenditure of supplemental energy, comparing it to Georges Bataille's doctrine of liberative expenditure: "Both Weil's decreation and Bataille's *dépense* draw their power from a loss of control. The person is no longer the self-centered, self-mastering subject but the site of his/her own violent overthrow. Moreover, this overthrow erupts *against the will* of the ego struggling for self-preservation. Neither decreation (equivalent to death) nor expenditure (whose horizon is death and horror) can be chosen. Decreation and Bataillean sacrificial excess seize us 'despite ourselves'" (*Saints of the Impossible* 176, emphasis in original).

77. Weil reflects on the absent presence of God in similar terms in her notebooks: "To feel that we love him, even if he does not exist. It is he who, through the operation of the dark night, withdraws in order not to be loved as the treasure is by the miser. Electra weeping for the dead Orestes. If we love God while thinking that he does not exist, he will manifest his existence" (PG 61).

78. The excessive love of Weil's Antigone is, furthermore, rooted in a profound religiosity, one of two key features of Meltzer's own reading of Sophocles's *Antigone*. The other feature is Antigone's foreignness, another aspect of the figure of excess in that it is unmappable: "If Creon confuses registers, Antigone falls outside all registers, realms, nomenclature. She is in herself *in excess*, a figural catachresis" (Meltzer, "Theories of Desire: Antigone Again," *Critical Inquiry* 37.2 [2011]: 176).

79. Weil's letter to her parents, December 16, 1942, in EL 218–19.

80. See Anne Carson's opera based on Weil's heedlessness of the mores and laws of society ("Part Three: Fight Cherries," of "Decreation: An Opera in Three Parts," *Decreation*).

81. Weil, "La Personne et le sacré," EL 25–26.

82. Carson, *Decreation* 162, 159.

83. See Simone Pétrement, *La Vie de Simone Weil* (Paris: Fayard, 1973); J. M. Perrin and G. Thibon, *Simone Weil telle que nous l'avons connue* (Paris: Fayard, 1967); T. S. Eliot, "Preface," *The Need for Roots: Prelude to a Declaration of Duties Toward Mankind* (New York: Harper and Row, 1971); and Georges Bataille, *Le Bleu du ciel* (Paris: Editions Flammarion, 1991).

84. Her first self-described "grand œuvre" was *Réflexions sur les causes de la liberté et de l'oppression sociale* (Paris: Gallimard, 1955).

85. See Weil's undated letter to Maurice Schumann from London. "Even when I was a child, and I believed I was an atheist and materialist, I always

had the fear in me of missing, not my life, but my death. This fear has never ceased to become more and more intense" (EL 213).

86. Included in a letter sent to Maurice Schumann on July 30, 1942, in EL 187.

87. "Mais elle est folle!" (see Simone Pétrement, *La Vie de Simone Weil II* [Paris: Fayard, 1973] 483).

88. That being said, Weil did her best to pitch the plan as eminently practical, including with it a report by the Red Cross that stated the significant drop in frontline casualties due to shock, exposure, and hemorrhaging when immediately treated, as well as a testimonial by Joë Bousquet, a soldier injured in World War I, endorsing the plan specifically for its perceived usefulness.

89. See chapter 4 for a discussion of debt and obligation.

CHAPTER 6: EMPTY PETITIONS: THE LAST LETTERS OF SIMONE WEIL

1. Maurice Blanchot, "L'Affirmation (le désir, le malheur)," *L'Entretien infini* (Paris: Gallimard, 1969) 178–79, trans. Susan Hanson, "Affirmation (desire, affliction)," *The Infinite Conversation* (Minneapolis: U of Minnesota P, 1993) 122.

2. See Simone Weil, *La Pesanteur et la grâce* (Paris: Plon, 1988) 273; hereafter cited as PG; translations are mine, with page numbers referring to the original.

3. Blanchot, "L'Affirmation" 176.

4. Weil, *Attente de Dieu* (Paris: Fayard, 1966) 38; hereafter cited as AD; translations are mine, with page numbers referring to the original.

5. According to Hélène Honnorat's account, Jacob's assessment was a "turning point" for Weil (as quoted in Simone Pétrement, *La Vie de Simone Weil* [Paris: Fayard, 1973] 608). However, as Robert Chevanier states in his introduction to Weil's *Écrits de Marseille*, that is "a bit exaggerated since Simone Weil knew for a long time that she could not but appear heretical in the eyes of Catholics; 'heresies' did not put her off since she declared to have found a truth 'in certain heresies, especially the Cathar and Manichean traditions'" (*Œuvres complètes*, Tome 4, Vol. 2: *Écrits de Marseille: Philosophie, science, religion, questions politiques et sociales (1940–1942)*, [Paris: Gallimard, 2008] 229; hereafter cited as EM; translations are mine, with page numbers referring to the original.)

6. Chevanier, "Introduction," EM 230.

7. Just as she had, shortly before (March 29, March 30, and April 1, 1942), addressed those same questions to Canon Fernand Vidal in Carcassonne. Weil's intention to continue her questioning about how her position aligned with that of the Church could not be clearer than in a questionnaire that she had prepared and asked Hélène Honnorat "to present it to all the priests she knew" (notes taken by Simone Pétrement from interviews with Hélène and Pierre Honnorat, Fonds Simone Pétrement, Bibliothèque Nationale de France).

Weil's "Questionnaire" is published in *Pensées sans ordre concernant l'amour de Dieu* (Paris: Gallimard, 1962). See also Weil, *Lettre à un religieux* (Paris: Gallimard, 1951); and Weil, "Le Dernier texte," *Pensées sans ordre concernant l'amour de Dieu* (Paris: Gallimard, 1962) 149–53.

8. See Weil, "À Propos du 'Pater,'" AD 215.

9. See Joseph-Marie Perrin, "Préface," AD 8. Weil also spoke of her encounter with Christ to Canon Fernand Vidal during one of their three meetings during Easter week, 1942. Vidal writes: "She then told me, clearly but without insisting, that Christ had seized her one day and had been revealed to her, so much did she believe in his divinity. On this point, her faith, her certitude, were absolute. I forbid myself to question her out of respect for the secret of her soul" (see "Témoignage d'un religieux," Don Clément, D'en-Calcat, Papiers Simone Weil, Boîte II: Documents autobiographiques, Bibliothèque Nationale Française, Paris; my translation).

10. Blanchot, "L'Affirmation" 173.

11. See also chapter 5 for a discussion of "the perfect demand."

12. That is the expression Weil uses in a letter addressed to Simone Pétrement (see Pétrement, *La Vie de Simone Weil*).

13. See chapter 4 for a discussion of the idea of "missing one's death" in Weil, *Venise sauvée: Tragédie en trois actes* (Paris: Gallimard, 1955); and Blanchot, *La Folie du jour* (Paris: Gallimard, 2002).

14. See chapters 1 and 3 for a discussion of preserving the other from harm.

15. I am modifying Judith Butler's brief reflection on the notion of the messianic within the performative: "If there is a sense of the messianic within the performative, it would doubtless be a way of thinking about this anticipatory form of positing that fails to achieve a final realization. If we think about this as part of what I was calling earlier the right to existence, then the performative would be an exercise of articulation that brings an open-ended reality into existence" (see Butler and Athena Athanasiou, *Dispossession: The Performative in the Political* [Cambridge: Polity, 2013] 129–30).

16. Martin Steffens, "La Figure du philosophe: Simone Weil, l'enracinée," in Simone Weil, *Les Besoins de l'âme, extrait de l'Enracinement: Prélude à une déclaration des devoirs envers l'être humain* (Paris: Gallimard, 2007) 90, my translation.

17. For a very good account of this trajectory, see Robert Chevanier, "Introduction," EM.

18. See chapter 5 for a discussion of the idea of a life at once expendable and necessary.

19. See chapters 1 and 5 for a discussion of need and objectless desire.

20. See chapter 5 for a discussion of supplemental energy.

21. Weil, *Écrits de Londres et dernières lettres* (Paris: Gallimard, 1957) 201; hereafter cited as EL; translations are mine, with page numbers referring to the original.

22. Papiers Simone Weil, Boîte I(I): Correspondance générale, Bibliothèque Nationale Française, Paris; hereafter cited as PSW; translations are mine.

23. Françoise Meltzer, "The Hands of Simone Weil," *Critical Inquiry* 27.4 (2001): 623.

24. Ibid. 623–24.

25. David Sylvester, *The Brutality of Fact: Interviews with Francis Bacon* (London: Thames and Hudson, 1988) 175.

26. Anne Carson, *Nay Rather* (London: Sylph Editions, 2013) 18.

27. The quotation used in the heading is from Blanchot, *Le Livre à venir* (Paris: Gallimard, 1959) 302, trans. Charlotte Mandell, *The Book to Come* (Stanford: Stanford UP, 2002) 222, translation modified.

28. Carson, *Decreation: Poetry, Essays, Opera* (New York: Knopf, 2005) 223.

29. Emmanuel Levinas, "Exercices sur 'La Folie du jour,'" *Sur Maurice Blanchot* (Saint Clément de rivière: Fata Morgana, 2004) 59, trans. Michael B. Smith, "Exercises on 'The Madness of Day,'" *Proper Names* (Stanford: Stanford UP, 1996) 159.

30. Papiers Simone Weil, Boîte XI: Lettres de Simone Weil à ses parents, Bibliothèque Nationale Française, Paris; my translation.

31. The quotation used in the heading is from EL 213.

32. Levinas, *Paul Celan: De l'être à l'autre* (Saint Clément de rivière: Fata Morgana, 2004) 25, trans. Michael B. Smith, "Paul Celan: From Being to the Other," *Proper Names* (Stanford: Stanford UP, 1996) 43; Weil, *Œuvres complètes*, Tome 6, Vol. 1: *Cahiers (1933-septembre 1941)* (Paris: Gallimard, 1994) 302.

33. PG 95.

INDEX